University Textbook Series

June, 1990

Especially Designed for Collateral Reading

HARRY W. JONES
Directing Editor
Professor of Law, Columbia University

ADMINISTRATIVE LAW AND PROCESS (1985)
Richard J. Pierce, Jr., Dean and Professor of Law, University of Pittsburgh.
Sidney A. Shapiro, Professor of Law, University of Kansas.
Paul R. Verkuil, President and Professor of Law, College of William and Mary.

ADMIRALTY, Second Edition (1975)
Grant Gilmore, Professor of Law, Yale University.
Charles L. Black, Jr., Professor of Law, Yale University.

AGENCY (1975)
W. Edward Sell, Dean of the School of Law, University of Pittsburgh.

BUSINESS ORGANIZATION AND FINANCE, Fourth Edition (1990)
William A. Klein, Professor of Law, University of California, Los Angeles.
John C. Coffee, Jr., Professor of Law, Columbia University.

CIVIL PROCEDURE, BASIC, Second Edition (1979)
Milton D. Green, Professor of Law Emeritus, University of California, Hastings College of the Law.

COMMERCIAL TRANSACTIONS, INTRODUCTION TO (1977)
Hon. Robert Braucher, Associate Justice, Supreme Judicial Court of Massachusetts.
Robert A. Riegert, Professor of Law, Cumberland School of Law.

CONFLICT OF LAWS, COMMENTARY ON THE, Third Edition (1986) with 1989 Supplement
Russell J. Weintraub, Professor of Law, University of Texas.

CONSTITUTIONAL LAW, AMERICAN, Second Edition (A TREATISE ON) (1988)
Laurence H. Tribe, Professor of Law, Harvard University.

CONTRACT LAW, THE CAPABILITY PROBLEM IN (1978)
Richard Danzig.

CORPORATE TAXATION, FEDERAL SECOND EDITION (1990)
Howard E. Abrams, Professor of Law, Emory University.
Richard L. Doernberg, Professor of Law, Emory University.

CORPORATIONS, Second Edition (1971)
Norman D. Lattin, Professor of Law, University of California, Hastings College of the Law.

CORPORATIONS IN PERSPECTIVE (1976)
Alfred F. Conard, Professor of Law, University of Michigan.

CRIMINAL LAW, Third Edition (1982)
Rollin M. Perkins, Professor of Law, University of California, Hastings College of the Law.
Ronald N. Boyce, Professor of Law, University of Utah College of Law.

CRIMINAL PROCEDURE, Second Edition (1986) with 1990 Supplement
Charles H. Whitebread, II, Professor of Law, University of Southern California.
Christopher Slobogin, Associate Professor of Law, University of Florida.

ESTATES IN LAND & FUTURE INTERESTS, PREFACE TO, Second Edition (1984)
Thomas F. Bergin, Professor of Law, University of Virginia.
Paul G. Haskell, Professor of Law, University of North Carolina.

EVIDENCE: COMMON SENSE AND COMMON LAW (1947)
John M. Maguire, Professor of Law, Harvard University.

JURISPRUDENCE: MEN AND IDEAS OF THE LAW (1953)
The late Edwin W. Patterson, Cardozo Professor of Jurisprudence, Columbia University.

LABOR RELATIONS The Basic Processes, Law and Practice (1988)
Julius G. Getman, Professor of Law, University of Texas.
Bertrand E. Pogrebin, Member, New York State Bar.

LEGAL CAPITAL, Third Edition (1990)
Bayless Manning.

LEGAL RESEARCH ILLUSTRATED, Fifth Edition with 1990 Assignments Supplement
J. Myron Jacobstein, Professor of Law, Emeritus, Stanford University.
Roy M. Mersky, Professor of Law, Director of Research, University of Texas.

LEGAL RESEARCH, FUNDAMENTALS OF, Fifth Edition with 1990 Assignments Supplement
J. Myron Jacobstein, Professor of Law, Emeritus, Stanford University.
Roy M. Mersky, Professor of Law, Director of Research, University of Texas.

PROCEDURE, THE STRUCTURE OF (1979)
Robert M. Cover, Professor of Law, Yale University.
Owen M. Fiss, Professor of Law, Yale University.

PROPERTY, PRINCIPLES OF THE LAW OF, Third Edition (1989)
John E. Cribbet, Dean, Chancellor, Professor of Law Emeritus, University of Illinois.
Corwin W. Johnson, Professor of Law Emeritus, University of Texas.

TAXATION, FEDERAL INCOME, Fifth Edition (1988)
Marvin A. Chirelstein, Professor of Law, Columbia University.

TORTS, Second Edition (1980)
Clarence Morris, Professor of Law, University of Pennsylvania.
C. Robert Morris, Professor of Law, University of Minnesota.

WILLS AND TRUSTS, THE PLANNING AND DRAFTING OF, Second Edition (1979) with 1982 Supplement
Thomas L. Shaffer, Professor of Law, University of Notre Dame.

WILLS, TRUSTS AND ADMINISTRATION, PREFACE TO (1987)
Paul G. Haskell, Professor of·Law, University of North Carolina.

Concepts and Case Analysis in the Law of

CONTRACTS

By

MARVIN A. CHIRELSTEIN
Professor of Law, Columbia University

UNIVERSITY TEXTBOOK SERIES

Westbury, New York
THE FOUNDATION PRESS, INC.
1990

Cover: The barque *Peerless,* by Richard Henry Nibbs (1816–1893), oil on canvas. Courtesy of the National Maritime Museum, Greenwich.

COPYRIGHT © 1990 By THE FOUNDATION PRESS, INC.
                    615 Merrick Ave.
                    Westbury, N.Y. 11590

Library of Congress Cataloging-in-Publication Data

Chirelstein, Marvin A.
   Concepts and case analysis in the law of contracts / by Marvin A.
Chirelstein.
       p.   cm. — (University textbook series)
   Includes index.
   ISBN 0–88277–803–X
   1. Contracts—United States. I. Title. II. Series.
KF801.C44   1990
346.73'02—dc20
[347.3062]   90–39102
                                                         CIP

Chirelstein Contracts UTB

To Ellen

*

PREFACE

My purpose in writing a brief Contracts primer is to offer first-year law students a reliable overview of the major themes and leading cases in the field. As the modest size of this book must suggest, I have made no effort to be comprehensive or to prepare a work that could possibly or even remotely qualify as a treatise. Very much more of the law of Contracts is omitted than included, and indeed two major topics—the Statute of Frauds and Assignment and Delegation—are touched upon only in passing. Some will feel that too much has been left out, but my own view is that omitting things is a good way to learn this or any other legal subject. At all events, my hope (and my hunch) is that less will actually turn out to be, if not more, then at least quite sufficient from the standpoint of a student reader.

I am very grateful to my colleague, Eben Moglen, who most generously read, commented upon and shook his head over the entire manuscript. Thanks are due, also, to Albert Rosenthal for answering questions and kindly allowing me to draw on his long experience as a Contracts teacher. Neither has any responsibility for the product.

MARVIN A. CHIRELSTEIN

Columbia University
May, 1990

*

TABLE OF CONTENTS

*

Concepts and Case Analysis in the Law of
CONTRACTS

*

Chapter 1

BACKGROUND ELEMENTS: THE CONTRACT CURVE AND EXPECTATION DAMAGES

Exchanging one thing for another—money for goods and services, typically—is a major preoccupation for most of us and for better or worse absorbs the greater part of our active lives. This being so, it is not surprising that Contracts—which is essentially the law of exchange—should have the status of a foundation course in law school. Any exchange relationship, even the simplest transaction at retail, is based on an agreement between the parties, and we naturally expect—though without thinking about it unless we have to—that legal rules in some way provide assurance that the agreement will be honored. Contract law is supposed to implement that expectation. In the process it chiefly asks and answers the following questions: first, whether the parties have behaved in such a way as to create legally recognizable expectations in one another; second, if they have, how those expectations should be characterized and understood; third, whether the understanding thus arrived at was faithfully carried out by the parties or somehow thwarted; and finally, if thwarted, what if anything the law should do about it. These questions can, of course, be presented in a fairly complex way and they may prove irritatingly difficult to answer. They are not very numerous, however, and quite often the difficulty results less from the need to frame complex legal principles than from uncertainty about what the parties really *did* expect and understand in the particular case under consideration. Judicial opinions, even the "great" opinions that have been chewed over for generations, are sometimes rather dream-like and opaque when it comes to explaining why the parties acted or expressed themselves as they did, and it is that "opacity," I believe, not the legal rules as such, that creates problems in many instances.

But before approaching the cases themselves, it may be worthwhile to say something about the economic framework in which contract law arises, admitting in advance that "economics," here, pretty well reduces to a set of truisms that are largely obvious to begin with. One such truism is that people enter into exchange relationships with one another—trading this for that—for the sole and sufficient reason that it makes them feel better off to do so. Thus, imagine a world consisting of only two commodities—apples

1

and oranges—and only two consumers—A and B—each with different preferences but each wanting to consume *some* quantity of both commodities. We can be quite sure that, unless already satisfied with the allocation of those commodities, A and B will at once commence to negotiate a trade, with A giving up some of his apples, say, in exchange for some of B's oranges and B doing the opposite. The effect, it is important to note, should be to make *both* parties feel richer than previously—not just A, not just B, but both. The trading process is not a poker game in which one player wins what another loses; rather, it is a kind of joint undertaking which increases the wealth of both parties and from which both emerge with a measure of enhanced utility. This is true, moreover, even though A and B are essentially in conflict, each seeking to drive the hardest bargain he can against the other and each having and cherishing the mentality of a shark. The act of making an exchange will (in the generality of cases) lead not only to individual but to mutual advantage despite a thoroughly self-centered outlook on the part of the traders. That being so, it would be unfortunate, even wasteful in economic terms, if the exchange did not take place.

All this is slightly banal, I admit, but it does describe the formal setting in which contracts calling for the exchange of one thing for another are made. A and B *both* trade up, so to speak, until one or the other feels that no further trading will lead to his advantage. They are not of course unique. The same formulation can be extended to a society more nearly resembling the real world—that is, a society in which there are many commodities and many consumers, including, I should add, not only consumers of outputs—households that eat up the apples and oranges—but consumers of inputs—business firms that buy and use labor and raw materials in producing goods and services. Once more, all of these individuals and entities will "naturally" engage in trading one thing for another—buying and selling, getting and spending—up to the point where such activity produces no further *mutual* advantage and the allocation of available resources—people as well as things—is classically "efficient."

Stressing economic efficiency leads to yet another important question (though, again, pretty easily answered). Thus, why should the law—as of course it does—go to the trouble of enforcing contract obligations between private parties? Why should our costly legal apparatus be used (in some way not yet specified) to *compel* people to keep their promises? As already noted, A and B are *both* presumed to be made better off by trading goods and services. If that is so, why shouldn't they be expected to keep their promises voluntarily—why add the element of legal compulsion to an arrangement which the parties entered into *without* compulsion and which each evidently regards as being in his own best interest?

The answer, of course, is that if all transactions took place instantaneously, as in the case of an everyday retail purchase, the need for enforcement rules would be slight. If you buy a book at the bookstore, the transaction is complete once the cashier has counted your money and you put the book under your arm. But retail sales are really the exception, although of course not without their own special problems. In most other situations, including almost all commercial dealings, the agreed-upon exchange is noninstantaneous; rather, it is intended to occur at some date in the future or is expected to take considerable time to carry out. An example of the former would be an agreement to pay $X for Y tons of steel to be delivered in ninety days. An example of the latter would be an agreement to build a factory for a stated price, construction to be completed in two years. In both cases vital terms are agreed to by the parties today, while performance—full payment on the buyer's side perhaps, and certainly delivery or construction on the seller's—is necessarily deferred.

Given a lapse of time between agreement and performance, it is possible that one of the two parties will come to regret the deal. Their agreement represents the parties' best estimates of future market conditions, but those estimates will almost never be perfectly accurate and it is easy to imagine that buyer or seller, owner or builder, will subsequently find that actual market prices have moved in a direction that makes performance in accordance with the terms originally agreed upon unprofitable. Considerations of reputation and standing might even then deter the disadvantaged party from breaking his promise, but if the financial loss that he confronts becomes substantial he might well prefer to tolerate the other party's hard feelings and back out of the deal altogether. Clearly, however, both parties *intended* to be bound by their agreement and would have found it difficult or impossible to carry on business in the first place without being able to count on the enforcement of their claims to performance. The steel buyer, for example, might have made an agreement to resupply the steel (perhaps after further processing) at a fixed price to a customer of his own; the builder would surely have made fixed-price agreements with various material suppliers and sub-contractors when calculating his costs for the factory building. Planning at all stages will have been carried forward on the assumption that the promises made by other actors will be kept or (if not) enforced. Unless that assumption *can* be made the process of exchange will obviously be discouraged or greatly complicated. While the legal system could leave each party to protect himself against breach by the other through the medium of insurance, bonding, hedging or the like, it is not easy to think of any self-protective device (other than violence or taking human hostages) that does not itself entail a contractual commitment by which the affected parties expect to be bound.

Accepting that legal enforcement is desirable, the next and in a sense the last really important question is what form such enforcement should take. One possibility, I suppose, would be physical compulsion: a person committing breach of contract would be *made* to adhere to his obligations by threat of force, just as a child is forced to live up to household obligations of various kinds. Where adults are concerned, however, this approach would convert contract law into criminal law—the breaching party would be arrested, tried, and then jailed or perhaps just flogged until compliance was forthcoming. But apart from the horrendous risk that would thus be added to everyday commercial dealings the fact is that we simply don't regard contract breach as so dangerous, anti-social or morally infected as to justify force. Indeed, as suggested later on, under certain circumstances our view may be that breach of contract is fully consistent with economic efficiency goals, even desirable, so that force or other compulsion would be seriously unwise.

Actually, the law does compel performance in certain situations, but these are isolated and relatively few in number. More generally, the common law deals and has always dealt with contract breach not by forced compliance but by compensating the injured party for his loss through an award of money damages. Our rule, briefly stated, is that the injured party may recover from the party in breach a dollar sum sufficient to put him in as good a position as he would have occupied had the contract been performed in full. This principle—easily the most important single idea in the whole contracts field—is referred to by convention as the "expectation damage" rule, and of course it is the injured party's "expectations" that are being compensated. To illustrate the rule as simply as possible, assume that Buyer and Seller contract for the sale of 1,000 barrels of oil (carefully specified as to grade or whatever) at a price of $20 a barrel, payment and delivery in 30 days. On the payment/delivery date, as it happens, oil is selling at only $14 a barrel and Buyer refuses to go through with the transaction. How much can Seller, the injured party, recover? A possible answer—but wrong—is $20,000. To be sure,

$20,000 is the aggregate purchase price due under the contract, and clearly Buyer has breached. If, however, we give appropriate recognition to the fact that there is an active market for oil, Seller would obviously be over-compensated if we awarded him an amount equal to the full purchase price. Having learned from Buyer that the agreement is being dishonored, Seller is free, if he chooses, to sell his 1,000 barrels on the market to any buyer at the prevailing $14 price. Assume he does. If he were *also* entitled to recover $20,000 from Buyer, Seller's total receipts would be $34,000 and the breach of contract would have been a piece of rare good fortune from his standpoint. Aimed at compensating, but not over-compensating Seller for Buyer's breach, the expectation damage rule limits Seller's claim to the difference between the contract price—$20—and the market value of the goods at the contract date—$14—or $6 a barrel. In effect, Seller is required to "mitigate" damages by accepting the best price then available in the market. Whether or not he really sells the oil doesn't matter for this purpose: since he could if he wished, he is presumed to have done so. The proceeds of such sale, actual or presumed, are then applied to Buyer's account, that is, are treated as if received by Seller from Buyer himself. It follows that Seller's claim against Buyer under the prevailing common law damage rule is limited to $6,000, the sum "needed" to satisfy Seller's original expectation. That expectation, of course, was to receive $20 a barrel for 1,000 barrels of oil.

The concept just described is a simple one, I know, but to make sure of it I might ask the following: In applying the expectation damage rule, should it matter whether Seller *later* disposes of his oil for more or less than its market value at the contract date? Suppose after shrewd calculation he decides to retain the oil in the hope that the market, which is apparently volatile, will go back up to $20 in the near future? And suppose it quickly does, so that Seller actually *gets* his $20 a barrel, say two weeks afterwards. Or suppose it drops still further and the oil is finally sold by Seller for only $10. Should either of these events make a difference in computing Seller's damage claim? The answer is no. Seller is not required to dispose of his oil at $14, but if he doesn't he is on his own both legally and in economic terms. The entitlements and obligations of the parties—and in particular Seller's rights against Buyer—are cut off and determined at the date set by the contract. The reason is plain. Market forecasts made by the parties when the contract was entered into were keyed to a date exactly 30 days forward, no later. Seller proved to be the better forecaster (this time). But Seller's decision to hold his oil off the market *after* that date—to retain his long position hoping for a price jump—is obviously a decision made solely for his own interest; the consequences, good or bad, are his alone. Hence, Buyer's breach gives Seller a claim to $6,000 in damages— no more, no less—without regard to subsequent events.

This very brief description of the expectation damage rule has focused on proper compensation to Seller, the injured party, but the implications for Buyer are equally notable. Given the rule, Buyer's act in breaching the contract gains him nothing in my illustrative case. From Buyer's standpoint the obligation to pay Seller $6,000 in damages leaves Buyer no better off than he would be if he completed the contract by paying Seller $20,000 as promised, took delivery, and then simply sold the oil in the market for $14,000. Whatever he does, whether he fulfills the contract or breaches, Buyer is poorer by $6,000. Accordingly, unless he thinks he has some legal defense to offer, Buyer might as well grit his teeth and carry out his obligations in accordance with the contract.

And very probably he would, which may suggest to the reader that the principal impact of the expectation damage rule is *prospective* rather than backward-looking and remedial. Viewed from the beginning rather than the end of the contracting process, it is obvious that both parties then considered themselves better off by (a) agreeing to exchange cash for oil and (b) fixing the price at $20 a barrel. Each party undoubtedly felt that the agreement was to his advantage despite an awareness that his market prediction might turn out badly. No doubt that judgment had something to do with limiting individual risk, and we will be more explicit about that factor in a brief Note, immediately below. For the moment, it is enough to state that Buyer and Seller (like A and B with their apples and oranges) each regarded the contract, including the fixed-price feature, as an opportunity to improve his wealth position. Plainly, however, that opportunity could be realized only if their agreement was seen to be fully reciprocal, that is, only if it was evident to both—at the outset—that neither could lose through one-sided compliance. If the legal rules permitted either party to breach without compensation to the other, then, probably, the best course to follow would be to avoid agreement altogether—regretfully, to be sure, because, as noted, the proposed exchange was otherwise thought by each to provide a material economic advantage.

But, of course, contracts calling for a forward exchange are entered into every day, and most are routinely performed, even though as to any single transaction one party is likely to prove a better forecaster of future market developments than the other.

The reason for this is that the expectation damage rule operates to deprive the "loser"—Buyer on this occasion—of any benefit from indulging in non-cooperative conduct and, reciprocally, gives the "winner" his due. The gamble is fair to both parties; neither can renege after the cards are dealt. In this respect the rule has a consistent and important role in making cooperative relations feasible [1] and, hence, in promoting what was described above as "efficient" resource allocation.

The foregoing, I hope, adequately explains the expectation damage rule in its simplest and most fundamental aspect, but I should caution that the subject of contract remedies is far more complex and extensive than my simple illustration suggests. If, for example, the transaction between a buyer and seller involved some product or service for which no active trading market existed, measuring damages by reference to daily price quotations would not be possible. In some situations, also, buyer and seller might have different expectations of benefit, so that the convenient element of symmetry would be lacking. Finally, my illustration entirely neglects the possibility that the parties may have incurred out-of-pocket costs in *reliance* on the contract—again, perhaps, in differing amounts—for which the injured party would presumably seek recovery as well. How should all or any of these circumstances be handled in fashioning a well-calibrated damage rule? These and other detailed remedy problems are examined in Chapter 8.

Calculation of damages is the final and culminating event in any contract litigation. Before reaching the damage question, as noted earlier, one needs first to determine whether a "contract" actually exists between the parties which the law recognizes and will enforce, then what the contract means, then whether the acts or omissions complained of by the plaintiff constitute a breach. Issues of this sort make up the bulk (the word is used advisedly) of most Contracts courses and are taken up at appropriate points in the Chapters that follow. Probably, though, the student's perspective will be clearer at each of these stages if he or she has some idea in advance of what is ultimately at stake for the parties, and this suggests that an overview of damages and remedies may be a suitable starting point in this field. ˙

Having praised the expectation damage rule as instrumental to the welfare-maximizing function of exchange, I should add, or concede, that in general (though with exceptions) contract law has nothing much to do with the larger question of who gets what in

---

    1. Birmingham, *Legal and Moral Duty in Game Theory: Common Law*   *Contract and Chinese Analogies,* 18 Buffalo L.Rev. 99, 105 (1969).

this world. The economist's model of efficiency is one in which all mutually beneficial trades have been carried out and executed, with the happy consequence that further changes that would benefit *all* individuals are impossible. But beware the syllogism: the fact that no further changes can be made that will make everybody happy does not mean that everybody *is* happy. A given society's resources may, for example, be allocated in such a way that 10% of the population owns 90% of all the apples and oranges and everything else, while 90% of the population must live on the 10% that is left. This seems inequitable, to put it mildly, but resource allocation is "efficient" in economic terms because no further exchanges are possible that will make someone better off without making someone else worse off. By contrast, a reallocative measure that produced a more equal distribution of resources would neither be compelled nor justified under a pure efficiency standard. The reason it would not is that some people (members of the minority) would be made worse off thereby, even though lots of other people would be made much better off. Those who are made worse off would obviously suffer a loss of "utility" (unless they are altruists) and hence would be very unlikely to regard such a measure as anything other than a forced exaction.

We might, nevertheless, and probably would, conclude that the distribution of resources in the society just described was inhumane and unfair and decide that something should be done about it. Plainly, however, the process of trading one thing for another, which assumes the pursuit of purely selfish motives, will not serve well as an instrument of "reform" unless we are sure that the people in the rich minority will be consistently wrong in their predictions about the economic future, like Buyer in my illustration. But that is implausible. It follows, I think, that Contracts, the law of *voluntary* exchange, has relatively little to say about equity and fairness in the large. Rather, its focus is on that multitude of commonplace, small-scale transactions by means of which private individuals seek to advance their personal well-being, each acting strictly in his own interest.

All this is pretty cold-blooded. Not liking it very much, some writers argue that contract law, with its emphasis on enforcement, is essentially a reactionary force, one that operates to preserve the status quo by treating the act of voluntary exchange as sacrosanct and inviolable, even though in some cases the parties to a contract may be unequal in bargaining power and education. Where such inequality exists (it is said) enforcement on the usual basis is unjustified and rules of amelioration should be developed. From the other end, some assert that strict enforcement of contracts is really a way of showing respect for the dignity and freedom of other individuals by taking them at their word. Hence, arguably, judicial or legislative interventions in the name of fairness—for example, excusing certain people from performance when it appears that the obligations they have assumed are especially harsh—amounts to creating one class of caretakers and another class of sheep. These viewpoints, which inevitably involve the proponent's ethical values, are brought into sharper focus in connection with the subject of unconscionability, which is taken up in Chapter 4.

One further (and concluding) set of observations should be made concerning the purpose and function of legal rules in the Contracts field. As has been seen, contracts are voluntary arrangements created by the parties themselves to carry out their own particular aims. People exchange things with one another because they want to not because they have to, and in fashioning the terms of exchange—who is obliged to do what for whom—they are likewise free, within broad limits, to invent their own rules of conduct and to structure their relationship in the way that best suits their personal interests. As usual, the structure finally adopted will be the product of negotiation—sometimes protracted, sometimes instantaneous—with each party seeking his own advantage but with both parties, presumably, feeling better off as a result of the exchange.

The role of legal rules in this setting—whether we speak of statutory rules, as in the case of the Uniform Commercial Code, or of common law rules—is important but, in a sense, subordinate. If the parties to a contract had the time and the vision to negotiate and articulate every element that could conceivably bear upon their relationship, weighing every contingency and imagining all possible future states of the world, there would be little need for contract rules as such. The resulting agreement, under these idealized circumstances, would be complete and self-contained; there would be no gaps of meaning and no ambiguity of language or expression, and hence nothing would be left for judicial interpolation or surmise. The courts, then, would function solely as an enforcement mechanism, automatically converting known obligations and entitlements into legal judgments.

The difficulty, of course, is that no contract, however detailed, can or will be wholly comprehensive. Apart from limitations on human foresight, the cost in time and money of sorting out all possible contingencies and then drafting the relevant contract provisions would be prohibitive even for large transactions, and the resulting contract would be as thick as the proverbial phonebook (actually, some are). For the smaller, routine transactions of daily business or personal life, anything more complex and time-consuming than a one- or two-page purchase order is obviously impractical.

Having this circumstance in mind, the primary function of legal rules becomes apparent. Thus, the presence of standing rules on which the parties can rely in the absence of a fully articulated agreement makes it unnecessary to burden every contractual undertaking with the costly process just referred to. By saying nothing in their agreement to the contrary, the contracting parties will be deemed to have adopted the legal rules supplied by statute or common law just as if those rules had been agreed to and written into the contract itself. In effect, the parties can go forward on the assumption that they have a complete contract *without* the need to reach express agreement on each and every question that might have bearing on their relationship, because the legal rules serve to fill in the gaps. This, in turn, means that the rules themselves, if well fashioned, should reflect the arrangements that the contracting parties, in the generality of cases, *would* have wanted and chosen had they actually gone to the trouble and expense of reaching an agreed position on the particular point at issue.[2] Most commentators, I think, would say they largely do.

Once again, however, we should be aware that the legal rules in this field are not obligatory elements of every contract. The parties are by no means bound to adopt those rules, and if their particular interests dictate otherwise, then, in general, they are free to create their own "rules" by explicit contractual provision. Their freedom in this regard is not unlimited—in a very few instances the legal rules are mandatory [3]—but for the most part the parties can either accept or "contract around" the standing rules at will.

———

Note on Risk–Aversion: As suggested above, a contract calling for future performance at a price fixed *currently* operates, in part at least, as a device for reducing risk. Thus, the parties to a

2. Goetz & Scott, *The Limits of Expanded Choice: An Analysis of the Interactions Between Express and Implied Terms,* 73 Calif.L.Rev. 261 (1985); Speidel, *Restatement Second: Omitted Terms and Contract Method,* 67 Cornell L.Rev. 785 (1982); Kronman, *Specific Performance,* 45 U.Chi.L.Rev. 351, 370 (1978).

3. See Ayres & Gertner, *Filling Gaps in Incomplete Contracts: An Economic Theory of Default Rules,* 99 Yale L.J. 87 (1989).

contract calling for a forward exchange of some commodity could elect instead to take a chance on the spot-market price for that commodity at the exchange date instead of committing themselves to a fixed price established today.   One or the other will probably wish he had, since the price-figure agreed to currently simply represents a "best guess" or estimate as to what the future price will actually be.   If market-price rises between now and then, the buyer will be pleased and the seller sorry; if it falls, the opposite. The reason the parties may choose to bind themselves to a fixed price rather than awaiting future market developments obviously relates to the more or less instinctive desire of both to avoid uncertainty.   Apart from recreational gambling, most people find uncertainty disagreeable and prefer to feel assured about the future, especially about the financial future.   Economists speak of this element of normal human psychology as "risk-aversion," and the general assumption is that it is universal, though no doubt differing in relative intensity from one person to another.

The compelling effect of risk-aversion in the formation of contracts calling for future performance is easily illustrated.   Suppose that Buyer and Seller enter into a contract today for the delivery in 6 months of a stated quantity of commodity X.   Assume that the price they agree upon after a little haggling is $100 per unit.   Of course, neither party knows what the spot-market price of X will actually be in 6 months and indeed they, together with other people who are active in the field, foresee a fairly wide range of possible future prices.   In particular, the general consensus of opinion is that the price of commodity X in 6 months will be $125, $100 or $75, depending on how market conditions develop, with each of the three outcomes being equally probable.   Assume further that at the $100 contract price each party is assured of a profit per unit of $10 on the deal.   Thus, Buyer has agreed to resell the commodity to a third party—perhaps after incorporating it into another product—at a price that will generate a $10 profit for Buyer, while Seller—based on labor and material costs that are also fixed by agreement—will similarly make $10 a unit.   The parties could have chosen to leave the purchase price open until the delivery date or not to have entered into a present agreement at all, with consequences that might be relatively favorable to one or the other.   But they didn't choose to do that (at least in my example) and the question is: why not?

Emphasizing the assumed element of risk-aversion, the answer, evidently, is that both prefer a *certain* profit of $10 to the *uncertain* prospect of a $35 profit, a $10 profit, or a $15 loss.

11

Under an open-price arrangement, the outlook for each is as follows:

Buyer/Seller

(1) Future Price	(2) Profit/(Loss)		(3) Probability	(4) Expected Profit/(Loss) (3) x (2)	
$75	$35,	($15)	⅓	$11.67,	(5.00)
100	10,	10	⅓	3.33,	3.33
125	(15),	35	⅓	(5.00),	11.67
				$10	$10

The "expected profit" (*i.e.,* the sum of Column (4)) from an open-price arrangement—$10 for each party—is thus just the same as the assured profit from a contractually agreed-upon price—also $10—but presumably both parties prefer the certainty that goes with agreement to the uncertainty of waiting. This is so, by hypothesis, because the possibility of making an additional $25 ($35–$10), while pleasant, is not *as* happy-making as the possibility of losing $25 ($10–($15)) is painful. For most businesses and individuals, dollar losses generate a greater *loss* of personal or institutional well-being than dollar gains of equal amount generate a *gain*. Hence, if both parties see the future more or less alike, and if both are averse to risk in roughly the same degree, they are likely to prefer a contractual commitment under which each is assured a $10 profit rather than being content to let uncertain nature take its course.

As usual, we can observe that the two parties, despite their arms-length relationship, are really acting in a way that leads to mutual benefit. Buyer desires protection against a sharp rise in market price and is ready to "pay" for such protection by giving up the opportunity to benefit from a sharp fall; Seller is prepared to do the opposite. Each party wants to minimize the risk that necessarily attaches to future events, and the contract, with its fixed-price component, is an effective means of attaining that objective.

Chapter 2

CONSIDERATION AND THE BARGAINED–FOR EXCHANGE

Chapter 1 makes the not very surprising point that the chief function of contract law is to provide a framework for the enforcement of promises. Since, however, the law cannot be concerned, even by implication, with every promise that people make in their daily lives, the first question that has to be faced is how to distinguish between those promises that merit enforcement by legal means and those that don't. The answer is largely (but, as it turns out, not exclusively) to be found in the common-law requirement of "consideration", which, in simplest terms, denotes the receipt by the promisor of "something of value" from the promisee. As already observed, contract law is centrally concerned with the everyday business of exchange—apples for oranges and all that—and hence legal enforcement is chiefly addressed to undertakings that arise in that context.

Section 17 of the Restatement * expresses the general understanding on this well-worn topic by stating that, except where special rules apply, the formation of a contract requires "a bargain" to which the contracting parties give assent, and "a consideration", which can take the form of either a return promise or an actual performance. Thus, most contractual arrangements that are made in a business setting involve an exchange of promises to do something in the future: Seller promises to deliver certain merchandise in 30 days; in return, Buyer promises to pay Seller $X when the merchandise is delivered. Here, the consideration for each party's promise is the promise made by the other. Once promises are exchanged, there is a "contract" and both parties are bound to perform accordingly. Less commonly, perhaps, consideration for a promise may consist *solely* of a "performance" by the promisee. C promises to pay D $10 if D mows C's lawn. D is not asked to say "I promise" but just to go ahead and mow. C's promise to pay becomes binding if and when the service is rendered by D (or, at least, commenced). In conventional terminology, contracts of the first sort—those involving an exchange of promises—are referred to as "bilateral"; contracts of the second kind—those involving an exchange of a promise for a perform-

---

* All Restatement references are to the Restatement of the Law, Second, of Contracts.

13

ance—are called "unilateral". As suggested in Chapter 3, the distinction between bilateral and unilateral contracts has legal and conceptual consequences that go beyond mere terminology, but for the moment we can simply note that the requirement of consideration may be met either by promising or by doing, depending on the context.

As stated, the aim of the consideration requirement, speaking very generally, is to tie legal enforcement to the common act of trading one thing for another. On the other hand, the ways in which people deal with each other are infinitely various and idiosyncratic, and for that reason it seems unlikely that any single doctrinal idea can succeed in being both broad enough and particular enough to cover every situation that arises. Consider, for example, a voluntary promise to pay retirement benefits. Thus, X Corporation, acting through its board of directors, promises to pay Z, a long-time employee, a monthly pension when Z retires. Taking X at its word, Z does retire after a short time and makes no effort to find another job. X pays the pension for a few years but then, having undergone a change in management, stops. Can Z enforce X's promise at that point? One certainly hopes so. To be sure, X received nothing measurable or tangible from Z in return for its promise to pay the pension. Yet it seems entirely plain that a failure to enforce Z's claim would work a fearful injustice, since Z, we can assume, is now too old and infirm to do anything but starve. To avoid this dire result, we (or a sympathetic court) could indulge in a little factual or semantic manipulation and find that Z's "early retirement" really was a valid consideration for X's promise. But if that is too farfetched, then we might frankly recognize that the consideration requirement operates too narrowly to promote fair outcomes in these and similar circumstances and conclude that an alternative basis for the enforcement of promises—here, obviously, the promisee's "induced reliance"—needs to be adopted.

As noted, Restatement Section 17 provides that a "contract" requires a "bargain" and a "consideration" *except* where "special rules" apply. It is, of course, the exceptions and the special-rule occasions that are of interest, and hence the discussion that follows is largely concerned with those cases in which the requirement of consideration does *not* apply. To keep perspective, however, we should remind ourselves that these "exceptional" situations are just that, and that in the common run of business and consumer dealings the element of consideration is present virtually by definition. I should add that the aim of this Chapter is merely to outline the traditional bases for the enforcement of promises in contract law—consideration, promissory estoppel, and moral obligation—and not by any means to canvass or exhaust the entire subject of consideration and its alternatives. Particular applications are to be found elsewhere—in Chapter 3, for example, in connection with firm offers and revocation, in Chapter 4 in connection with contract modification and duress, and in Chapter 5 in connection with exclusive agency agreements and requirements contracts. In each of those contexts, as it happens, the formal nature of the consideration requirement has sometimes made it harder, rather than easier, to reach sensible results, and not infrequently it has had to be subordinated to other legal criteria.

A final introductory note may be in order. It has often been observed that lay persons—non-lawyers—sometimes seem to think that an agreement has to be in writing in order to be legally binding. That, of course, is not true. A spoken promise is no less effective as a matter of law than a written promise, and indeed most, or at least many, of the transactions that people enter into in daily life—small-scale retail purchases, short-term employment arrangements—are based on "contracts" and entail binding promises even though there is no "writing" that embodies the parties' understanding. Going further, Restatement Section 19 confirms that a promise may be expressed "in acts", that is, without words, and indeed, as indicated in the next Chapter, the commencement of performance may by itself constitute a "return promise" that is sufficient to create a bilateral contract.

The point should not, of course, be overstressed. Almost any exchange that involves substantial outlays or complexity of detail is likely to be reduced to writing and to be signed by the parties, although in many instances the cost of formalization is held to a minimum through the use of standardized contract forms. As a safeguard against spurious claims, moreover, the Statute of Frauds, applicable with minor variations in every State, forbids the enforcement of certain classes of contracts—among others, sales of land, suretyships, and service contracts not to be performed within one year—unless evidenced by a "written memorandum". UCC 2–201 contains a like restriction applicable to sales of "goods" for a price of $500 or more. Neither the Statute nor the UCC means that oral agreements within the affected classes cannot be made and performed—they are not in any sense illegal—but only that enforcement may be unavailable if one party or the other refuses to fulfil her obligations. A sizable body of relatively uninteresting jurisprudence has grown up around the Statute of Frauds, much of it aimed at confining and limiting the application of the Statute. Some of this is adverted to at various points, but the Statute and its case-law progeny are not otherwise systematically discussed in this volume.

A. Promises to Make a Gift

Donative promises—parent, for example, promising to give child a new car when child graduates from college—would appear to fall entirely outside the "bargain" configuration that underlies the formation of a binding contract. The parent's promise may create a happy expectation in the child, but the parent is obviously free—without, as a legal matter, risking anything more than the child's hard feelings—to change her mind. For the reason, I suppose, that a disappointed donee suffers relatively little in the way of measurable damages, the general rule is that a promise to make a gift in the future is not enforceable.

But suppose that the promisor demands specific conduct from the promisee as a condition of the gift; or suppose the promisee, counting on the promisor to keep her word, incurs irreversible obligations of her own. A promisor who reneges under these circumstances can certainly be criticised for having behaved in a misleading fashion. The question here, however, is whether, apart from recriminations and other forms of personal revenge, the promisee has any strictly legal recourse. Are there situations in which the promise to make a future gift is actually treated as enforceable, either on the ground that promisor and promisee have in some sense struck a "bargain" or because the promisee has made commitments in reliance on the promisor's good faith?

In *Hamer v. Sidway,*[1] Uncle William promised to give young Willie, his nephew and namesake, the sum of $5,000 if the lad, then 15 years old, would refrain from smoking, drinking and gambling until he reached the age of 21. Willie evidently did refrain and on reaching his majority wrote to his Uncle requesting the promised sum. In a letter of reply, Uncle William stated that he would carry out his promise by placing $5,000 in a bank account for Willie's benefit and would keep the fund "on interest" until he thought his nephew capable of using it wisely. "I would hate very much," wrote Uncle, a self-made man, "to have you start out in some adventure that you thought all right and lose this money in one year." Getting the money in the first place, he explained, "cost me a heap of hard work . . . ." Willie apparently made no objection to this decision, at least none that was recorded.

1. 124 N.Y. 538, 27 N.E. 256 (1891).

A dozen years then passed into history, during which time (as recounted by the court below) Willie borrowed from Uncle, but lost and never repaid, some $13,000 in money and merchandise. Willie finally declared bankruptcy, though without disclosing to his creditors any interest in the $5,000 bank account, having previously (so he said) transferred that interest to his wife. Uncle died at the end of this period, and the plaintiff, to whom Willie's claim was hastily reassigned, demanded that the defendant, as executor of Uncle's estate, pay over the $5,000 account (plus accumulated interest) to her. Defendant refused on the asserted ground, among others, that as Uncle had received no consideration for his original promise to Willie, no contract existed which the assignee of Willie's wife could now enforce.

Reversing the lower court, which had characterized the claim as an assault on the estate by dissatisfied relatives, the New York Court of Appeals held for the plaintiff. In promising to "pay" Willie $5,000 for being abstemious until he reached age 21, Uncle had in fact induced Willie to "forbear" from doing things he had a legal right to do. Willie *used* to smoke and drink occasionally, it appeared, but he stopped like a good fellow when offered a monetary inducement by his uncle. Under settled law, said the Court, surrendering one's freedom of action is sufficient consideration for a promise; in effect, Willie "performed", even though performance consisted of a forbearance rather than an affirmative act. It was of course true that Uncle, intending Willie's good more than his own, received no tangible benefit himself. But the courts do not, as a general rule, inquire into the "adequacy" of consideration—that being a matter for the private judgment of the parties—and if Uncle thought it worth $5,000 to get Willie to avoid bad habits, then there was "nothing . . . that would permit a determination that the uncle was not benefited in a legal sense."

Solely from the standpoint of doctrine—and putting aside one's less than favorable view of young Willie himself—the decision in *Hamer v. Sidway* is generally regarded as correct. There *was* a bargained-for consideration of sorts, and apparently Uncle got the result he sought. As compared with other things Uncle might have bought with his money, I suppose good behavior on Willie's part ranked reasonably high, and there can be little doubt that Uncle, if asked, would have *wanted* Willie to believe that the money would finally be his. In social terms, the transaction was a bit unusual—senior family members do not typically "buy" good conduct from juniors—and we might doubt whether it is really worthwhile to invoke costly legal processes in support of Uncle's moral standards. On the other hand, if a donor-promisor actually wishes to make his gift the subject of a "deal", and particularly if the amount involved is not trivial, then, arguably, there may be no more reason in this context than in a conventional setting to deny the parties an opportunity to capture welfare gains through trade.

But suppose the underlying arrangement lacks the "bargain" feature said to be present in the *Hamer* case, or that the element of benefit to the promisor is simply too remote to be recognized. Is the absence of consideration always fatal from the standpoint of a disappointed donee-promisee, or are there other grounds on which the enforcement of a future gift-promise might be justified? In *Ricketts v. Scothorn*,[2] a kindly grandfather, eager to make life easier for a granddaughter who was slaving away in a shop at a salary of $10 a week, gave the granddaughter his demand note for $2,000 with annual interest at 6%. Grandfather expressed the hope that the yearly interest would enable granddaughter to quit her miserable job if she chose. While quitting the job was not a requirement or condition of the gift, granddaughter did abandon her employment at that point, although she went back to work a year later, apparently because grandfather was unable to keep up the interest payments. At grandfather's death, granddaughter demanded that his estate pay the principal amount of the note and on being refused brought suit against the executor.

Drawing on decisions involving the enforcement of pledges to charity, the Supreme Court of Nebraska held for the plaintiff. The Court conceded, indeed it emphasized, that there was no consideration to support the grandfather's promise. Ordinarily, it said, a mere promise to make a gift in the future is not enforceable. But where a donee, relying in good faith on the donor's promise, is led thereby to spend money, incur debts or take some other costly and irreversible step, the donor may be "estopped" on grounds of equity and fairness from asserting "want of consideration". This is true, at least, where the promisor's object is

2. 57 Neb. 51, 77 N.W. 365 (1898). Compare Kirksey v. Kirksey, 8 Ala. 131 (1845), another casebook standby in the field of family gifts. Having learned of his brother's death, the defendant wrote to his bereaved sister-in-law inviting her to give up her current residence and come with her children to live in a more comfortable house on his ample property. His reason: "I feel like I want you and the children to do well." The plaintiff accepted the invitation and happily moved into the comfortable house, but after two years the defendant changed his mind and forced the plaintiff to pack up and move to a miserable hut "in the woods". Subsequently, he threw her out altogether. The explanation for this apparent cruelty is unknown (to us), but I suppose we might guess that the two former in-laws at some point formed a "relationship", that the relationship later broke down, and that the defendant then took steps to eliminate all ties.

In any event, the Court, holding that the defendant's promise was a mere gratuity and lacked consideration, refused to award the plaintiff damages for breach despite the obvious element of reliance.

reasonably clear at the time the promise is made. In the case of a charitable pledge, the promisor's aim might be to support the construction of a facility—say a hospital wing—or to fund a research project. In the present case, the donor's object was to free his granddaughter from the obligation to continue her employment, and in fact she did give up her job at his suggestion. "Having intentionally influenced the plaintiff to alter her position for the worse on the faith of the note being paid when due, it would be grossly inequitable to permit the maker, or his executor, to resist payment on the ground that the promise was given without consideration. The petition charges the elements of an equitable estoppel, and the evidence conclusively establishes them."

The concept of "estoppel" based on the promisor's representations to the promisee—now generally referred to as promissory estoppel—is reflected, with refinements and enlargements, in Section 90 of the Restatement, discussed in more detail below. Briefly, Section 90 provides that a promise which is expected by the promisor to induce the promisee to take some action, and which does induce such action, is binding and enforceable if necessary to avoid injustice. Reliance by the promisee may thus be sufficient to create an enforcement right against the promisor, even though the transaction does not involve a "bargain" between the parties and even though the promisor receives no "consideration". Grandfather Ricketts sought neither a return promise nor a performance from his granddaughter; his promise was nonreciprocal in the sense that it imposed no obligation on the promisee. Grandfather did, however, intend and expect that granddaughter would quit her job and opt for a life of leisure. She understood his purpose and she opted, confident of his support. There was no element of exchange, but there was foreseeable reliance, and that, in the Court's view, justified enforcement.

Taken together, the *Hamer* and *Ricketts* cases suggest a threefold classification of family gift-promises, which can be illustrated as follows:

(1) A promises to pay B, her niece, $10,000 if B, now employed as a bartender, will quit her job and go to law-school, payment to be made on graduation day. A, a lawyer herself, thinks law is a nobler profession than tending bar and wants B to continue in the family tradition.

(2) A is told that B is sick of tending bar and wishes to go to law-school but will have to borrow heavily to meet expenses. Eager to forward B's ambitions, A promises that when B graduates she, A, will pay off B's student loans up to a limit of $10,000.

(3) A, glad that B wants to give up bartending and go to law-school, promises to give B $10,000 as a graduation present.

Assume in each instance that B does go to law-school and graduates, but that A refuses to come across with the $10,000. If the matter is actually litigated, I suppose we might expect the following results: enforcement of A's promise in Case (1), because, as in *Hamer v. Sidway,* there was a "bargain" and a "consideration"; enforcement in Case (2), because, as in *Ricketts,* A's promise should reasonably have been expected to induce, and did induce, action on B's part that involved a significant cost; but no enforcement in Case (3), because A merely promised B a gratuity and was always free to change her mind.

To be sure, the outcomes just suggested assume that we can tell with some degree of confidence just which of the three cases is actually up for decision. A has put nothing in writing, however, and hence the parties' understanding would have to be derived by reconstructing the conversation that took place between them when they discussed the matter across the kitchen table. The quality of the evidence, therefore, is likely to be rather doubtful—especially so if, as in *Hamer* and *Ricketts,* A is no longer among the living at the time of the trial—and there is the obvious possibility of selective recall. But even if we knew exactly what had been said, the fact is that the three cases, although distinguishable in formal terms, are really very much alike at bottom. Quite simply, A wished to help B to a better future, and B persuaded herself that law-school was marginally preferable to mixing drinks. Whether viewed as a "bargain", an "inducement", or a "gratuity", all that was really involved was A's desire to act generously towards B and B's confidence in A's good will. Essentially, and in common understanding, the relationship between the parties was based not on legal commitment, but on trust and family feeling. The notion that B would ever regard herself as rendering a service to A for which she could later claim compensation is, despite *Hamer,* quite absurd; and while B doubtless hoped that A would continue in a generous frame of mind, the possibility that A might be unwilling—or, as in *Ricketts,* unable—to make the promised gift would surely have been considered by B and would temper her reliance.

In any event, and although approved by the Restatement, the decisions in *Hamer* and *Ricketts* appear to be fairly singular. The courts, perhaps concerned about the risk of false claims, have seldom enforced donative promises in a family setting, being unwilling, on the whole, either to construe such promises as bargained-for or to find significant reliance on the part of the promisee. The two decisions themselves, really, are little more than casebook curiosities and can probably be explained on the ground that neither of the promisors actually revoked or withdrew the future gift-promise during his lifetime. The litigation in both cases was not (as it would be in the hypotheticals above) between a promisee and a promisor attempting to resist enforcement, but between the promisee and the promisor's executor, the latter acting on behalf of other relatives named in the promisor's Will. In practical terms the question was not whether the promisor himself should be made to pay, but how to divide the promisor's estate among his quarreling descendants. Doctrinal issues aside, I think it may have appeared to the respective courts that each of the promisors (certainly Grandfather Ricketts, but probably Uncle William as well) went to his final rest wanting and intending that his gift to the plaintiff be completed ahead of other bequests; indeed, both promisors may actually have assumed that their gifts *had* been completed during life—in Uncle's case by placing the money in a designated bank account, in Grandfather's, by delivery of a demand note to the donee. Possibly (even probably) the court in each case felt that it was effectuating the decedent's true testamentary purpose by enforcing his promise, and it may well have been *that* perception, rather than the element of consideration or of reliance (both pretty much trumped-up and artificial), that ultimately led to the results described.

Given the strictures of the consideration requirement, some writers have argued that donor-promisors who specifically wish to be liable to their donee-promisees ought to be free, by purely formal means, to *render* their promises enforceable.[3] If Uncle William actually wants to obligate himself (or his estate) to his nephew, why make things difficult by requiring the nephew to show, later on, that Uncle's promise had been supported by consideration? In earlier times the seal served the purpose just mentioned, because a promise made under seal, even though it was a gift-promise and without consideration, was generally regarded as binding. This, of course, is no longer true: the legal efficacy of hot wax and engraved signet rings has been eliminated by decision or statute in almost every state, although legal stationers can still provide you with gummed wafers and red ribbons if you want them. Actually, however, the place of the seal has been taken by yet another type of formal observance, namely, the recital of nominal consideration. Thus, in exchange for "one dollar in hand paid, receipt whereof is hereby acknowledged", X makes a promise

3. Posner, *Gratuitous Promises in Economics and Law,* 6 J.Legal Studies 411 (1977).

of some sort to Y. As already noted, apart from allegations of fraud or legal incapacity, the courts do not ordinarily inquire into the adequacy of consideration. It is the *existence* of a bargain that matters, not whether the bargain is equal or unequal from the standpoint of an objective observer. Accordingly, it is at least arguable that a future gift promise is enforceable if it is in writing and is given the form of a bargain, even though there is no consideration for the promise in fact.

But should the law treat mere formality (whether by seal or recital) as sufficient to support a gift promise? The answer, one would think, depends on why we hesitate about enforcing future gift promises in the first place. If our reason is a worry about false claims, misunderstandings and the like, then the affixing of a seal or a recital of nominal consideration might be taken as proof that the donor's promise had been made in a conscious and deliberate frame of mind, although the existence of a signed "writing" by itself seems sufficient to show that. On the other hand, if our reason for withholding enforcement is that we think donee-promisees are unlikely to be much harmed when unrelied-upon gift promises are not kept, or if we feel that donors really *ought* to be free to change their minds (e.g., because later the donor either goes broke or loses her affection for the donee), then mere formality at the time the promise is made would appear to be insufficient if not irrelevant.[4]

Without quite knowing where to look for a definitive statement of policy on donative promises, I take some comfort from the rather confident hunch that the whole problem, despite its casebook prominence, cannot really be very important. As in *Ricketts,* promises that are relied upon by the donee to her detriment will be enforced on that ground even though consideration is lacking, so that donees who are truly harmed by the donor's failure to keep her word are to that extent protected. But even where there is no reliance factor, donors who wish to make gifts which the donee will *receive* in the future can easily do so by transferring their property in trust for the donee's benefit. The trust instrument would direct the trustee to distribute the property to the donee on the occurrence of some future event—when the donee reaches age 21, say, or graduates from law-school—but to return the property to the donor if the future event fails to occur. The donor's intention to make a future gift would be largely realized by this device, yet the transfer in trust would be regarded as a *present*

4. See Eisenberg, *Donative Promises,* 47 U.Chi.L.Rev. 1 (1979); Goetz & Scott, *Enforcing Promises: An Examination of* the Basis of Contract, 89 Yale L.J. 1261 (1980).

gift—completed when made—and the question of consideration would not arise.

B. Reliance and Promissory Estoppel

Whatever one thinks of the *Ricketts* decision, it has long seemed evident that the bargain-theory of consideration operates too narrowly and too inflexibly to do equity in all circumstances. One way to put the point is to say that there appears to be a mixed set of "interactive dealings" that stands midway between conventional swap transactions, in which consideration is present by definition, and wholly nonreciprocal gift-promises, in which consideration is plainly lacking. What characterizes such dealings, as suggested, is a promise on one side and a cost—but neither a "return promise" nor a "performance"—on the other. An automatic application of the consideration requirement under these circumstances would preclude enforcement and would excuse the promisor from financial accountability. Yet it is obvious that the promise and the cost are causally related—there is at least an inference of reciprocity—and simple fairness suggests that the law would be deficient in reflecting reasonable expectations unless a remedy of some sort were made available to the promisee.

As already mentioned, the task of supplying flexibility in this area is largely entrusted to the doctrine of promissory estoppel, which treats the promisee's "reliance" as an independent and sufficient basis for enforcement. The Restatement continues to adhere to the requirement of a bargained-for consideration in general terms. By way of exception, however, Section 90 provides that—

> "(1) A promise which the promisor should reasonably expect to induce action or forbearance on the part of the promisee or a third person and which does induce such action or forbearance is binding if injustice can be avoided only by enforcement of the promise. The remedy granted for breach may be limited as justice requires."

In effect, a promisee acting in reliance can obtain enforcement even though consideration for the promise is lacking, although the promisee's remedy may be "limited"—may be less in amount, presumably, than the customary measure of expectation damages.

The doctrine of promissory estoppel has been applied to charitable subscriptions, to cases involving gratuitous bailments in which the bailee undertakes to preserve or insure the property delivered to her care, to oral promises to convey land on which the promisee then enters and makes improvements, and, as indicated, occasionally to family gifts. The courts have divided on the voluntary payment of retirement benefits to employees: thus, as noted earlier, a promise to pay a pension to a long-time bookkeeper—out of friendship, but perhaps also as a way of encouraging her early retirement—has been held enforceable under Section 90 even though not bargained for by the promisee [5], but enforcement was denied where the promisee was an independent sales agent and the promise to continue paying partial commissions following the termination of his agency was found to be gratuitous [6].

While Section 90 authorizes the enforcement of a promise solely on the basis of the promisee's reliance, the question of whether, in the first place, there has been a communication that actually *qualifies* as a promise may itself present some difficulty. In *East Providence Credit Union v. Geremia*,[7] the plaintiff-bank made a standard car-purchase loan to the defendants, the loan being secured by a chattel mortgage on the car itself. The loan agreement required the defendants to carry collision insurance, naming the bank as payee, and provided that if defendants failed to keep the policy in force by paying the premiums when due, the bank could pay such premiums and add the amount thereof, with interest, to the principal of the defendants' debt.

Having received notice that defendants' insurance was about to be cancelled for non-payment of premiums, the bank sent the defendants a nasty form letter that said:

"We are in receipt of a cancellation notice on your Policy. If we are not notified of a renewal Policy within 10 days, we shall be forced to renew the policy for you and apply this amount to your loan."

Defendants reacted by calling the bank and telling a clerk that they were broke and that the bank should therefore go ahead and pay the premium. A few weeks later, and at a time when the defendants still owed the bank about $1,000 on the original loan, the car was totally demolished in an accident. Had the insurance policy still been in effect, the proceeds would have been paid to the bank and would presumably have satisfied the defendants' debt in full. In fact, however, the bank never did pay the overdue premium and the policy was cancelled before the accident. The loan then being in default, the bank applied to principal some $200 which the defendants had in a savings account and sued for

5. Feinberg v. Pfeiffer Co., 322 S.W.2d 163 (Mo.App.1959).

6. Pitts v. McGraw–Edison Co., 329 F.2d 412 (6th Cir.1964).

7. 103 R.I. 597, 239 A.2d 725 (1968).

the $800 balance. Insisting that they owed nothing because the bank had bound itself to renew the policy in a timely fashion, defendants counterclaimed for their $200 savings account.

The Supreme Court of Rhode Island, though saying relatively little about the particular facts of the case itself, enthusiastically adopted Section 90 as the law of the State and held for the defendants. The doctrine of promissory estoppel, said the Court, provides "a much needed remedy to alleviate the plight of those who suffer a serious injustice as a result of their good-faith reliance on the unfulfilled promises of others." Citing an Arkansas decision in which promissory estoppel was praised as "an attempt by the courts to keep remedies abreast of increased moral consciousness of honesty and fair representations in all business dealings", the Court declared that it gladly subscribed to "those sentiments." As a sort of back-up or reinforcement, however, the Court also found that there really *had* been a consideration for the bank's promise, because the loan agreement gave the bank the right to add the renewal premium to the principal of the defendants' loan and to charge additional interest on the recomputed balance.

Was the decision in the *East Providence* case correct or merely compassionate? The Court's holding, and particularly its application of the promissory estoppel doctrine, seems justified *if* we accept what appear to have been its factual premises, namely, (a) that the bank really did "promise" to renew the policy and (b) that the defendants "relied" on that promise in some material way. But did the bank actually promise anything? The language of the bank's form letter—"If we are not notified . . ., we shall be forced to . . ."—sounds more like a threat than a promise to me, and I think anyone receiving such a letter would at once understand that the sender's purpose was not to make a commitment but to collect a debt. In effect, the letter warned the defendants that, unless they did as *they* had promised, the bank would feel compelled to protect its own interest in the loan collateral at their expense. To construe that warning as a "promise"—one that entitled the defendants to hop in their car and drive about without even checking to *see* if the insurance problem had been taken care of—is to convert what was supposed to be a club into a boomerang. The bank probably did plan to renew the policy and simply slipped up. Pretty plainly, however, it had no intention either of obligating itself to renew or of inducing reliance in the defendants, and the phrase "we shall be forced to . . ." hardly justified the latter in believing otherwise.

The question raised in the *East Providence* case—whether there has been a "promise" and a justified reliance within the meaning of

Section 90—comes up again, as will be seen, in connection with the important subject of offer-and-acceptance. Thus, A offers to sell Blackacre to B at a stated price. B spends time and money investigating the proposal, but before she can accept A withdraws the offer. Does Section 90 afford B a remedy in these circumstances, or should we consider that B simply took a risk when she failed to accept A's offer at the time it was made? Going further, suppose C tells D that she will offer D a franchise to sell certain merchandise if D can raise a stated amount of investment capital. D raises the capital by selling various assets that she owns, but C then decides that D's funds are insufficient and refuses to make the franchise available. Again, does D have enforcement rights against C under the rule of Section 90, or should D have nailed the matter down in some way at the very beginning? These and related issues receive an airing in Chapter 3.

C. Moral Obligation and Past Consideration

Promissory estoppel—the concept of reliance-based enforcement—represents the principal exception to the standard requirement of consideration, but not the only exception. Yet another class of promises that sometimes appear to call for enforcement despite the absence of consideration (at least of present consideration) consists of promises made in recognition of a benefit received in the past. As a general proposition, a person who performs unrequested services for another does not thereby acquire a right to compensation or restitution, even though the performance entailed a cost to the former and a benefit to the latter. In effect, if you do somebody a favor, you cannot convert your generosity into an enforceable contract claim; services that were intended to be voluntary and gratuitous remain so as a matter of legal presumption. There are, of course, limits to this "rule". Thus, a doctor who gives emergency treatment to an accident victim is assumed to be responding to the latter's request and can therefore recover the fair value of her professional services [8]. In general, however, one who makes a gift, including a gift of services, cannot afterwards withdraw her gift by reconstituting herself a creditor.

But suppose that the beneficiary of the voluntary service—grateful, perhaps embarrassed—subsequently *promises* to compensate the volunteer for the value of the benefit received. Should that promise be treated as binding on a sort of hindsight view of events, or should it simply be regarded as a future-gift promise—returning the favor, so to speak—and hence, on general principles, be held unenforceable if the promisor later changes her mind?

8. Cotnam v. Wisdom, 83 Ark. 601, 104 S.W. 164 (1907).

In *Mills v. Wyman*,[9] the plaintiff, as an act of kindness, gave shelter, food and some sort of medical attention to the defendant's son, who, having returned from a "voyage at sea," was found by the plaintiff wandering the lonely streets of Hartford ill and destitute. The son, age 25, died after a couple of weeks and the plaintiff then wrote to the defendant (who lived in Massachusetts) telling him what had happened and requesting reimbursement for the plaintiff's added expenses. Although he had no legal obligation to pay his son's bills, the son being an adult, the defendant instantly wrote back promising to reimburse the plaintiff in the amount requested. Later, however, apparently after some reflection (and perhaps after making further inquiries), the defendant changed his mind and refused to pay. His reason for refusing— whether just cold-hearted stinginess or something else—we never learn.

At all events, the Supreme Court of Massachusetts, with evident regret, held for the defendant on the ground that there had been no legal consideration for the defendant's promise. The defendant obviously hadn't asked the plaintiff to care for his son— the plaintiff had "acted the part of the good Samaritan" and had simply volunteered his services. Accordingly, there was no present consideration for the defendant's promise. While past consideration might sometimes be sufficient—as, for example, where a debtor promises to pay a debt previously contracted but now discharged in bankruptcy or barred by the statute of limitations— here there was no pre-existing obligation because the son was of full age and lived independently of his father's family. Having received nothing from the plaintiff, the defendant's promise must be regarded as gratuitous, a promise to make a gift. The defendant's moral duty to keep his promise would be recognized by everyone; but as there could be no legal enforcement absent some "gain" to the promisor, the matter would have to be left "to the interior forum, as the tribunal of conscience has been aptly called". There was, in the Court's view, an overriding need to protect the security of those "honest and fair-minded men, who may inconsiderately make promises without any equivalent", even if the consequence here was to relieve a promisor whose behavior should be regarded as "disgraceful".

The decision in *Mills* can be (always is) contrasted with that in *Webb v. McGowin*,[10] where the promisor himself was the beneficiary of the plaintiff's rescue efforts. According to the allegations in the complaint, Webb, a workman employed by a lumber mill,

9. 3 Pick. 207 (Mass.1825).

10. 27 Ala.App. 82, 168 So. 196 (1935).

had been on the point of dropping a huge pine block from an upper floor of the mill to the ground below when he perceived that the falling block would be likely to crush McGowin, who had suddenly appeared from nowhere and now stood directly beneath him. To prevent this catastrophe, Webb elected to go over the side along with the block, in that way diverting the block away from McGowin but sustaining crippling injuries to himself. Subsequently, and allegedly in consideration of the plaintiff's act of self-sacrifice, McGowin, who also happened to be president of the company, promised to pay Webb $15 every two weeks for the rest of his life. McGowin did make such payments on a regular basis during his own lifetime, but following McGowin's death his executors refused to continue the payments, claiming that McGowin's promise to Webb had been without consideration.

Reversing the lower court, which had granted the defendant-executors' motion to dismiss, the Alabama Court of Appeals held that the plaintiff's allegations of fact sufficed to state a legal basis for the enforcement of McGowin's promise. Admittedly, McGowin had no strictly legal obligation to Webb at the time he made his promise: having behaved as a "volunteer", Webb evidently had no claim against McGowin for restitution, and it was not suggested that McGowin had himself caused Webb's injuries through any act of personal negligence. In that sense McGowin's promise was gratuitous. Plainly, however, McGowin had realized a material benefit in being saved by Webb from death or serious harm; equally plainly in view of Webb's resulting disability, McGowin had a moral obligation to compensate Webb for his loss. While he could have ignored it, McGowin chose instead to affirm and ratify that obligation by promising to pay Webb a lifetime annuity. "Material benefit" plus "moral obligation" added up to a "valid consideration", and hence McGowin's promise was enforceable even though made after the event.

Taken together, *Webb v. McGowin* and *Mills v. Wyman* obviously suggest that moral obligation may support a promise in the absence of traditional consideration, but only if the promisor has been personally benefited or enriched by the promisee's sacrifice and there is, as a consequence, a just and reasonable claim for compensation. No clearer case of an enrichment-and-sacrifice can be imagined than that in *Webb v. McGowin* (at least that alleged [11]). The decision in *Mills* is painful (unless, again, there was

11. The executors apparently settled with Webb instead of going to trial. It is, of course, just possible that the latter's injuries were the result of an ordinary, if dreadful, workplace accident; that McGowin simply took pity on a disabled employee to whom no other compensation was available; and that the life-saving "story" was exactly that

more to the story than we are told), but presumably it can be accepted on the ground that the defendant's promise was simply a shock-reaction to the news of his son's death and was given without forethought or deliberation. Actually, "moral obligation" does not appear to have been a logically necessary criterion in either case. Thus, moral obligation by itself entitled the respective plaintiffs to nothing whatever *until* a promise had been made. But once there *was* a promise moral obligation became irrelevant, because the decisive question then, indeed the only question, was whether the promisor had received a personal benefit for which the plaintiff could justly demand compensation.

Rescue cases like *Webb* and *Mills* are uncommon, as has been observed,[12] and perhaps we ought to try to test the benefit-received principle in a more conventional setting. Under ordinary circumstances, someone seeking to purchase a service would offer—that is, promise—to pay the service-provider a stated sum for the service that she wants. The offer to pay, made after due deliberation, invites a consideration in the form of a performance (or perhaps a promise to perform), and once the consideration has been supplied by the promisee there is a "contract" and the promisor is bound. But suppose the process is *reversed* in time, with the performance actually preceding the promise to pay. D mows C's lawn while C is away on vacation and then asks C to pay her whatever C thinks the service is worth. D presumably has no legal claim on C at this point because C never requested the service and obviously cannot return it as if it were a misdelivered package. But suppose C, perhaps feeling embarrassed and somewhat cornered, promises to pay D $10 on the following Tuesday. Subsequently, however, C changes her mind and refuses to pay. Is C's promise binding even though she was under no legal obligation to D when she made it, or should the promise be treated as gratuitous and unenforceable even though the lawn was, in fact, neatly mowed?

The answer, probably, is that enforcement would be denied. To be sure, C has received a benefit and $10 appears to be a reasonable price for the service. But D's act in imposing the service on C without C's request is obviously a high-pressure sales tactic which one hesitates to reward or encourage. Section 86 of the Restatement provides that a promise made in recognition of a benefit previously received is binding to the extent necessary to prevent injustice (the additional requirement of moral obligation

(McGowin no longer being available to confirm or deny).

12. S.D. Henderson, *Promises Grounded in the Past: The Idea of Unjust En-* *richment and the Law of Contracts,* 57 Va.L.Rev. 1115 (1971).

is simply dropped) *unless* the benefit was conferred "as a gift or for other reasons the promisor has not been unjustly enriched". Reflecting the decision in *Drake v. Bell* [13], the explanatory comment indicates that C's promise would be binding if D, having been employed to mow a neighbor's lawn, had simply mowed C's lawn by mistake. In that circumstance, D's motives are innocent and the benefit-received principle justifies treating C's subsequent promise to pay as a kind of ratification or approval of the transaction. Curiously, the pure "imposition" case is not illustrated in the Restatement commentary, although, as in the mistake case, both a promise and a benefit-received are present. In the end, however, I suppose we can conclude that an imposed-upon promisor would be regarded as having been victimized rather than *unjustly* enriched, while the promisee would be viewed as having taken a conscious risk that her unrequested service might earn her nothing. It follows, I think, that neither the courts nor the Restatement would treat a promise made under these conditions as binding.

I should add that the foregoing by no means exhausts the subject of restitution, unjust enrichment and "quasi-contractual" relief. The topic comes up again, and in a more significant context, under the general heading of Remedies in Chapter 8.

13. 26 Misc. 237, 55 N.Y.S. 945 (1899).

Chapter 3

CONTRACT FORMATION

The formation of an enforceable contract involves a two-step procedure with which everyone is instinctively familiar. Thus, we offer our legal services to a prospective client for cash; the client, one hopes, accepts. We ourselves are besieged with offers of consumption goods and investment opportunities, and *we* accept if the exchange seems beneficial. The critical process elements—offer and acceptance—are learned quickly and early on by almost everyone, and at the level of daily conduct they require little more than an exercise of intuitive preferences.

On occasion, however, the question of whether an "offer" has been made that the law will recognize as such, and if so whether it has been "accepted", becomes the subject of dispute. The reason, most often, is that one party or the other has changed his mind. Having taken steps that seem to evidence an intention to offer or accept, the individual or the firm suddenly has second thoughts: the price initially proposed now seems too high or too low, or the terms of sale now seem too generous or too burdensome, or perhaps a better deal is proposed by someone else. Since an enforceable obligation attaches only if there has been an "offer" and an "acceptance" in legal terms, one avenue of escape may be to argue that the putative transaction is lacking in either or both of those vital supports. The problem, then, in general, is to determine whether the reluctant party went so far in the direction of the other party, whether by word or conduct, as to generate an irreversible undertaking. The answer, I think, while partly to be found in the doctrinal elements discussed in Section A of this chapter, ultimately depends on how the circumstances of the particular case are perceived and interpreted by a court or a jury.

The problem just mentioned—whether the parties have in fact struck a deal—is greatly complicated by the long-standing common law rule that an offeror may revoke his offer at any time prior to its acceptance by the offeree. Except as limited by the doctrine of promissory estoppel and, in some instances, by statute, the offeror is free, in effect, to terminate the offeree's power to accept by exercising his own power of revocation. Such termination may result also if the offeree takes action that can be interpreted, even if not really intended, as a rejection of the original offer—for example, by making a counteroffer in reply.

31

The consequence of all this, as the discussion in Section B should suggest, is to raise vexing questions about which party acted first, what was meant or understood by the words used or the action taken, and so on.

In this connection, and before getting involved in details, it may be worthwhile to remind oneself, very briefly, that the offer and acceptance rules do have a larger purpose. As noted in Chapter 1, the principal function of contract law (at least as things stand) is to provide an enabling framework within which private parties can carry out a mutually beneficial exchange of goods and services—A and B, again, trading apples for oranges. However, the fact that the parties can improve their respective wealth positions by making an exchange does *not* mean, even theoretically, that there is only one single point—*just* so many apples for *just* so many oranges—at which the mutually beneficial swap must or should take place. Rather, there exists a number of possible trading points—a range of "efficient outcomes"—at any one of which an exchange will be beneficial to both. A will, of course, prefer that the rate of exchange be more favorable to him while B will prefer the contrary, and it is this circumstance that inevitably prompts the two parties to commit a certain amount of time to the tedious process of haggling. Which of them is the better haggler we cannot know in advance, but at some stage in the process each of the parties should reach the conclusion that the returns to additional bargaining are too small to justify further struggle. They will then, presumably, make a deal. In a very general sense, the role of contract law in this context is (a) to distinguish the culminating moment of agreement from all the bargaining activity that has gone before and (b) to protect the agreement thus arrived at from any effort by either party to start the bargaining process up again.

Apart from the need for a recognizable offer and acceptance, there is a kind of overriding legal requirement that the parties to a contract evidence by some discernable means their intention actually to be bound by the terms of their agreement. It must appear (in the scriptural language of Restatement Section 17) that there has been "a manifestation of mutual assent." Assent would normally be "manifested" by the execution of a written document, or by an oral expression of agreement, or perhaps simply by commencement of the performance that the offer calls for. As one possible complication, however, suppose a contract is entered into purely in jest (at least by one of the parties) or as a dare or in a mood of drunken boasting? Should the law take account of personal intent in this connection, or should it take the spoken or the written word as literally meant? In *Lucy v. Zehmer*,[1] the defendant claimed (a) that he was drunk, (b) that he was kidding, and (c) that the plaintiff knew the defendant was (a) and (b) when he offered to sell the plaintiff his farm for $50,000 (apparently a reasonable price for the property). A 12–word contract of sale was drawn up on the back of a counter check and signed by both parties. Arguing that the whole thing had been intended and understood as a joke, the defendant later refused to transfer the farm and the plaintiff sued for specific performance.

Reversing the trial court, the Supreme Court of Virginia held for the plaintiff. The Court seemed to believe that the defendant hadn't been all *that* drunk (it was defendant who wrote out the contract) and had been at least partly in earnest when he offered the property for sale. But even if Zehmer truly did intend the contract to be a joke, Lucy apparently never got the point and instead considered the execution of the contract to be a serious commitment that was binding on Zehmer as well as on himself. He scurried about the very next day and arranged (with his brother) to put up half the purchase price, then engaged an attorney to examine title, and thereafter advised the defendant in writing that he was ready to close the deal. Since the plaintiff reasonably thought that the defendant was serious, and since the language of the contract was plain and unmistakable, the parties' mutual promises were enforceable despite Zehmer's "undisclosed intention" to regard these doings as buffoonery.

The trial court in *Zehmer*, it can be noted, apparently took a different view of the parties' conduct and probably "found" that Lucy actually knew, or had reason to know, that Zehmer was joking about the farm sale. If Lucy had been aware that Zehmer was joking (assuming Zehmer *was* joking), then clearly there should have been no contract. While the law normally treats a promisor as having been sincere in his spoken or written utterances, it would be absurd and ritualistic to hold a party to his promise if both he *and* the promisee understood the matter to be a joke. The larger object of the law, after all, is to provide a basis or framework in which the exchange of goods and services can be made with some assurance by persons who more or less consciously expect to be better off as a consequence. No reason whatever can be suggested for enforcing a "contract" that neither party intended or expected to be fulfilled, though it is presumably fair enough to impose the burden of proof on the alleged joker. A slightly harder question—that presented by *Lucy v. Zehmer* if, with the Court, we assume a somewhat humorless Lucy—is what

1. 196 Va. 493, 84 S.E.2d 516 (1954).

to do when the promisor's joke is taken seriously by the promisee. At that point, I suppose, we might as well draw down the corners of our mouths and hold the promisor. It is not so much a matter of being tough-minded and "objective" in our approach to the language of the contract as it is a need to resolve the clash between the two parties' individual expectations. This need seems especially compelling if (as was allegedly true in *Zehmer*) the promisee spent time and money in reliance on the promisor's misleading statement. Since the jesting promisor created the problem and evidently failed to make his attitude clear to the promisee, the responsibility for the apparent misunderstanding is pretty plainly his. Conceding that minds never met (i.e., the promisor was joking), it is really impossible to ignore the element of relative fault in this context, and one is led finally to insist either that there has been constructive assent on the part of the promisor or that actual assent is here unnecessary.

On a slightly different front, suppose the parties clearly and consciously manifest assent, but each has in mind an object or an act that is wholly different from the act or object contemplated by the other. In the famous *Peerless* case,[2] decided by the Court of Exchequer in 1864, the plaintiff agreed to sell to the defendant, and the defendant agreed to buy, 125 bales of Surat cotton at a stated price. The cotton thus sold was to arrive on the ship Peerless sailing from Bombay, but when the Peerless, or at least *a* Peerless, reached port at Liverpool the defendant refused to accept and pay for the merchandise. As it turned out, there were two ships named Peerless sailing from Bombay, and while the plaintiff clearly had in mind the Peerless that sailed from Bombay in December, the defendant just as clearly meant to designate the Peerless that sailed from Bombay in October. The contract contained nothing that clarified the matter because neither party had any idea that there were two ships Peerless in the world. It may be supposed that the December Peerless arrived in Liverpool some weeks or months after the October Peerless and that the market price for cotton had fallen between the earlier date and the later. Apparently conceding that he and the defendant had had different Peerlesses in mind, the plaintiff argued that as 125 bales of Surat cotton had in fact arrived from Bombay aboard a ship called "Peerless", the agreement between the parties was in all respects satisfied and the defendant was bound. In any event, said plaintiff, the time of sailing was not expressly mentioned by the parties in their agreement and, hence, should not be viewed as material to their understanding.

2. Raffles v. Wichelhaus, Court of Exchequer, 1864, 159 Eng.Rep. 375, discussed in Simpson, *Contracts for Cotton to Arrive: The Case of the Two Ships Peerless*, 11 Cardozo L.Rev. 287 (1989).

Finding that there had been no "consensus ad idem"—no agreement on the same thing, presumably—the Court held for the defendant. Since the defendant intended to buy one lot of merchandise—the cotton goods carried by Peerless–October—while the plaintiff intended to sell another—the cotton goods carried by Peerless–December—there was no contract or agreement which the Court could enforce. Thus, Pollock, C.B., intending to highlight the weakness of plaintiff's position, observed that "It may as well be said that if there is a contract for the purchase of certain goods in warehouse A., that [contract] is satisfied by the delivery of goods of the same description in warehouse B." Plaintiff's counsel apparently withered in the face of this incisive riposte, but perhaps he should have grasped the nettle. Assuming the "goods" stored in Pollack's warehouses were indeed of "the same description", a buyer could hardly reject them on the ground that they had been drawn from one location rather than another, unless place of storage had an effect on quality, physical condition or the like. For the same reason, everything else being equal, the defendant in the *Peerless* case should reasonably have been indifferent to the mere identity of the vessel that was employed to carry his merchandise across the seas.

Quite obviously, however, much more was at stake for both parties than the name of a ship. As with other commodities, the market price of cotton in Liverpool no doubt fluctuated from week to week, perhaps widely, so that in offering to sell December-shipment cotton at a predetermined price the plaintiff was making a bet on the state of the market at the anticipated arrival date. The defendant, by contrast, was betting on the market price for October shipments and thus, in effect, took or thought he was taking a very different gamble. Presumably, neither party knew or had reason to know of the other's intention. Having wagered their money on two different events—the value of October cotton-futures in one case, of December cotton-futures in the other—the only possible conclusion was that there had been no wager to start with. Although the parties probably did not suffer equally (plaintiff, unlike defendant, may have had unrecovered shipping costs plus the drop in market price to grieve over), the Court was limited to an all-or-nothing result. Either a contract for the sale of cotton had been formed by mutual assent or it had not. Without a consensus ad idem, there was simply no agreement to which the parties could be bound.

The *Peerless* case is mentioned again in Chapter 5 in connection with the problem of contract interpretation, and it has bearing as well on the subject of "mistake," which is taken up in Chapter 7. More generally, the requirement of mutual assent once more becomes an issue—this time with implications for social policy—in connection with so-called contracts of adhesion, discussed in Chapter 4.

A. Offer and Acceptance

1. *Offers.* When is a communication to be regarded as an "offer" and when is it to be taken merely as an invitation to engage in bargaining and negotiation? The distinction, obviously, is important to both the offeror and his offeree. A property-owner who is interested in selling his property requires current market information before deciding on an offering price. Such information may be available from brokers or other middlemen, but if the property is more or less unique—say, an operating business—then it may be that prospective buyers themselves will be the only real source of reliable market data. In the latter event, the owner needs to issue some sort of communication that will induce buyers to go to the trouble and expense of valuing the property and submitting bids. The question, I suppose, is how he can do that— what he can legally say to signify the reality of his intentions— without actually offering the property for sale. Buyer-offerees are, of course, equally concerned with the legal significance of the property-owner's utterances. A buyer who accepts what he believes to have been an "offer" will necessarily assume that his economic position has changed materially. He may then be led to take some costly and irreversible step—borrow money, sell property of his own, reject other opportunities—in reliance on what he thinks is a binding agreement. He will of course be disappointed, perhaps seriously disadvantaged, if the communication which he confidently regarded as an offer was really, or at least legally, just a feeler.

The words "I hereby offer to sell you Blackacre for $1,000 cash" could hardly be clearer and plainly constitute a promise to convey Blackacre if the offeree agrees to pay the offering price. But suppose the message waffles slightly: "I am eager to sell Blackacre but would not take less than $1,000 for it. Please let me know promptly if you are interested." Is this an "offer" that will become a binding contract if the addressee says "I accept," or is it merely an invitation to *make* an offer which the owner can then take under advisement? The subject-property is designated and a price is mentioned; hence all the operative terms are present that a true offer would be expected to include. While the phrase "would not take less" lacks the firm promissory smack of "I hereby offer", one cannot entirely fault the addressee for thinking that Blackacre will be his if he agrees to the $1,000 figure.

In the end, as usual, it is the surrounding circumstances that really matter. If the two parties mentioned above have been bargaining over Blackacre for the past six months, steadily trading proposals and counter-proposals in an effort to find a mutually acceptable price, then "would not take less" or "would not pay more" might well be taken as an offer. If there has been no prior bargaining, a different inference seems plausible. Given that a seller's constant aim is to get the highest price he can for his property, the quoted communication probably should be seen as nothing more than the first step in an open auction. The words "would not take less than. . . ." fairly imply that Blackacre is up for sale to the highest bidder, with the number "$1,000" intended to be understood as the *minimum* selling price—equivalent to an auctioneer's "upset price"—rather than the figure which the owner is now prepared to accept as final. The decided cases (what few there are) generally support the latter construction. Absent special facts (e.g., a history of party-to-party negotiations), the courts are likely to conclude that a communication which advises interested parties that designated property is for sale at a price not below $X merely establishes the basis of an auction, but does not constitute an "offer".

Dealings between merchants—manufacturers and retailers, for example—can present the same problem of ambiguous intent, although it may be supposed that general familiarity with trade custom and practice reduces the occasions for dispute to a minimum. In *Fairmount Glass Works v. Grunden–Martin Woodenware Co.*,[3] the plaintiff, Grunden–Martin, wrote to the defendant requesting "the lowest price you can make us . . . for ten carloads of Mason green jars, complete, with caps, packed one dozen in a case. . . ." Defendant promptly answered, saying "we quote you Mason fruit jars . . .: Pints $4.50, quarts $5.00, half gallons $6.50 per gross, for immediate acceptance, and shipment not later than May 15. . . ." Plaintiff next day sent a telegram ordering "ten carloads as per your quotation. Specifications mailed." At this point, apparently, defendant became aware that its inventory of Mason jars had already been cleaned out—not a single jar in the warehouse—and at once communicated the bad news to the plaintiff: "Impossible to book your order. Output all sold. . . ." Unable to find another source of supply at the same favorable prices, plaintiff sued for breach.

3. 106 Ky. 659, 51 S.W. 196 (1899).

Holding for the plaintiff, the Court found that the defendant's initial communication constituted an "offer" in legal terms rather than a mere invitation to deal. The price quotations were issued by defendant in response to a specific inquiry, one which, significantly, made clear the particular quantity of Mason jars that plaintiff had in view. Most important, perhaps, defendant's request for "immediate acceptance" implied that the next and *last* step in the transaction was expected to be plaintiff's yes or no. In effect, plaintiff was entitled to assume that inventory sufficient to cover its order had been earmarked by defendant, provided only that plaintiff's reply should be, as it was, immediate. Finally, the Court was not much troubled by the fact that plaintiff's telegram failed to specify pints, quarts, etc., since the defendant's offer appeared to confirm that merchandise was available in each category.

Although easy to approve on its own facts, the *Fairmount* case does *not* stand for the proposition that the circulation of price quotations by a supplier of goods constitutes an offer, or a set of offers, that can be "accepted" and thus converted into a binding contract by prospective purchasers. To be sure, such circulations are intended to generate business in the form of purchase orders, but as a general rule it is the order itself that constitutes the "offer" and the purchaser who plays the role of offeror. Even when prices are quoted in response to a specific inquiry, the normal understanding, which may or may not be made explicit, is that orders are solicited subject to available stocks or to change of price without notice. In commercial usage, the word "quotation" implies the reservation of a right on the supplier's part to accept or reject customers' orders more or less at will, and in a sense the real question in the *Fairmount* case was whether the language of the defendant's initial communication—"we can quote you . . . ."—should not have been understood to include that reservation. As suggested, the additional words "for immediate acceptance" presumably convinced the Court that the defendant actually intended to depart from the customary pattern of solicitation and, hence, that "quote" meant "offer" under the circumstances.

Perhaps the last serious issue that comes up under the heading "offer" concerns the effect of retail advertisements. In the silly but never-to-be-forgotten case of *Lefkowitz v. Great Minneapolis Surplus Store,*[4] the defendant put an ad in the local newspaper which said:

4. 251 Minn. 188, 86 N.W.2d 689 (1957).

"Saturday.   Each. . .$1.00

1 BLACK LAPIN STOLE

BEAUTIFUL

worth $139.50. . .$1.00

First Come

FIRST SERVED"

Lefkowitz, though a male person, was first in line on Saturday and demanded the beautiful stole for a dollar. The Store refused to sell, asserting that the garment was available to women customers only and reminding Lefkowitz that it had thrown him out when he tried to pull the same stunt on an earlier occasion.

Holding that the advertisement must be construed as an "offer" because it invited a particular performance—getting in line first on Saturday—the Court awarded Lefkowitz damages of $138.50 and thus taught the Store a painful lesson, i.e., beware of cranks and monomaniacs. The Store may have intended to restrict its offer to women (or, at least, to shoppers having a bona fide intention to look at other merchandise as well), but that restriction did not appear in the advertisement itself and it could not be added after the offer had been accepted.

The *Lefkowitz* case aside, it is obvious that public advertisements, like the merchant's price quotations, are not to be regarded as offers in a legal sense. Intentionally misleading advertising may be punishable or enjoinable under local consumer protection statutes—and of course the advertiser's reputation for fair dealing is at stake—but in general advertisements are regarded as nothing more than invitations to deal. This is true even though the advertisement is specific as to price, quantity, time-limit ("Big Sale! One Day Only!") and other details. Shoppers are presumed to understand that advertised goods may or may not be available by the time they get ready to buy. In legal terms, therefore, it is the customer, not the advertiser, who occupies the status of "offeror".

2. *Acceptance.* Assuming an "offer" has been made, the next and final step in the formation of a contract is, obviously, acceptance by the offeree. Once accepted, the offer becomes a contract: both parties are bound and neither can renege without liability to the other. At the same time, as noted, an offeror is free to revoke his offer and terminate the offeree's power to accept, provided only that he acts before the offeree has recorded his acceptance. If the offeree acts first, and if his action qualifies as an acceptance under

relevant legal standards, the deal is done. Inevitably, cases arise in which the offeror, faced with an apparent acceptance by the offeree, seeks to revive or restore his power of revocation by arguing that the effort to accept was ineffective. What constitutes an effective acceptance may thus, in a given case, become a question of considerable importance.

The answer, it turns out, depends upon the requirements of the offer itself. The offeror is master of his offer (in the standard phrase), and just as the offeror can set and insist upon the substantive terms of the deal—price, quantity, time of payment and so on—so the offeror can dictate the form and manner of the offeree's acceptance. In an ordinary commercial setting, the offer (itself a promise by the offeror to do or pay something in exchange for something else) seeks a reciprocal promise from the offeree. This is evident and unambiguous, I suppose, where an offeror seeks to purchase goods or services to be delivered or performed in the future. The offeror presumably plans to make a variety of contractual commitments himself—to lenders, suppliers, customers, etc.—and therefore requires an undertaking from the offeree that can be relied upon today. Whether the offeree does or doesn't perform in the future is of course important, but it is not the question of the moment. What matters for present purposes, and matters critically, is that the offeror be able to commit himself to others on the basis of the offeree's commitment to him. Accordingly, the offeror seeks a promise from the offeree at this stage, nothing else and nothing less.

A promise constituting an acceptance would normally be stated in appropriate language, whether written or oral. On some occasions, however, especially where the offer is a routine or recurring event, the accepting offeree might simply skip the formality of verbal expression and proceed directly to perform the act that the offer calls for. Thus, a purchaser sends a seller an order (i.e., offer, see above): "Please ship promptly 1,000 units of [merchandise] at your quoted price of $10 per unit." The seller-offeree could respond by mailing the purchaser a notice of acceptance—in effect, a promise to deliver—in which event, no doubt, there is a contract to which both parties are bound. Suppose, however, that the seller, a man of action, says nothing but "promptly" loads the merchandise on a truck with appropriate instructions for delivery. Can the purchaser—asserting that his offer sought (but never got) acceptance from the seller in the form of an express promise to deliver the goods—revoke the offer before (maybe even after) the truck arrives? One would hardly think so: the purchase-order could have required written notification of acceptance, but in fact it didn't. Instead, the order appeared to contemplate that performance itself would suffice as an act of acceptance and that a separately stated promise was unwanted or unnecessary.

UCC 2–206 makes it clear, where sales of goods are concerned, that an offer—usually a purchase order—can be accepted by any reasonable "medium", including the commencement of performance. In particular, unless otherwise unambiguously indicated, an offer to buy goods for "prompt shipment" is to be construed as inviting acceptance either by promise or by the act of shipment itself. Restatement Sections 32 and 62 announce a similar principle and establish also that acceptance by performance is a two-way street. Thus, performance by the offeree is regarded as equivalent to an expressly stated promise: in effect, having shipped the goods or otherwise commenced performance, the offeree becomes a promisor in his own right; he is legally bound to the terms of the offer and no more free than the offeror to treat his contractual obligations as terminable short of completion.

What qualifies as the "commencement of performance" for these purposes? In *Ever–Tite Roofing Corp. v. Green,*[5] the defendant-homeowners submitted a written order to the plaintiff-contractor for the re-roofing of defendants' residence. The order form, furnished by the plaintiff's salesman, stated among other things that "This agreement shall become binding only upon written acceptance [by] . . . the Contractor, or upon commencing performance of the work." Since the work itself was to be done entirely on credit, Ever–Tite requested a credit-report on the Greens from a local lending institution, a procedure which apparently took some ten days to complete. A favorable report having been received, Ever–Tite sent a crew of workmen and a truck loaded with supplies to the Greens' house for the purpose of starting the job. On arriving, however, the Ever–Tite people found another crew hard at work on the roof and were told by the Greens that their services were not required. The Greens, it appeared, having waited a week and heard nothing from Ever–Tite, made a deal with another roofing company which was willing to, and did, begin the work at once.

Ever–Tite thereupon sued for breach, claiming damages of $85.37 for the workmen's transportation and wages plus $226 for lost profits. Resisting, the defendants argued that the plaintiff never actually commenced performance—and, hence, did not "accept"—before being told that the defendants' offer had been withdrawn.

5.   83 So.2d 449 (La.App.1955).

Reversing the trial court, which had held for the defendants, the Supreme Court of Louisiana directed that judgment be entered for the plaintiff-contractor. Under general rules, said the Court, an offer that does not specify a time-limit remains open for a reasonable time (unless revoked). Given the necessity of a credit-check, of which defendants were presumably aware, ten days was plainly reasonable in the circumstances presented. More critically, the Court held that plaintiff's act in loading its truck and transporting men and materials to the Greens' residence must be viewed as "commencing performance"; hence, the plaintiff had accepted before becoming aware (indeed, before it *could* become aware) of the Greens' intention to hire another roofer. In effect, there was a binding contract once the truck got underway, presumably because it was then, and at that point, that Ever–Tite began to incur unrecoverable expenses—$85.37—on the Greens' account. The amount was small, to be sure, but it would have cost the defendants even less—the price of a single phone call—to have notified the plaintiff of their decision to revoke.

Although a bit tough on the Greens (who, in effect, paid more than once for the same roof), the decision in *Ever–Tite* may ultimately have been beneficial both for the home-repair industry and for individual homeowners generally (at least in Louisiana). Thus, why should a company like Ever–Tite insist on being free to accept a repair contract *either* by formal written communication to the customer *or* by "commencing performance of the work"? As indicated, the company really cannot accept the customer's order until a favorable credit report is received (unless the customer is prepared to pay in advance), because repair contracts, like most consumer obligations, are routinely assigned to a lender which provides the funds to finance the work. On the particular day it receives notice that the buyer's credit has been cleared, however, the company may find that all of its work-crews are engaged on other repair jobs. Alternatively, it may find that it has a crew that is not so engaged. In the former event, the company would wish to transmit a written acceptance to the customer in order to lock up the contract; but in the latter event, instead of taking time to write a letter, it would prefer to send out the crew itself at once. The company's larger aim is to maintain a relatively constant work-force and to keep its workers busy at all times. This, in turn, presumably means lower costs and a resulting benefit to consumers. While the Greens' roofing job amounted to little in itself, the company obviously thought that an important practice was at stake both from its own standpoint and that of the industry.

42

The Court may have thought so as well. In practical terms, the *Ever–Tite* decision means that home-repair customers can avoid commitment only if they act before the necessary credit-check is completed. Thereafter, by one means or the other, they are almost certain to be bound.

The contract held to have been entered into in the *Ever–Tite* case was, of course, a bilateral contract—that is, a contract based on the exchange of one promise for another. The offeree's promise in *Ever–Tite*, as has been seen, was made by commencing performance rather than saying 'I promise,' but the legal effect was the same. In some situations, by contrast, the offeror seeks nothing *but* a performance—a promise or commitment by the offeree to do something in the future is unwanted or irrelevant. Contracts of this sort—referred to as unilateral—are uncommon and probably not very important, yet they do present an issue that commentators have at times found challenging. Briefly stated, if an offer seeks a performance, and only that, is the offeror free to revoke the offer before the performance has been completed, even though the offeree, acting in reliance, has already begun performance and made a sacrifice of time and effort? Thus (and the illustration may well be representative of the class [6]), suppose X offers to pay Y $5 if, by nightfall, Y will find and return X's cat, which has somehow strayed away. Y says, "Okay, I'll start looking." He spends all day searching through the neighborhood and at last locates the cat at the top of a tree. Not having a ladder, Y climbs the tree with great difficulty and crawls out on a shaky limb to grab the cat. At that moment, X, watching from the sidewalk below, yells up: "Forget it, Y! I've found that life is simpler without a cat. Leave him up there."

Can Y recover against X? Taken literally, X promised to pay only when the cat was found *and* returned; the offer could be accepted only by a completed performance and until accepted could be revoked. But the idea that Y could be induced to put in a long day's work, perhaps relinquishing other income-producing opportunities, and then be denied his reward just when the goal was in sight is shocking and ignominious. Still, there is a certain symmetry in the positions of the parties. Not having been asked for a promise and not having given one, Y can presumably stop searching if he tires of the effort. X has no right to claim performance from Y; Y can quit whenever he likes and leave X to find the cat and climb the tree himself. The parties could have protected themselves by placing their agreement on a bilateral

6. But see Pettit, *Modern Unilateral Contracts,* 63 B.U.L.Rev. 551 (1983).

footing—X promising to pay Y $5 in return for Y's promise to search diligently—but apparently neither was prepared to make the commitment that an exchange of promises would have entailed.

All this is fairly silly, I concede, but it probably remains true, in general, that unilateral offers of the sort just illustrated are revocable by the offeror at any time prior to completion of performance. To be sure, a court determined to escape the latter conclusion probably can find a way. Possibly (though with difficulty on the "facts" given), X's offer might be treated as seeking a series of completed performances—(1) searching, (2) finding, (3) returning—so that some compensation would be due to Y at the end of each segment rather than only on final recovery of the cat. In the alternative, X's offer, unless entirely unambiguous, might be construed as seeking a promise *through* the commencement of performance. As in *Ever–Tite,* Y's act in beginning the search could then be viewed as the acceptance of an offer to form a bilateral rather than a unilateral contract. Section 45 of the Restatement moves some distance in the latter direction by treating the commencement of performance in response to a unilateral offer as conferring an "option contract" on the offeree—a right to complete the performance that has been commenced if he chooses to do so. In effect, X is regarded as having made a twofold offer to Y: (a) to pay $5 if Y finds and returns the cat, and (b) to treat the offer as irrevocable if Y begins the search. The Restatement stops short of converting all unilateral contracts into bilateral contracts, however. While barring revocation by the offeror once the offeree has commenced to perform, Section 45 does not bind the offeree to complete the performance. The offeree can abandon the undertaking short of completion without incurring liability to the offeror, although of course in that event the offeror's duty to perform (pay the $5) does not arise. In *Ever–Tite,* by contrast, the commencement of performance by itself constitutes a "promise"; accordingly, the contractor-offeree, now a promisor, has a binding obligation to complete what it began.

One final problem in the acceptance area—that of timing—deserves brief mention. As in *Adams v. Lindsell,*[7] suppose an offer to sell certain merchandise is sent to an offeree by mail and is duly accepted, also by mail. Before the offeree's letter of acceptance is received, however, the offeror changes his mind and writes (calls, wires) the offeree to say that he has decided to revoke. Since it is clear in most cases that an offeror can revoke

---

7. 106 Eng.Rep. 250 (King's Bench, 1818). And see, Restatement Section 63; Macneil, *Time of Acceptance: Too* *Many Problems for a Single Rule,* 112 U.Pa.L.Rev. 947 (1964).

his offer at any time prior to acceptance, the question is whether that power has been foreclosed by the offeree's action in mailing his letter or whether the offeror's power to revoke survives until actual receipt. The answer, approved by the Restatement and by a good many decisions, is that the mailing of an acceptance is effective to create a contract and binds the offeror. The offeree may have taken important and costly steps (including, perhaps, the rejection of significant offers from others) on the plausible assumption that the unrevoked offer was his to accept, and it would pretty plainly be unreasonable to ask him to await notification of receipt by the offeror before feeling free to regard the deal as done. Without trenching on the offeror's general power to revoke, the effect of the "mailbox rule" is to limit the duration of that power and to give the offeree some protection once he has taken action by accepting.

B. Revocation and Counteroffer

1. *Revocation and Reliance.* The discussion just above deals with the question of what action on the part of an offeree is to be regarded as "acceptance" such that the offeror is bound thereby to complete the transaction in accordance with the terms of his offer. Our assumption has been that *until* the offeree accepts—whether by making a return promise or by commencing performance—the offeror is free to revoke. The question to be considered here is whether that assumption is always valid—or, rather, what significant exceptions should be attached to it. At stake from the offeror's standpoint is the ability to regain control of the economic interests that are affected by the offer. The offeror may have changed his mind about selling or buying, he may be dissatisfied with the offeree for some reason, or he may simply want to return to the auction market in the hope of a better price. In any such event his aim will be to shut down the outstanding offer at once. The offeree presumably sees the matter in opposite terms: from his standpoint there is plainly an advantage, and perhaps some urgency, in keeping the offer alive and available until he, rather than the offeror, has made the final decision to take it or leave it.

In *Dickinson v. Dodds,*[8] the plaintiff received a memorandum from the defendant on Wednesday offering to sell him certain real estate—land and buildings—for £800. The offer was to be "left over until Friday, 9 o'clock A.M." On Thursday the plaintiff learned from his agent that the property had been offered or sold to another investor (one Allan, also named as a defendant), where-

---

8. Court of Appeal, Chancery Division, 1876, 2 Ch.Div. 463.

upon the plaintiff raced to the house in which defendant was staying and handed to defendant's mother-in-law a written acceptance of defendant's offer—which, however, she somehow afterwards forgot to give him. Early Friday morning, apparently having lain in wait all night, plaintiff and his agent intercepted the defendant at a railway station leaving town and again tried to hand him a copy of the acceptance. "You are too late," cried the defendant, ducking into his compartment, "I have sold the property."

Reversing the trial court, the Court of Appeal held that plaintiff was not entitled to specific performance and likewise not entitled to restrain conveyance of the property or to impress a trust upon the property if it had already been conveyed. Despite his written assurance that the offer to sell would be "left over until Friday, 9 o'clock A.M.", the defendant was free to revoke at any time prior to the plaintiff's acceptance. A promise to hold an offer open, being a mere *nudum pactum*, is not binding—that, said the Court, is "one of the clearest principles of law"—and can always be withdrawn on notice to the offeree. To be sure, defendant never actually notified the plaintiff that the offer had been revoked or that the property had been sold to someone else; indeed, judging by his attempt at a hasty get-away on Friday morning, defendant pretty plainly thought himself bound to hold the offer open. In fact, however, plaintiff admitted that he knew about the prior sale, and that knowledge, though circumstantially derived, was equivalent to being told by defendant "in so many words, 'I withdraw the offer' ".

Postponing for a moment our own judgment of the merits, I think it is easy to see why the Court in *Dickinson* would have been most reluctant to affirm the lower court's decree for specific performance. In effect, it couldn't: no matter what the plaintiff's rights might have been, the contract entered into between the two defendants (by which Dodds conveyed the real estate to Allan) was entirely valid and enforceable; even if the plaintiff had been wholly ignorant of the prior sale, no legal basis existed (at least no contract rule) for treating Allan's title to the property as defeasible. For the same reason, Dodds had nothing left to convey once the deal with Allan was done. Accordingly, there was no one to whom a decree for specific performance could have been directed who either could or would have had a duty to obey it.

Money damages, however, remained a possibility, so that the doctrinal issues in the case—(i) whether the offer should have been viewed as irrevocable at all events until Friday at 9 A.M., and (ii) if not, whether indirect knowledge of a prior sale should be

46

regarded as equivalent to a direct communication from the offeror—still need to be sorted out. As to the first issue, I think everyone would agree that the bare language of the defendant's offering memorandum—"This offer to be left over until Friday, 9 o'clock"—was insufficient by itself to establish the defendant's true intent (whatever inference we might make from his later behavior) with perfect clarity. One possible reading—that stressed by plaintiff—is that the phrase "left over until" means that the offer is "firm," or irrevocable, up to the date and hour given. The other reading, no less plausible I think, is that the offer, though at all times revocable *with* notice to the offeree, will expire without notice once such date and hour have passed. Conceding that Dodds may have *thought* himself bound, the Court nevertheless chose the second construction on the ground that consideration for the defendant's promise was lacking. Any sense in this? Not much, perhaps, in the particular circumstances of the case itself, but if we contemplate term offers generally, the likelihood that consideration *will* be present where an offer is intended to be irrevocable is obviously great. Thus, suppose the term for which Dodds' offer was "left over" had been 90 days instead of only Wednesday-to-Friday. If such offer were irrevocable, then Dickinson would find himself in the enviable position of being able to benefit from any appreciation in the value of the underlying property during the 90-day period, while leaving the risk of any decline with Dodds. Generally, if property subject to an irrevocable option goes up in value during the relevant term, the option-holder will exercise his option and eliminate the offeror's interest. If the property goes down in value, the optionee will allow the option to lapse and the loss will fall on the offeror. Options thus being valuable economic rights in themselves, it is presumptively unlikely that the owner of marketable investment property would actually grant an irrevocable option (otherwise known as a "call") to another investor without demanding and receiving from the latter a premium—that is, a monetary consideration—in return. He might, of course, but since doing so entails a significant economic detriment, the *presumption* is plainly contrary.

The practical issue that confronted the Court of Appeal in *Dickinson v. Dodds* was simply *which* of the two commercial arrangements mentioned above the offeror and offeree had intended to create—a revocable offer subject to a deadline, or an option. On the one side, as stated, there is the very considerable probability that Dodds actually thought himself bound to keep the offer open until Friday at 9. On the other is the stark fact that Dodds received nothing whatever from Dickinson for giving up a valua-

ble (however short-lived) economic interest. Presumably recognizing that property sellers do not customarily grant irrevocable
options without getting paid for them, the Court resolved the
ambiguity that resides in the words "left over until Friday" by
finding the promisor's undertaking to be *nudum pactum*—a promise without consideration—and hence unenforceable as an option
contract. What the Court meant, simply, was that offers must be
presumed to be revocable unless a fee or premium is paid to the
offeror. Adding a deadline for acceptance means that the offer
expires automatically on the date named, but nothing more.

As to the second issue in *Dickinson v. Dodds*—whether indirect knowledge of the prior sale should be regarded as equivalent
to direct notice of revocation—I suppose we could begin by wondering why *any* notice of revocation was required on the part of the
offeror. Why not imply the term "revocable without notice" since
in fact Dodds' written offer contained nothing either way on that
subject? The answer, in addition to a kind of intuitive sense of
fairness, no doubt derives from the obvious consideration of comparative costs. Having sold the property to Allan, it would have
cost Dodds very little to send Dickinson a message notifying him
that the offer was withdrawn. Until notified, however, Dickinson
would presumably continue to spend time and money on investigation, appraisal, arrangement of financing, etc., all of which would
be halted once notice of revocation was received. Imposing a
notice requirement on the offeror would be expected to minimize
the combined cost of revocation to the parties and helps to justify
the fundamental decision to treat the offer as revocable by the
offeror at will. It follows, I think, that the means or the source of
notice to the offeree is relatively unimportant as long as he
actually gets the information. While direct notification is obviously the norm, it may not always be the quickest mode of
communication and the object, after all, is to avoid wasteful
outlays, not to observe formalities.

The use of a consideration test to distinguish revocable from
irrevocable offers seems natural and apt where transactions in
investment property—securities, real estate—are concerned, but of
course it may be that in a given case a property seller actually
perceives advantage in making an irrevocable offer *without* consideration. Thus, suppose an individual owns land that is worth
either a lot or a little depending on whether it has substantial
mineral content. A mining company indicates that it may be
willing to undertake the necessary geological testing if the landowner will make an irrevocable offer to sell the property for a
price of $1 million. On the assumption that he can't do the

geological work as well or as cheaply himself, the landowner might be very glad to grant the mining company an option to buy for a limited period.   In these circumstances, as Restatement Section 87 recognizes, the law ought to, and in general presumably does, accept a recital of nominal consideration—"$1 in hand paid, receipt whereof is hereby acknowledged, plus other good and valuable consideration"—as adequate to bind the offeror.   More generally, in the case of an offer of goods by a "merchant", UCC 2–205 rejects the rule of *Dickinson v. Dodds* and provides that a firm offer can be made by means of a signed writing, no consideration being required, if the offer is limited to a reasonable time not exceeding three months.

As suggested, the rule of *Dickinson v. Dodds* seems plausible despite its formalism where one-shot property transactions are concerned.   But in cases involving what might be called cooperative relationships—offeror and offeree being linked in a joint undertaking of some sort—the question of revocability takes on a different color.   Here the most familiar context is that of the routine construction bid.   Thus, the Lancaster School District invites contractors to submit bids on a school construction job, all bids to be in by July 28 at 8 P.M.   Drennan, a licensed general contractor, sits in his office on the afternoon of July 28 preparing a bid for last-minute submission.   The telephone rings constantly as various subcontractors call in their own bids for specialty work—plumbing, electrical, etc.—each of which Drennan posts on a master-sheet for use in making his final submission to the School District.   Among his callers is Star Paving Co., which offers to do the paving work for $7,131.   Star's figure turns out to be the lowest bid for paving received that afternoon, and Drennan therefore includes it in his own bid to the School District.   When the bids are opened on July 29, Drennan proves to be low-bidder and is awarded the contract.   Happy with this outcome, Drennan drops in next morning to say hello to the good folks at Star only to be greeted with the news that their paving bid was a great mistake— too low by half—and that they have now decided to withdraw it. Apparently unwilling to renegotiate, Drennan later contracted with another paving concern to do the work for $10,900, and then sued Star for the difference.

Finding for the plaintiff, the Supreme Court of California held in *Drennan v. Star Paving Co.*[9] that Star's offer to do the paving work for $7,131 included a "subsidiary promise" not to revoke until "plaintiff should have at least an opportunity to accept [that offer] after the general contract had been awarded to him."   It

9.   51 Cal.2d 409, 333 P.2d 757 (1958).

was true, the Court said, that consideration in a conventional sense was lacking—Drennan paid nothing to Star in exchange for the latter's surrender of its ordinary right of revocation. Where, however, the offeror's aim is to induce the offeree to rely on the offer and to make commitments of its own on the basis of such reliance, Restatement Section 90, applicable in California, waives the requirement of consideration and turns the offer into a binding promise. Star, of course, knew that Drennan would rely if its bid for the paving work was the lowest, and "it is only fair," said Justice Traynor, that Drennan should have a reasonable chance to say yes thereafter.

The *Star Paving* decision is inevitably to be contrasted with the Second Circuit's decision in *James Baird Co. v. Gimbel Bros.*,[10] in which, on roughly similar facts, Judge Learned Hand held that the subcontractor's offer could be revoked even after the general contractor had submitted its own bid (the winning bid, as it turned out) using the subcontractor's price-quotation. The subcontractor's offer, said Hand, looked for an acceptance from the offeree in the form of a return promise, not merely "reliance" through the submission of a bid. Even if adopted as a general rule of law, therefore, the doctrine of promissory estoppel would not apply: the offeree plainly based its bid-submission on the offeror's price-quotation, but that was not "the act" by which the offeror expected to be bound.

Comparing *Gimbel* with *Star Paving*, the elements of fairness and orderly conduct pretty plainly weigh in favor of the latter. The most compelling feature, quite obviously, is the circumstance that the general contractor—Drennan or Baird—is bound by its own bid once the contract has been awarded, and indeed in most cases it cannot withdraw its bid without a substantial penalty even if the subcontractor's revocation is received before the award is made. If the *Gimbel* rule were followed, general contractors would be obliged to add a premium to their bids in order to reflect the risk that one or another of their subcontractors might revoke before acceptance. The law would then have operated, in effect, to increase the overall cost of ordinary construction projects without adding anything of positive value to the process. Both Star Paving and Gimbel asserted that a "mistake" had been made in submitting their quotations to the general contractors; presumably, however, as Justice Traynor pointed out, the burden of care and resulting loss is more suitably imposed on the offeror who originated the price-quotation than on the offeree.

10. 64 F.2d 344 (2d Cir.1933).

While it seems easy, thus, to come down on the side of *Star Paving,* the somewhat troubling fact remains that promissory estoppel is a one-way street in this context. Having been awarded the Lancaster school contract, Drennan was free, if he wished, to make a new round of phone calls in order to determine whether any of Star's competitors would care to go a little lower than $7,131 for the paving work. Neither Drennan nor Baird was bound, even conditionally, to award the subcontract to the defendant; use of a subcontractor's figure in submitting its own bid—often, as in *Baird,* on a lump-sum basis—does not constitute acceptance on the general contractor's part of any particular subcontractor's offer; and the subcontractor cannot claim to have "relied" since it would have incurred the cost of working up its bid even if the general contractor had finally used the figure submitted by a different subcontractor. Worried about this problem but unable to escape it, Justice Traynor asserted that the general contractor was simply *not* at liberty to delay acceptance in the hope of getting a better price—meaning, presumably, that Drennan's claim to promissory estoppel would be forfeited if it were shown that he had gone on to make inquiries of other paving companies after the main contract was awarded. But even so, Drennan might well think it worthwhile to shop around a bit before communicating his acceptance—and might even think it quite legitimate to do so given the last-minute pressure under which general contractors are obliged to act in preparing their final bids. *Star Paving* thus tilts the balance of advantage to the general contractor, though even in this rough-and-tumble context considerations of business standing and reputation are likely to count more than legal rules in promoting fair dealing on both sides.

In *Star Paving* the doctrine of promissory estoppel was applied to convert a revocable offer into an option contract, ultimately allowing the offeree to trump the offeror's hasty effort at withdrawal. Enforcement meant compensating the plaintiff's expectation interest, which was measured by the difference between Star's bid and the greater amount Drennan was finally obliged to pay to another paving contractor for the same work. Restatement Section 90 provides, however, that the remedy for breach "may be limited as justice requires", and in a few instances—*Hoffman v. Red Owl Stores, Inc.*[11] is among the best known—the courts have concluded that "justice" required compensating the plaintiff's reliance interest instead. In *Red Owl,* the plaintiff was an ambitious small-town bakery owner who, in 1959, contacted a representative

---

11.   26 Wis.2d 683, 133 N.W.2d 267 (1965).

of the Red Owl chain with a view to getting a Red Owl supermarket franchise. In the course of discussions plaintiff stated that all the capital he had available for investment was $18,000, to which the Red Owl people replied that that sum would be quite sufficient to set up in business as a Red Owl store. Subsequently, at the urging or at least with the active encouragement of Red Owl, plaintiff (a) sold his bakery building at a loss of $2,000, (b) bought a small grocery store in order to gain experience as a grocer, (c) shortly afterwards sold the grocery store for an amount roughly equal to his cost, (d) put $1,000 down on land in a neighboring town where the new Red Owl would be constructed, and (e) incurred $265 in personal moving and rental expenses. All this preparatory activity took place over a period of about three years, during which Red Owl steadily maintained its promise that a franchise would be offered once all conditions had been met. Not much, however, was ever said by either party about the specific terms of the expected franchise and no final plans to build the new store were actually made. Finally, in 1962 Red Owl indicated that the plaintiff's capital investment requirement had been raised to $34,000 and that a proposed equity investment by plaintiff's father-in-law would have to be made in the form of a gift or subordinated loan. Plaintiff thereupon abandoned the whole undertaking and sued Red Owl for breach.

The case was tried to a jury, which found that Red Owl had represented to the plaintiff that he would get the franchise if he met certain conditions and that plaintiff had relied on those representations and fulfilled all the conditions required. The jury then awarded damages of $3,265 for items (a), (d) and (e), above, plus an additional $16,735 to reflect an alleged loss on the sale of the grocery store mentioned in (b) and (c). On appeal, the Supreme Court of Wisconsin ordered a new trial with respect to the last-named item on the ground that so large an award of damages from the sale of the grocery store was not supported by the evidence. As to the three smaller items, however, the Court upheld the jury award solely on the basis of promissory estoppel. The "promissory representations" made by Red Owl in the course of their negotiations induced the plaintiff to take the steps described above, and the consequence, when such representations failed, was to leave the plaintiff with fairly heavy reliance losses. Since promissory estoppel contemplates a "remedy . . . limited as justice requires," the jury's action in compensating him for those losses was (except as noted) sustained.

It should be stressed that Hoffman made no claim against Red Owl for expectation damages based on anticipated profits from the proposed franchise. If he had, he almost certainly would have failed, because Red Owl never actually offered him a franchise in terms that were definite or clear enough to be accepted, even under an induced reliance or estoppel theory. Indeed, no offer of a franchise was made in any form—Red Owl merely promised that it *would* make such an offer if the stated conditions were satisfied. In affirming the jury's damage award, the Court did not and presumably could not find a conventional breach of contract on Red Owl's part. Instead, it identified an actionable course of conduct—leading Hoffman on, obviously—for which Restatement Section 90 and the doctrine of promissory estoppel were held to provide independent grounds for relief. As applied in *Red Owl,* promissory estoppel was not merely a substitute for consideration or a device for converting an offer into a binding contract—in effect, there *was* no offer. Rather, Section 90 was made to "serve as a distinct basis of liability, without regard to theories of bargain, contract, or consideration",[12] and with its own special damage standard. So viewed, the doctrine would appear to have come a long way from its origins: having begun as a rationale for the enforcement of future-gift promises, it then developed into a rule equally applicable in a commercial setting, and now operates (at least it did in *Red Owl*) to impose fair-dealing requirements on parties engaged in *pre-contractual* negotiations, with no offer having yet been made by either.

The *Red Owl* decision is approved by the Restatement and, apparently, by most commentators, but I think one can legitimately be concerned about the resulting risk to prospective offerors. It would obviously be inappropriate and unwise to treat failed negotiations—an everyday event—as an occasion for assessing damages against one party for costs incurred by the other in taking steps to rearrange his affairs, even if such steps were foreseeable and recommended by the former. Contract law presumably ought not to be turned into a kind of generalized guarantee against personal or financial disappointment. But where an element of inducement is present in the form of positive assurances, and the disappointed party, reasonably relying, takes action that is costly and irreversible—sells a business, quits a job, demolishes a building—it may be suitable to follow *Red Owl* and like decisions in holding that promissory estoppel creates an actionable claim. That claim, however, as noted, seems to derive from the doctrine itself—operating as a kind of free-standing legal principle—rather than from conventional contract concepts.

12. Henderson, *Promissory Estoppel and Traditional Contract Doctrine,* 78 Yale L.J. 343 (1969).

2. *The Mirror–Image Rule: Counteroffers and Qualified Acceptance.* If an offeree purports to accept an offer but in doing so adds various conditions and qualifications of his own, is the acceptance binding on the offeror, at least in part? Generally speaking, the answer is no: the common law rule, reflected in Restatement Section 59, is that a statement of acceptance is effective only if it is a mirror image of the offer and expresses unconditional assent to all of the terms and conditions imposed by the offeror. A purported acceptance which alters those terms or adds qualifications does not bind the offeror, even if the changes or additions are minor. As indicated below, the mirror-image rule has been specially adapted by the UCC for routine merchandise transactions, but in situations not affected by the Code its application as an all-or-nothing principle is largely unquestioned. The rational basis of the rule, I think, is evident: in making an offer to exchange one thing for another, the offeror empowers the offeree, by accepting, to terminate or constrain the offeror's interest in the subject-matter of the offer. Plainly, however, it would be improper to allow the offeree to bind the offeror to pay a higher price or accept a lower price in the proposed exchange than the offeror has promised to pay or accept, and for the same reason we can't permit the offeree to add or eliminate conditions. This is so because the elements of an offer must be assumed to be interconnected: the price, quantity and character of the property or services to be exchanged are obviously primary, but the terms of payment, the security arrangements required of the offeree, the indemnities, warranties and representations to which the offeree is asked to commit himself—each of these features has a positive dollar-value in the mind of the offeror. The rejection or dilution of any one of them by the offeree, or the addition of other features, presumably increases the offeror's cost or adds to his risk, so that the offeror would then be prompted, in his own interest, to recalculate the value of the transaction as a whole. The added or rejected feature may or may not be a deal-breaker—the offeror may be willing to agree to it—but that decision is obviously up to the offeror. In effect, there *is* no deal, and nothing to which the offeror is bound, until all of the dependent conditions on which the offeror finally insists have been accepted by the offeree.

The mirror-image rule yields a further implication. If an offeree responds to an offer by making a counteroffer—in effect, proposes terms *other* than those contained in the original offer—the common law treats that response as the legal equivalent of an outright rejection. The consequence is that a subsequent effort by the offeree to accept the original offer is ineffective. The offeror can simply disregard the counteroffer and go on to make a deal with someone else on whatever terms he likes. While the rule, so stated, is well settled and is echoed by Restatement Section 39, I think one's first reaction is to feel slightly troubled at the notion of treating counteroffer and rejection as legal equivalents. Faced with an express rejection, an offeror would naturally conclude that he was at liberty to make a deal with another buyer and would consider it unnecessary to direct any further communication to the offeree. But a counteroffer—essentially, a bid below the offering price—is rather different psychologically and might well be thought to shift the burden of response to the offeror. To be sure, offerees have no affirmative duty to respond to offers and are generally free to disregard them; but a counterofferee—who, after all, initiated negotiations by making the original offer—would seem to have a further obligation to the process itself; indeed, silence on the counterofferee's part is more likely to suggest that the counteroffer is being studied than that the original offer has been dropped or withdrawn.

Reduced to an isolated problem of communication, the issue—whether a counteroffer should be viewed as a rejection or as a kind of inquiry on the part of the original offeree—seems pretty close. But perhaps the common law rule can be understood and supported if one envisions an offeror and offeree dealing with each other at a distance and by correspondence rather than face to face or by telephone. Thus, suppose a seller writes to a prospective buyer offering to sell Blackacre for $1,000. The buyer writes back offering $800. Evidently, offeror and offeree appraise Blackacre differently. Seller's highest priority is, of course, to locate somebody who more nearly agrees with *his* appraisal, and if a second buyer promptly appears and is willing to pay $1,000, seller may be compelled to make the deal at once or risk losing his price by taking time to notify the first offeree. If, next day, seller receives a purported acceptance from the first offeree, that communication has simply got to be treated as ineffective: as in *Dickinson,* no legal basis exists for discharging seller's obligation to convey Blackacre to the second buyer, yet there is only one Blackacre. Moreover, in view of the second buyer's willingness to pay $1,000 without haggling, we can assume that Blackacre had a higher value to him than to the first offeree, so that any legal rule that conferred a superior claim on the latter would presumably be inefficient.

As noted, Restatement Section 39 adopts the common law rule on counteroffers. The same section adds, however, that a counteroffer shall not be treated as a rejection if the offeree "manifests a contrary intent"—if, for example, the offeree's aim was merely to "inquire" about the possibility of different terms. But how can we tell? Again, suppose Seller offers to sell Blackacre to Buyer for $1,000. Buyer's response: "I'm willing to buy for $800—would you take that much?" Seller's reply: "No." The meaning and legal effect of the original offer is plain, but the same cannot be said of Buyer's response—or, indeed, of Seller's one-syllable reply. Is "I'm willing . . . would you take . . .?" a counteroffer or a mere inquiry? The differences in consequence are obviously great. If it is a mere inquiry, then (a) Seller cannot bind Buyer to the $800 figure by simply saying "Yes" at that point, and (b) Buyer's power to accept the original offer of $1,000 is not terminated. If it is a counteroffer, the contrary is true as to both elements. But in any case Seller said "No," which seems clear enough. But is it? On one reading, "No" could mean, "No, and I withdraw my original offer." But on another: "No, but my offer to sell at $1,000 still stands." Apart from a resort to the surrounding circumstances for clues to the parties' intent, the quoted words, few and simple as they are, raise problems of interpretation that are fairly difficult to handle with confidence.[13]

The problem of ambiguous expression in this context is illustrated by the Supreme Court's decision in *Minneapolis & St. Louis Railway Co. v. Columbus Rolling–Mill Co.*[14] The plaintiff, Railway, on December 5th wrote a letter to the defendant, Rolling–Mill, requesting a price-quotation "for 2000 to 5000 tons 50 lb. iron rails, March . . . delivery." On December 8th, Rolling–Mill wrote back advising that it would "sell 2000 to 5000 tons of 50 lb. rails for fifty-four . . . dollars per gross ton . . . If our offer is accepted, shall expect to be notified of same prior to Dec. 20th . . . ." On December 16, Railway directed Rolling–Mill by telegram to "enter our order for twelve hundred tons rails . . . as per your favor of the eighth", and on that day also sent a letter to the same effect. On December 18th, Rolling–Mill wired back, saying, "We cannot book your order at present at that price." On December 19th, Railway fired off another telegram instructing Rolling–Mill to "enter our order for two thousand tons rails, as per your letter of the [eighth]." This, apparently, was followed by a long, dead silence, until, on January 19th, Rolling–Mill informed Railway that it denied the existence of any contract between the parties. Insisting that its second telegram—that of December 19th—constituted an acceptance of Rolling–Mill's offer of December 8 to supply "2000 . . . tons", Railway sued for breach.

The Supreme Court held for the defendant. The applicable rule of law, said the Court, is that a purported acceptance which

13. See Restatement Section 39, Illustration 1.

14. 119 U.S. 149 (1886).

varies the terms contained in the offer to which it responds is equivalent to a rejection by the offeree. In consequence, negotiations are at an end. The offeror can renew the original offer if he cares to, but if he doesn't, it cannot be revived thereafter through a tender of acceptance by the offeree. Rolling–Mill having offered to sell not less than 2,000 tons, Railway's telegram of December 16th, in which it proposed to purchase only 1,200 tons, must be viewed as a counteroffer and hence a rejection, and this entitled Rolling–Mill to treat the original offer as withdrawn. In effect, Rolling–Mill need not have responded at all to the December 16th wire. Once that telegram had been sent, the original offer was dead.

Accepting the Court's enunciation of the common law in this area, I think it is possible to detect rather more ambiguity in the correspondence between Railway and Rolling–Mill than the opinion itself seemed willing to allow. One doubts, for example, that Railway understood the offering letter of December 8 as anything other than an echo of its own inquiry; nothing in that letter suggests that Rolling–Mill meant "2000 tons" to be taken as an absolute *minimum* quantity-limit, below which the selling price would be higher than $54 a ton. For the same reason, when it ordered 1,200 tons of iron rails on December 16th Railway probably thought it was accepting the offer of December 8 and never imagined that it would be seen as "negotiating" or proposing a variation in the original terms. As it turned out, of course, by December 18th Rolling–Mill no longer wished to honor its $54 offer at *any* quantity level, and it almost certainly intended its December 18 telegram to be an outright revocation of the offer of December 8. Had it plainly so stated, the case would have been an easy one: lacking an acceptance that mirrored the express terms of its offer, Rolling–Mill would have been *entitled* to revoke at that point under the general rule of *Dickinson v. Dodds*. Yet the language of its own telegram was ambiguous—it did not simply say "We revoke" (or the equivalent) and I suppose one *possible* reading is that Rolling–Mill actually meant to renew its offer while continuing to insist upon the 2,000–ton minimum.

Clearly, however, it meant just the opposite. Given its unwillingness to sell at $54 even after Railway had increased its order to 2,000 tons, the words "We cannot book your order at present at that price" were almost certainly intended by Rolling–Mill to mean "any order you may now or hereafter submit." No doubt the Supreme Court very well understood that the real purpose of the December 18th telegram was to withdraw the original offer, and on balance the Court probably felt that Rolling–Mill's intention to revoke deserved to be respected and placed ahead of Railway's subsequent effort to accept. Finding it difficult to convert the December 18th telegram into a specific act of revocation, however, the Court may finally have concluded that the simplest course was to treat Railway's prior communication as a counteroffer having the same effect.

The mirror-image rule presumably continues to reflect the common law generally, but in one significant context—routine merchandise transactions—the rule has been supplanted and substantially modified by UCC 2–207. The setting is one in which a purchaser—say a retailer—orders a quantity of goods from a supplier at a stated price and for delivery at or by a certain date. Often, the order would be communicated orally to the supplier's sales representative, face-to-face or over the phone, and similarly accepted, with a written confirmation from the supplier to follow. The confirmation repeats the main elements of the transaction— price, quantity, etc.—but also adds some further data—shipping information, for example—that weren't mentioned when the order was discussed. Alternatively, the purchaser's order may have been submitted to the supplier on a printed order form and then accepted or acknowledged by the supplier on a printed confirmation form of its own. The two forms agree as to the main elements of the transaction, but each form also includes (presumably on the back and in small print) a dozen or more paragraphs drafted by counsel and specifically designed to protect and favor the sender in the event of a dispute between the parties. We can assume that no one on either side actually takes time to read and study the boiler-plate material—it is the front of the forms that carries all the operative data. Yet the fine-print provisions are undeniably there; at least formally, they are part of the bargained-for exchange.

The consequence, if the common law mirror-image rule applies, is that there is no contract at all. The purchaser, having apparently placed a firm order for merchandise, could subsequently refuse to accept delivery on the ground that the supplier's confirmation was really a "counteroffer" and rejection. And even if the transaction were carried out as planned, with the merchandise being delivered and paid for, there might be troublesome questions as to *whose* boiler-plate actually governed if a dispute arose between the parties afterwards and the respective forms were found to be in conflict. Pretty plainly, however, these legally generated uncertainties have no place in the field of day-to-day sales of merchandise; purchaser and supplier never really intended or expected that the boiler-plate provisions would be taken into account in determining the acceptability of the deal on either side, and it is unlikely that the substance of those provisions was consciously "priced" into the transaction.

UCC 2–207 largely overthrows the mirror-image rule in this context by separating the boiler-plate provisions from the primary and agreed-upon elements of the transaction. Having made this separation, the section treats the latter as "the contract" and relegates the former to the lesser status of mere "proposals". Very briefly,[15] 2–207 begins by treating the offeree's (typically, the supplier's) written acknowledgement or confirmation as an "acceptance" even though it contains terms that add to or differ from those that were orally agreed to or appear in the purchaser's written order. As stated, such additional terms are treated not as a counteroffer on the part of the offeree, but as "proposals" for addition to "the contract", which is assumed to consist of those terms, presumably the main ones, on which the parties have agreed. If the additional terms are more or less harmless and do not "materially alter" the contract, then, unless the offeror objects, they become part of the contract and binding on the offeror. If the additional terms *are* material, or if they conflict with terms contained in the offeror's purchase order, then unless expressly accepted by the offeror such terms are simply excluded from the contract and regarded as binding on neither party. As a result, "the contract" consists of those terms that were agreed to by the parties or are deemed to have been adopted, plus such terms as may be supplied by other provisions of the UCC in the absence of agreement. The offer and apparent acceptance survive as an enforceable agreement, therefore, despite the presence of additional or conflicting terms in the written or printed documents.

UCC 2–207 presents a fair number of interpretative problems—what constitutes a "material" alteration is only the most obvious—and has generally been criticized as confusing and clumsily drafted. What is notable, however, even assuming that such criticism is just, is how infrequently litigation under 2–207 appears to have arisen and, by implication, how rarely the "battle of the forms" has actually led to court-room controversy. The reason (if the latter observation is correct) is that businesses rely very little on contract formalities in conducting their day-to-day affairs. Standing, reputation and the desire of buyer and seller for further profitable dealings and continuing commercial relations are obviously more important than the vindication of legal claims; hence, disputes are usually resolved informally, and there is seldom a

15. For a full discussion, see White & Summers, *Uniform Commercial Code* (Second Ed.1980) sec. 1–2.

need to invoke the statute. When legal controversy does arise, 2–207 wisely supports recognition of "the contract" by placing agreed terms in the forefront and discarding the stricter standards of the common law.

Chapter 4

UNFAIRNESS AND UNCONSCIONABILITY

A. Traditional Elements: Duress, Incapacity and Misrepresentation

Contracts, as noted, are voluntary, self-inspired arrangements by which private individuals seek to enhance their personal interests through the familiar process of arms-length exchange. In general, we can assume that each of the contracting parties acts without coercion (no gun to her head), that each is reasonably clear about her own preferences (knows what she likes), and that each has sufficient information about the world to distinguish intelligently among alternative goods and services (can tell a hawk from a handsaw). Possessing these common attributes—free will, self-knowledge and a modicum of practical information—an individual who makes promises on which others place reliance is normally bound by contract even if the commitments she has made seem improvident or idiosyncratic. The legal system obviously cannot undertake to assess the comparative wisdom of the parties as a general precondition to the enforcement of contract obligations.

If, on the other hand, either party lacks or can be presumed to lack the attributes of informed volition, then the customary basis of contract is in doubt. Recognizing this, the law has traditionally regarded contracts as void or voidable if made by persons lacking legal capacity, including "infants" (generally, persons under 18), drunks and the mentally ill, or if entered into under conditions of duress, or if induced by fraud or misrepresentation. The intuitive basis for treating a promise as non-binding under such circumstances is clear, I think, but inevitably there are borderline definitional issues—particularly in the areas of "duress" and "misrepresentation"—that test the limits or the application of the concept. Some of these are sorted out briefly in the discussion that follows. The much larger and infinitely more contentious question of consumer safeguards and so-called contracts of adhesion is reserved for Section B.

1. *Duress.* Promises extorted by violence or threat of violence are obviously not enforceable. Formation of a contract requires "assent" on the part of each of the contracting parties, and while a gun to the head will almost always compel an

61

affirmative response from the victim, the law, for reasons too plain to require discussion, treats the resulting "agreement" as void. Economic duress—a threat to discharge an employee, for example, unless the employee agrees to release a valid claim she has against the employer—may likewise vitiate a contract, though in these circumstances the contract is likely to be regarded as voidable at the victim's option rather than void at inception.

Perhaps the most interesting question in the duress field—one that may actually require us to articulate our rationale more carefully—concerns the enforceability of a promise to modify an *existing* contract, agreed to (perhaps) as a consequence of the promisor's threat to breach.[1] Thus, A promises a performance to B. Before the performance has been completed, A asks B to agree to a change of some sort in the terms of their contract—perhaps an increase in compensation. Eager for A's performance, B agrees, but later reneges. The rule at common law—referred to as the "preexisting duty" rule—is that the performance of an act which the promisee is already bound by contract to perform is not "valid consideration". The enforcement of B's subsequent promise would accordingly be barred on the ground that a fresh consideration for that promise was lacking. Although sometimes criticized as formal and "scholastic",[2] on one view the preexisting duty rule can be commended for protecting B from what may have been an effort at coercion or at least undue pressure on A's part. On the other hand, applying the rule in an automatic fashion, and without some sense of why they actually did propose and agree to the modification, might result in the frustration of the parties' real interests by making it difficult or impossible to carry on cooperative relations in the future. Especially in the case of long-term contracts—the construction of a building would be an obvious example—circumstances affecting performance could change, as time passed, in ways that were not anticipated when the agreement was entered into, and the parties might very well think it

1. For discussion, see Narasimhan, *Of Expectations, Incomplete Contracting, and the Bargain Principle.* 74 Cal.L.Rev. 1123 (1986); Muris, *Opportunistic Behavior and the Law of Contracts,* 65 Minn.L.Rev. 521 (1981); Hillman, *Policing Contract Modifications under the U.C.C.: Good Faith and the Doctrine of Duress,* 64 Iowa L.Rev. 849 (1979).

2. See, e.g., Schwartzreich v. Bauman–Basch, Inc., 231 N.Y. 196, 131 N.E. 887 (1921). The plaintiff, having entered into a 1–year employment contract with the defendant at a stated salary, later prevailed on the defendant to make a new contract increasing the salary to meet a competitor's offer. *Held,* judgment for the plaintiff affirmed. The parties effectively rescinded the first contract by mutual consent. They then went on to form a second contract in which their exchange of promises constituted valid consideration. The fact that the rescission of the old contract and the creation of the new contract took place simultaneously was "unimportant".

better now to modify the terms of the agreement than to allow their relationship to sink into conflict and litigation. Where the modification of a contract has positive elements for each of the parties—a creditor, for example, agrees to extend the maturity date of a loan; the debtor, in turn, consents to a higher rate of interest—then, as a technical matter, there is consideration on both sides and the new promises are mutually enforceable. But if the modification runs in favor of one party only, a strict application of the consideration requirement would prevent enforcement even though the change is reasonable and acceptable to the promisor.

Recognizing a certain tension in policy goals, the Restatement first affirms the preexisting duty rule, stating in Section 73 that the "performance of a legal duty owed to a promisor. . . . is not consideration", but then in Section 89 (under the topic-heading Contracts Without Consideration) provides that a promise modifying a contractual duty will be binding on the promisor "if the modification is fair and equitable in view of circumstances not anticipated by the parties when the contract was made". Going somewhat further, but essentially reflecting the same tension, UCC 2–209 simply eliminates the need for consideration in this context, requiring only that the modification be made in "good faith" and for a "legitimate commercial reason". Where there is "extortion" or "coercion", on the other hand, or "the use of bad faith to escape performance", both the Code and the courts regard the modification as ineffective and will permit the promisor to treat her consent to it as voidable.

While the distinction between "legitimate" commercial conduct and "extortion" looks like a garden-variety line-drawing problem, the issue may actually be a bit more subtle than that. Thus, we could imagine a case—perhaps *Austin Instruments,* discussed below, is one—in which the threat to breach exhibits both elements at once: it is legitimate from the standpoint of the party doing the threatening, but coercive or extortionate in its impact on the party under threat. In deciding whether or not to apply the doctrine of duress, we would then have to determine which of the two parties' interests to treat as paramount. No equivalent dilemma is presented in the case of a physical threat, obviously, because the outcome is the same whether our focus is on the threatening party or the party threatened.

In the well-known *Alaska Packers* case [3], the defendant, owner of a salmon cannery, had a contract with the plaintiffs, a group of

3. Alaska Packers' Ass'n v. Domenico, 117 Fed. 99 (9th Cir.1902).

hearty sailors, to operate its fishing boats in certain remote northern waters. The sailors signed "articles" under which each was to be paid $50 for the "season" (the season, apparently, being short) plus 2 cents a fish. At the very last moment, however, and when it was plainly too late for the defendant to hire replacement personnel, the sailors threatened to stop work and jump ship unless the defendant agreed to sign new articles doubling their pay to $100. The defendant did agree, but then later, the catch being in, refused to pay more than the $50 originally promised. Finding that the plaintiffs' conduct was willful, arbitrary and "without any valid cause", the court held that the defendant's promise to come through with an extra $50 had been given for no consideration and, hence, need not be performed. While the defendant might, theoretically, have chosen to sue the sailors for breach instead of consenting to the modification, as a practical matter it had no choice since the sailors would obviously be unable to respond in damages.

As in the gun-to-the-head case, the result in *Alaska Packers* probably can be accepted without pausing to distinguish between the parties' respective interests. Plainly, the defendant's consent to the pay raise was a forced consent, the alternative being the loss of much of its investment in the cannery itself. Plainly, also, the plaintiffs timed their threat so as to maximize the defendant's vulnerability—plaintiffs had received no competing offer and no change had occurred in the market for their services or the conditions of their work that would explain or legitimate an effort to get an increase in compensation. As suggested, therefore, the outcome is the same whether we emphasize the absence of a "legitimate reason" on the plaintiffs' part or the defendant's lack of choice; under either test, there appears to have been considerable justification for applying the doctrine of duress.

By contrast, *Austin Instrument Co. v. Loral Corporation*[4], a four-to-three decision of the New York Court of Appeals, is a case in which choice of rationale may finally become impossible to avoid. In *Austin*, the defendant, Loral, having been awarded a $6 million contract by the Navy for the production of radar equipment, entered into a subcontract with the plaintiff for the manufacture of various precision gear components. The Navy contract contained a strict delivery schedule—the radar equipment was for use in Viet Nam—and imposed liquidated damages for late deliveries or cancellation. After shipping some of the gear parts but not all, Austin apparently realized that it was going to lose money

4. 29 N.Y.2d 124, 324 N.Y.S.2d 22, 272 N.E.2d 533 (1971).

on the subcontract, and it thereupon notified Loral that it would cease further shipments—would, in effect, breach the contract— unless Loral agreed to a retroactive price increase. Equally important, Loral had meanwhile been awarded a second Navy contract for radar equipment and announced that it proposed to subcontract with another component manufacturer. Having presumably tooled up for the first Navy contract, Austin demanded that Loral give it the right to make all the gear components to be furnished under the second as well. Unable to reach a settlement after three or four weeks of discussion, Loral finally agreed to both demands because (as it told Austin in a letter written by counsel) "We have feverishly surveyed other sources of supply and. . . . they could not even remotely begin to deliver on time. . . . Accordingly, we are left with no choice or alternative but to meet your conditions." Subsequently, Loral refused to pay at the increased price levels for the parts shipped under the first contract, and Austin sued.

Finding that money damages would have been inadequate and that Loral could not have obtained the gear parts from other sources in time to meet its obligations to the Navy, a majority of the Court of Appeals, reversing the court below, held for the defendant. Austin's threat to stop deliveries confronted Loral with the danger of liquidated damage claims or cancellation by the Navy as well as loss of standing as a defense contractor, all of which "deprived Loral of its free will". Hence, the contract modification was voidable on grounds of duress. The dissenting judges would have affirmed the decision of the lower court, which had found that Austin's demand for renegotiation during a "time of continual rising of material and manufacturing costs" [5] was by no means uncommon or improper. Doubting whether Loral had been truly diligent in canvassing alternative suppliers, the dissenters evidently felt that Austin's request for a price increase was "a commercially understandable renegotiation" rather than "an exercise of duress."

Just how to weigh the disputed facts in *Austin Instrument* is, of course, a matter of debate. On the whole, however, the approach taken by the dissenters—emphasizing Austin's motives in demanding a price increase rather than the impact of that demand on Loral's "free will"—seems the more plausible and consistent of the two. The critical issue, I think, should not have been Loral's state of mind, which would always have been fiercely hostile to any proposal for a price increase, but whether Austin's

5. Quoted from the majority opinion of the Appellate Division; 316 N.Y.S.2d 534.

insistence on renegotiating was the sort of hold-up move that the contract law should refuse to encourage. The question, really, is whether or not Austin's behavior should be seen as strictly "opportunistic"—whether, like the sailors in *Alaska Packers,* Austin consciously and deliberately chose to threaten breach at a time when it knew that true renegotiation was impossible. On this score, however, and no matter how the facts are viewed, it seems pretty clear that Austin's threat to breach was triggered *not* by Loral's vulnerability but by its own loss experience under the first subcontract and its disappointment over the second.

Where market changes—sharply rising labor and material costs in *Austin*—confront one of the contracting parties with the prospect of substantial losses, the other contracting party ought not to be greatly surprised by demands for modification and by threats of breach, express or implied. The "Official Comment" to UCC 2–209 (nowhere mentioned in the *Austin* opinion, incidentally) states that "such matters as a market shift which makes performance come to involve a loss may provide [a good faith] reason" for the disadvantaged party to seek modification, even though failure to perform will constitute an actionable breach. In these circumstances, presumably, the disadvantaged party (Austin) regards it as less costly, and hence more efficient, to pay damages than to meet its contract obligations. The advantaged party (Loral), faced with a demand for modification, is then obliged to choose between (i) suing for damages, which may or may not be adequate in amount and will in effect be reduced by unrecoverable litigation expenses, and (ii) renegotiating and making financial concessions of some sort to the disadvantaged party. The equation is a painful one (painful for both parties, really), but the process, which is otherwise known as compromise, would not usually merit application of the doctrine of duress, because it is precisely what the Code provision mentioned above appears to contemplate. This is so, I think, even where defense contracts are involved, and even in war-time.

2. *Misrepresentation and Concealment.* The requirement of "assent", which is fundamental to the formation of a binding contract, implies in a general way that both parties to an exchange shall have a reasonably clear conception of what they are getting and what they are giving up. If the identity or the character of the property or service being bought or sold is overtly misrepresented by one of the contracting parties, then the other party's assent is obviously less than meaningful and any agreement that results will be regarded as voidable. This follows as a matter of law even though there is no specific intent to defraud—

that is, even if the misrepresenting party is unaware that her statement or representation is false. Representations of fact, at least if material and if relied upon in good faith, constitute an "inducement" to the receiving party for which the representing party is deemed responsible. If the inducement is worthless, then, whether she acted fraudulently or innocently, the party responsible for having offered it will, in effect, be obliged to restore the offeree to status quo.

All this is standard fare. What is less clear under the decided cases is whether, or in what circumstances, *non-disclosure* of a material fact—mere silence—should be treated as the legal equivalent of misrepresentation. Thus, A offers to sell her house to B for $100,000. There are termites in the basement and it will cost $5,000 to get rid of them. Having lived in the house for years, A knows about the termites. B doesn't. Does A have a legal duty to bring the matter to B's attention? If she says nothing, can B afterwards rescind? Or can A simply leave it up to B to check out the condition of the house for herself before she buys?

In *Swinton v. Whitinsville Sav. Bank* [6], the Supreme Court of Massachusetts held that the seller of a home "infested with termites" had no legal obligation to disclose this circumstance to the buyer, even though the seller knew about the termites and knew the buyer didn't. A property-seller cannot, of course, make false representations about the property—can't tell lies and get away with it—but "bare nondisclosure" is a different matter and creates no liability. Were the rule otherwise, the Court reasoned, "every seller [would be] liable who fails to disclose any nonapparent defect known to him in the subject of the sale which materially reduces its value and . . . [s]imilarly . . . every buyer would be liable who fails to disclose any nonapparent virtue known to him . . . which materially enhances its value . . ." Given the frailties of human nature, a standard "so idealistic", if imposed as a strict requirement of law, would be unworkable. Accordingly, buyers and sellers dealing at arms-length must each look out for themselves—caveat emptor, caveat vendor—at least in Massachusetts.

The *Swinton* decision has been followed by some courts but it has been rejected by others on the ground that it no longer reflects "American mores", and it is specifically disapproved by Section 161 of the Restatement, about which a further comment is made below. In making our own evaluation, we should of course bear in mind that the effect of the *Swinton* decision—that is, its conse-

6. 311 Mass. 677, 42 N.E.2d 808 (1942).

quence for *future* home-buyers and sellers—is simply to require the buyer to conduct her own investigation of the house, hiring a plumber to inspect the water-pipes, an electrician to examine the wiring, and an exterminator to look for bugs, rather than relying for such information on the seller. All this costs money, however, so that if, as in *Swinton,* the seller *already* knows about a defect in the premises, it will be cheaper for the seller to disclose it than for the buyer to have to discover it for herself. From the standpoint of efficiency, therefore, a rule that requires disclosure may be superior to caveat emptor.

But does it really matter? Not much, I think, in the generality of cases. Even if the law required the home-seller to disclose everything she knew, the buyer could never be sure in advance that the seller actually *had* accurate knowledge about the state of the water pipes and the wiring, and it seems virtually certain that she would want to undertake her own investigation before making a commitment to buy, whatever the expense. Where a casual transaction between nonprofessionals is in view—the sale of a residence, a used car, a diamond ring—the buyer would almost never be satisfied to act on the basis of the seller's disclosures, since the buyer would have no reason to assume that the seller actually knew all there was to be known about the property. In this context, therefore, the disclosure rule, whether contrary to *Swinton* or in accord, probably has little significance in practice.

At all events, as noted, the *Swinton* decision is rejected by Section 161 of the Restatement, which treats non-disclosure as equivalent to misrepresentation where the undisclosed fact concerns a "basic assumption" made by the other party to the contract and where the non-disclosure "amounts to a failure to act in good faith". The good-faith condition, otherwise rather mysterious, is evidently intended by the Restatement to distinguish between cases that involve a seller's knowledge of hidden defects— the *Swinton* case itself—and cases involving so-called market information which is typically the product of research and special expertise on the part of a potential buyer. In general (and as observed at greater length in Chapter 7 in connection with the related subject of "mistake"), an individual who spends time and money developing information about the intrinsic value of certain property does not and should not have a legal duty to disclose her findings to the property's present owner. Just as an inventor is rewarded with a patent or an author with a copyright, so, in effect, the developer of market data is rewarded with the right to keep the information to herself until she can acquire the property for her own account. Thus, fancifully, if the buyer in the *Swinton* case had been a geologist whose research convinced her that there was a gold-mine under the seller's residence, she would surely have had no obligation to tell the seller that the property was actually worth a thousand times the asking price. While the seller could be said to have made a "basic assumption" that the property was intended for residential use only, there would be no "failure to act in good faith" on the geologist's part if she bought it without disclosing, i.e., surrendering, the fruits of her research.[7] Hence, the Court in *Swinton* was pretty clearly wrong in supposing that a decision that required a seller to reveal a "nonapparent defect" would similarly require a buyer to reveal a "nonapparent virtue". The two cases may be alike in respect to the element of concealment. In respect to the obligation of disclosure, however, they can be, and presumably would be, treated differently even if the Court had succumbed to its "moral sense" and had required the home-seller to come clean about the termites.

B.　Standardized Forms and Unconscionability

Consumer transactions of all kinds—purchasing a car, renting an apartment, applying for an insurance policy—are regularly carried out on the basis of printed, standard-form contracts prepared by the seller or by the industry-group to which the seller belongs. In addition to price and merchandise description, the contract form includes various technical provisions that purport to define the rights and duties of the parties in some detail. Drafted from the seller's perspective, these standardized clauses are generally intended to minimize the seller's risks and responsibilities—for example, by narrowing the scope of the seller's warranties or by expanding its legal remedies in the event the buyer fails to make installment payments when due—and, by the same token, to impose burdens or other limitations on the buyer.

The buyer, we can safely assume, is unaware of the detailed content of the standard-form agreement at the time she signs it. She is given no real opportunity to read the document, and as the technical provisions are written in legal language, she couldn't fully understand them if she studied the agreement all day. In any case, even if read, understood and loudly objected to, the standard-form contract terms are simply not negotiable. The buyer may in some instances (say a used car purchase) bargain with the seller over price, but the remaining contract terms are

---

7. Kronman, *Mistake, Disclosure, Information, and the Law of Contracts,* 7 J. of Legal Studies 1 (1978).

offered on a take-it-or-leave-it basis. Indeed, the seller's representative—salesman, rental agent—would usually have no authority
to alter the document. To be sure, the buyer can always shop
elsewhere; but she is likely to assume, often correctly, that the
same or a similar standard-form contract is employed by other
sellers in the field, so that dragging herself from one office or
showroom to another in search of better terms would be a wasted
effort.

In this familiar setting, are there, and should there be, any
limits on the seller's legal ability to enforce the contract against
the buyer? Before answering, I suppose we ought to acknowledge
that where ordinary consumer transactions are concerned there is
really no practical alternative to the use of standard-form purchase agreements, whatever their shortcomings. Sellers of mass-
merchandise products (cars, apartment space, insurance policies)
obviously cannot take time to negotiate a detailed contract for
each individual transaction, and the buyer herself would not wish
to incur the heavy expense (e.g., legal fees) that such negotiations
would entail. The rights and obligations of seller and buyer do
need to be spelled out in writing, but both parties have a real
interest in minimizing the cost of contracting. Standard-form
agreements are the best and probably the only way of avoiding
transaction costs that might otherwise overwhelm the transaction
itself, and since it is the seller, not the buyer, for whom such
transactions are a constant and repeated event, the drafting of the
contract form quite naturally becomes the seller's responsibility.
The result, however, as stated, is a document which thoroughly
favors the seller's interest—one, moreover, to which the buyer is
compelled to "adhere" if she wants the merchandise, because the
seller will not make the goods available on any other basis.

In *Henningsen v. Bloomfield Motors, Inc.*[8], the plaintiff bought
a new Plymouth from the defendant-dealer. The steering mechanism failed ten days after the car was delivered and the plaintiff's
wife was injured. Plaintiff and his wife brought suit against the
defendant and against Chrysler, the manufacturer, for breach of
an implied warranty of merchantability, that is, a warranty
against defective manufacture. Absent any contractual disclaimer, an implied warranty of merchantability would, under the law,
entitle a car-buyer to damages for personal injuries even if (in the
Court's words) "due care were used in the manufacturing process".
Seeking to avoid such liability, the defendants pointed out that the
purchase agreement did, in fact, specifically disclaim all warranties, express or implied, other than liability to replace defective

8. 32 N.J. 358, 161 A.2d 69 (1960).

parts for a period of 90 days following purchase. While the
defendants presumably stood ready to replace the defective steering mechanism, they contended that the contract effectively eliminated any further liability, including liability for personal injuries.
The contract was, of course, a standardized purchase agreement,
with the warranty disclaimer printed in small type on the back of
the form.

The Supreme Court of New Jersey, in a decision generally
regarded as path-breaking, held for the plaintiffs—meaning, in the
circumstances, that the contractual disclaimer, insofar as it sought
to immunize the defendants from personal injury claims, would be
regarded as void. It was true, said the Court, that competent
parties are free, in general, to make any lawful agreement (of
which this was surely one), and that anyone who signs a contract
without reading it does so at his peril. Here, however, overriding
considerations of public policy—in effect, the need "to protect the
ordinary man against the loss of important rights"—made it
appropriate to disregard the conventional premises of laissez-faire
and to treat the warranty-disclaimer as a nullity. Need for
protection—really, special protection—for "ordinary" men arose
for several reasons, in the Court's view, of which the most important appeared to be the monopoly position occupied by the Big
Three auto manufacturers (GM, Ford and Chrysler), which together produced 93.5% of the passenger cars sold in this country (in
1958). The same standard form warranty-disclaimer was used by
all three, or by their dealers, so that a car-buyer could neither
negotiate nor shop elsewhere for better terms. Free of the compe-
tition that exists in other fields, car makers would be less concerned with safe construction, would feel less of an "urge to be
careful", if they could also, by contract, insulate themselves from
liability for personal injuries resulting from defective manufacture. Apart from public policy, the Court apparently detected an
element of misrepresentation in the dealings between the defendants and the car-buyer. The warranty-disclaimer, as noted, was
a fine-print provision which the buyer could not have been expected to read with any care unless actively called to his attention
by the dealer. And even if he had read it, or should be deemed to
have read it, the true significance of the disclaimer would almost
certainly have escaped him. Thus, an "ordinary layman" would
be likely to read the warranty clause as meaning merely that
Chrysler would replace defective parts (not substitute a whole new
car) within a period limited to 90 days after purchase. But the
same ordinary layman would never conceive that the clause was
designed as well to deprive him of the right to claim damages for
personal injury, because that was a right which he would other-

wise regard as "the most important and fundamental one arising from the relationship". The challenged clause was skillfully drafted to avoid "drawing too much attention" to the defendants' effort to escape their customary warranty obligations; in fact, it drew too little.

As noted, the Court in *Henningsen* took emphatic notice of the alleged monopoly position of the Big Three auto-makers (foreign imports being virtually non-existent at the time the case was decided) and the resulting inequality in bargaining power between car-sellers and buyers. A car-buyer, said the Court, "must take or leave the automobile on the warranty terms dictated by the maker. He cannot turn to a competitor for better security." There was, in effect, a kind of "duress" in the sense that the desired goods would simply have been withheld by the alleged auto cartel had the plaintiff been unwilling to swallow the boiler-plate contract terms as well.

But suppose the factor of market dominance is lacking; suppose the seller operates in a strictly competitive economic environment and has plenty of business rivals eager for the buyer's trade. While a seller—say a department store—would usually have greater resources and possess more commercial sophistication than its customers, even the simplest consumer knows that there are many places to shop and that close substitutes for the brand she wants are readily available. Is "unconscionability" confined to the relatively rare monopoly situation said to exist in *Henningsen,* or should it apply to consumer transactions generally, even though in most circumstances the ordinary consumer is not without a "meaningful choice" both among competing sellers and among alternative goods?

In *Williams v. Walker–Thomas Furniture Co.*[9], decided by the D.C. Court of Appeals in 1965, the Company, a retail store, sought to repossess various household items that it had sold to Williams, a welfare recipient, over a period of some five years. Each sale (including the last, a stereo set sold for $514.95) was on credit, Williams being obligated to make monthly installment payments, called "rent", until the full purchase price was satisfied. The printed form purchase agreement contained a so-called cross-collateral or "dragnet" provision of which the purpose was to secure the customer's indebtedness by empowering the Company, in the event of a default, to repossess not only the particular item (say the stereo set) to which the indebtedness related, but every other article purchased from the Company on which any balance remained due at the time the latest purchase was made. In

9.   350 F.2d 445 (D.C.Cir.1965).

mechanical terms, this purpose was accomplished under the contract by assuring that a balance would be due on each previous installment sale until the customer had paid off her indebtedness to the Company for *all* purchased articles, current and past. The cross-collateral clause read as follows:

"[T]he amount of each periodical installment payment to be made by (purchaser) to the Company under this present lease shall be inclusive of and not in addition to the amount of each installment payment to be made by (purchaser) under such prior leases, bills or accounts; and all payments now and hereafter made by (purchaser) shall be credited pro rata on all outstanding leases, bills and accounts due the Company by (purchaser) at the time each such payment is made."

Williams having defaulted on the stereo installments, the Company, pointing out that under the above provision she still owed 3 cents on one item and 25 cents on another, sought to "scoop up" all the merchandise it had ever sold her,[10] presumably leaving behind nothing but a couple of orange crates and the empty stereo carton. Represented by the legal assistance office of the bar association, Williams resisted on the ground that the cross-collateral provision was unconscionable and therefore not enforceable. Finding no legislative authority for the defense of unconscionability—the UCC, and with it Section 2–302, had not yet been made applicable in the District of Columbia—the District Court reluctantly held for the Company. In so holding, however, it did not hesitate to express its opinion of the Company's aims and methods:

". . . at the time of this and the preceding purchases, appellee was aware of appellant's financial position. The reverse side of the stereo contract listed the name of appellant's social worker and her $218 monthly stipend from the government. Nevertheless, with full knowledge that appellant had to feed, clothe and support both herself and seven children on this amount, appellee sold her a $514 stereo set . . . We cannot condemn too strongly appellee's conduct."

On appeal, the Circuit Court held that the defense of unconscionability was available in the District of Columbia as a matter of common law and required no specific statutory authorization. Accordingly, the District Court's decision was reversed and the case remanded for a finding on the "possible unconscionability" of the contract provision at issue. By way of guidance to the court

---

10. Skilton & Helstad, *Protection of the Installment Buyer of Goods under the UCC,* 65 Mich.L.Rev. 1465 (1967).

below, Judge Wright indicated that "unconscionability" meant or included two salient factors: an absence of meaningful choice on the buyer's part (in effect) and the presence of contract terms "unreasonably favorable" to the seller. Meaningfulness of choice might be negated by the "manner" in which the contract was entered into, and with respect to "manner" the question was: "Did each party to the contract, considering his obvious education or lack of it, have a reasonable opportunity to understand the terms of the contract, or were the important terms hidden in a maze of fine print and minimized by deceptive sales practices?" If the latter were the case, then, where the contract terms were also found to be "commercially unreasonable" and "so unfair", enforcement should be refused.

The "unconscionability" principle, now reflected in UCC 2–302 and represented by a fairly substantial body of recent case law, has been discussed at greater length and with more intensity, I think, than any recent issue in the contracts field.[11] Legal scholars tend to divide across quite a broad spectrum in their evaluation of that principle, with ethical premises playing an unmistakable part in the debate. One difficulty, as the *Henningsen* and *Walker–Thomas* courts candidly acknowledged, is how both to apply and to contain the concept of unconscionability— how to protect people from being dealt with by car-dealers and furniture companies in ways that violate their expectations as consumers, while at the same time continuing to honor "freedom of contract" as a fundamental tenet of the legal system. The answer furnished by the cases, and presumably accepted by the UCC, is that a contract entered into by competent adults is binding without regard to anyone's opinion of its fairness; but where the circumstances indicate that one party did not, or could not, fully comprehend the meaning of the contract, then the court is free to use its own judgment to determine whether the contract terms are fair. Thus, the threshold issue in *Walker–Thomas* is whether the Company made the cross-collateral provision clear to Ms. Williams at the time she signed the form contract. If so, there can be no "unconscionability". If not—if, in effect, the bargaining process was tainted by non-disclosure and incapacity— then, and presumably only then, the reviewing court can deny enforcement to those contract terms which it finds to be unfair.

11. See, e.g., Rakoff, *Contracts of Adhesion: An Essay in Reconstruction*, 96 Harv.L.Rev. 1173 (1983); Leff, *Unconscionability and the Code—The Emperor's New Clause*, 115 U.Pa.L.Rev. 485 (1967); Eisenberg, *The Bargain Principle and its Limits*, 95 Harv.L.Rev. 741 (1982); Epstein, *Unconscionability: A Critical Appraisal*, 18 J. Law & Econ. 293 (1975); Slawson, *Standard Form Contracts and Democratic Control of Lawmaking Power*, 84 Harv.L.Rev. 529 (1971).

But while plausible in theory, in fact and application the unconscionability defense usually reduces itself to the single question of "substantive fairness". It is, after all, basic to the problem of unconscionability that form language is seldom understood or even read. The shopper in a store or a showroom does not take time to pore over the contract, and the salesman (who probably couldn't make one if he tried) would rarely attempt an explanation of its terms. The law could respond by insisting on the classic principle that "one who does not choose to read a contract before signing it cannot later relieve himself of its burdens. . . ." But that "rule" having been discarded in the present context, consumers are almost always free to seek relief from contract terms which they regard as oppressive and unreasonable by asserting that they did not "knowingly assent" to those terms when the contract was entered into. In the end, therefore, it is likely to be substantive fairness, rather than defects in the bargaining process, with which the reviewing court will be concerned.

Shifting our attention to the fairness issue itself, I suppose the first point we would agree upon is that the challenged contract term—say the cross-collateral provision in *Walker–Thomas*—must be considered and appraised as of the time the contract was entered into by the parties—before the fact, so to speak—rather than afterwards and in hindsight. The question to be asked is not whether Ms. Williams *now* feels oppressed by the repossession of her household goods—she obviously does—but whether it was unconscionable to include that term in the purchase agreement at the time she bought the stereo set. Would she have agreed to the cross-collateral provision if she had fully understood it, or would she have attempted to negotiate different terms with Walker–Thomas? If the latter, what *are* the terms to which she would finally have given her full, conscious assent?

The answer, unfortunately, cannot simply be that Ms. Williams would have preferred a purchase agreement that omitted the cross-collateral clause. No doubt she would, but I think we have to assume that if cross-collateralization were eliminated, the store would then insist (and in future *will* insist) on some adjustment to the credit terms that it offers to its low-income customers. Thus, Ms. Williams "borrows" $514—the price of the stereo set— from Walker–Thomas. The cost to Ms. Williams, i.e., the interest rate she pays on the loan, obviously reflects her credit-worthiness as a borrower. The more property she puts up (or is led to put up) by way of security, the lower the cost of credit to her and to others at the same modest income-level. If the cross-collateral provision is held to be unenforceable, so that the lender's only security in the event of a default is (as I guess it would be) the stereo set itself, then, no doubt, the interest rate demanded by the lender will increase correspondingly and Ms. Williams' monthly installment payments will be that much higher. In finding, or at least strongly suggesting, that the cross-collateral provision should be regarded as unconscionable, the Court in *Walker–Thomas* also in effect decreed that Ms. Williams and other low-income people who want to buy home-appliances on time must in the future pay more for credit.

We can now restate the question asked just above—whether Ms. Williams would have agreed to the cross-collateral clause had she understood its meaning—in the following way. Assuming full awareness on Ms. Williams' part, which of the two alternative credit arrangements should we suppose that she would actually have preferred—easier security terms and higher interest charges, or harsh security terms and lower interest charges? The Court (wittingly or unwittingly) decided that Ms. Williams would choose the former combination—easier terms and higher interest—if she, and presumably other low-income consumers, were able to make a conscious choice. By contrast, Walker–Thomas (and probably most of the other retailers in that neighborhood) evidently believed that customers would react more favorably to the opposite pattern—strict security requirements and lower interest—because monthly payments would be smaller. As to who was "right"—the Court or Walker–Thomas—we will of course never know. The strict-security component was in no real sense "chosen" by Ms. Williams; rather, it was slipped into the transaction and hidden from view.

Decisions like *Walker–Thomas* are sometimes criticized on the ground that they represent an unwanted and improper intervention in the lives of poor people (who, it is said, ought to be as free as the rest of us to throw their money away), but I think that this may somewhat overstate the issue. While everyone agrees that the use of standard form contracts is a necessary incident of mass-merchandising, it is also undeniably true that consumers (not just poor consumers) do not and cannot know all that the contract contains at the time they make their purchases. Where there is reason to doubt that the consumer would actually prefer the terms contained in the form contract (if she understood them) over an alternative set of terms, there may be some sense in the notion that a court (agency or legislature) should act to supply the missing element of conscious volition, rather than leaving that decision to producers and sellers who draft the contract forms.[12]

---

12. Goldberg, *Institutional Change and the Quasi-Invisible Hand,* 17 J. of Law & Econ. 461 (1974).

The question, ultimately, is whether Judge Wright or the Walker–Thomas Furniture Company is in a better position to make a "meaningful choice" on behalf of Ms. Williams and other consumers. The choice *will* be made, in effect, by one or the other. Hence, arguably, the unconscionability doctrine operates not as a means of controlling or intervening in people's lives, but as a device by which the choice-function is allocated to a court, rather than to the other contracting party, where the circumstances show that the consumer cannot choose for herself.

Chapter 5

CONTRACT INTERPRETATION

A good deal has been said already—more or less by the way—
about contract interpretation, and I somewhat doubt whether a
bare recital of general principles, apart from the particular contexts in which they might apply, is really very useful. Restatement Section 201(1) quite sensibly provides that where the parties
attach the same meaning to the terms used in their agreement,
the interpretation of the agreement should be in accordance with
that meaning even if a third party, presumably viewing the
matter from an objective standpoint, might interpret the contract
language differently. The converse is also true: whatever an
objective observer might think, if the contracting parties attach
different meanings to the same term, then neither is bound by the
understanding of the other unless one of them knew or had reason
to know what the other understood the disputed term to mean.
Apart from these "rules"—which properly emphasize a subjective,
party-oriented approach to contract interpretation—neither the
Restatement nor the decisional law or commentary offers much
that goes beyond the invocation of ordinary good sense in dealing
with the vagaries of language. In any case, as is often pointed out,
problems of contract interpretation are far more likely to arise
because of clumsiness and ineptitude on the part of the draftsmen
or the contracting parties themselves than because of philosophic
differences about the meaning of meaning.

In *Frigaliment Importing Company v. B.N.S. International
Sales Corp.,*[1] the issue (the Court said) "is, what is chicken?" The
plaintiff, a Swiss importer, sent an order to the defendant, an
American poultry exporter, for 75,000 pounds of "Grade A Chick-
en" at $33 per 100 pounds. The defendant, allegedly a newcomer
to the poultry trade, accepted the order and promptly shipped.
When the merchandise arrived in Switzerland, however, instead of
the tender young "broilers and fryers" which plaintiff intended to
resell to its customers—presumably retailers and restaurants—
and which plaintiff clearly had in mind when it forwarded its
purchase order, the shipment was found to consist of stringy old
stewing chicken—good for boiling up in a soup with noodles and a
chunk of carrot, but entirely unsuitable for the grill or the lightly
buttered frying pan. A second shipment, also of stewing chicken,
was apparently aborted by the defendant when it realized that

1. 190 F.Supp. 116 (S.D.N.Y.1960).

plaintiff would not accept the merchandise. Plaintiff sued for breach of warranty under the equivalent of UCC 2–313(1)(b), which provides that "Any description of the goods which is made part of the basis of the bargain creates an express warranty that the goods shall conform to the description."

Holding for the defendant, Judge Friendly found that the term "chicken", not otherwise specified, could properly be taken to refer to "stewing chicken or fowl," and that the defendant, in accepting the original order, actually believed that stewing chicken was the product it was asked to deliver. Defendant's subjective belief would not be significant, said the Court, if it did not coincide with an objective meaning of the disputed term, but in fact the regulations issued by the Department of Agriculture included six classes of poultry under the heading "Chicken"; to-wit, Broiler or fryer, Roaster, Capon, Stag, Hen or stewing chicken, and Cock or old rooster. Since defendant's subjective intent thus agreed with the relevant definition—or at least with one such definition— there was no breach of warranty. To be sure, the plaintiff wanted and expected broilers or fryers (not Hen, Stag or anything else). However, the burden was on the plaintiff to show that it had used and communicated the term "chicken" in the narrower rather than the broader sense; and that burden it failed to carry.

Accepting (since we must) that the defendant did not know and had no reason to know what sort of merchandise the plaintiff customarily imported, the reasoning (if not the outcome) in *Frigaliment* still seems rather doubtful. The Court did not really answer the question, "what is 'chicken'?" Rather, it answered the question, "is stewing chicken 'chicken'?", which is a wholly different question. Thus, stewing chicken *is* "chicken" under the Department regulations, but so are broilers and fryers, and no real explanation is given in Judge Friendly's opinion for preferring the defendant's subjective/objective understanding to the plaintiff's. Plaintiff was no more or less accurate and precise than defendant in its understanding of the critical term, and its own subjective intent was just as firmly fixed. The Court may have meant to imply that offerors generally bear a heavier obligation to be clear and specific about contract language than offerees, but the respective roles of offeror and offeree in a fast-moving commodities market are difficult to separate and the opinion does not suggest any particular reason why a greater "burden" should be imposed on one market operator than the other.

Probably (as Judge Friendly indicated in a later decision), the *Frigaliment* case should have been regarded as another instance of the *Peerless* problem and decided by reference to the doctrine of

Raffles v. Wichelhaus.[2] Importer and exporter obviously attached different meanings to the term "chicken," neither (apparently) having reason to know about the particular meaning intended by the other. The legal result, then, is simply a failure of mutual assent and neither party has a claim based on "contract". Under these circumstances, if the *Peerless* doctrine applies, the consequence should be to nullify all outstanding obligations: there is no breach of warranty on defendant's part, but plaintiff has no duty to accept and pay for any undelivered merchandise. The actual outcome in *Frigaliment* is thus, probably, unobjectionable. Since the first shipment of stewing chicken was apparently accepted, paid for and resold to customers, that transaction as a practical matter was irreversible and any resulting loss (e.g., refunds to customers) had to be borne by the plaintiff. With respect to shipping costs, spoilage, etc. incurred in connection with the second shipment, the dollar loss no doubt fell on the defendant. Both parties thus suffered some financial damage, and that is sad, but as neither had a contract claim against the other—there being no contract—the law itself provides no remedy.

Rightly or wrongly reasoned, *Frigaliment,* like *Peerless,* highlights the fallibility or variability of language itself and the possibility that the parties to a contract may use the same words to express quite different aims and expectations. At some point, it appears, the element of misunderstanding or ambiguity is simply overwhelming and there is nothing sufficiently common or mutual to make a contract out of.

That said, I should emphasize that the latter outcome is rare and unusual. Generally speaking, contract law dislikes breakdown and frustration and prefers instead, where reasonable, to construct an enforceable contract out of whatever raw materials of intention the parties have made available. Where, for example, the parties have failed or omitted to specify a "term" in what would otherwise be a binding agreement—even so vital a term as price—the courts may supply the missing element by resorting to trade usage or to any prior course of dealing between the parties "which is fairly to be regarded as establishing a common basis of understanding . . . "[3] While the courts will not enforce a mere "agreement to agree", there is a tendency—supported by both the UCC and the Restatement—to find an understanding by reasonable reference to custom or to the parties' previous conduct. In *Frigaliment,* by contrast, there had been no prior course of dealing

2. Discussed in Chapter 3, above.

3. Restatement Section 223; and see UCC 2–204(3).

between plaintiff and defendant, and evidently trade usage was too various to be relied upon.

The discussion that follows takes up two further problems of contract interpretation (out of many that could be chosen) which likewise involve ambiguity of expression and intent. The first—the parol evidence rule—concerns the relationship between spoken agreements and written contracts. The issue, briefly stated, is whether written documents clear on their face should be subject to expansion or contraction by reference to prior oral agreements which are, of course, invisible. The second—exclusive dealing arrangements and other flexible commitments—returns once more to the question of how to enforce agreements that are indefinite with respect to the parties' obligations or that fail to make provision for a critical change in circumstances.

A. The Parol Evidence Rule

When applicable, the parol evidence rule renders unenforceable oral agreements entered into prior to the adoption of a written contract. Restatement Section 213 expresses the substantive concept in terms of "discharge": a written agreement that is found to be "completely integrated"—that represents a full and final embodiment of the parties' understanding—effectively discharges any prior agreement that falls within its scope. The consequence in evidentiary terms is that proof of the alleged prior agreement is inadmissible and cannot be placed before the trier of fact, which might of course be a jury otherwise inclined to sympathy for the alleged promisee. The judge himself makes the first and critical determination as to whether the written contract is in fact an integrated agreement. If it is, then, as stated, the prior oral agreement is discharged and evidence thereof is excluded for lack of relevance.

The purpose of the rule is apparent. Since the completion and execution of a written contract is typically the concluding point in the bargaining process, one's ordinary expectation is that the document itself will contain all the conscious and important elements of the deal. All sorts of things might have been said in the course of negotiations; tentative understandings might have been reached on particular issues but then later dropped or traded away or even forgotten. Once reduced to writing, however, the terms of agreement can be reviewed and revised more or less at leisure and finally articulated to everyone's satisfaction. The parol evidence rule assumes that the formal writing reflects the parties' minds at a point of maximum resolution and, hence, that duties and restrictions that do not appear in the written document, even though apparently accepted at an earlier stage, were not intended by the parties to survive. In addition, and quite apart from the survival of matters discarded in the course of negotiations, there is the obvious danger of outright fraud. If the contracting parties are entirely free to introduce evidence of prior oral agreements, what is there to stop an unscrupulous party from offering, or threatening to offer, evidence of a prior agreement that is altogether specious?

But suppose that none of these illicit factors is present. Suppose the parties used the written contract to express the central elements of their agreement—price, delivery date, identity of the property to be transferred—but assumed that various other obligations, mutually agreed upon and very much part of the deal, would be met in good faith and without a need for lengthy written elaboration. Even more simply, suppose they have a written agreement covering one transaction and a prior oral agreement on another. If applicable in these circumstances, the parol evidence rule would operate not as a safeguard against false or erroneous claims but as a rule of forfeiture, which would clearly be unfair and undesirable. While it might be simplest to adopt a very strict exclusionary rule where prior oral agreements are concerned, the consequences in a given case—one in which there really is no doubt about the parties' intent—could be harsh. It is not obvious, moreover, what a very strict rule would actually consist of, unless it took the form of a universal statute of frauds which permitted enforcement *only* with respect to written contracts. Short of doing that, the need is for an exclusionary principle that leaves room for judgment, good sense, sound discretion and similar sterling judicial attributes. As the cases next discussed should illustrate, the parol evidence rule, in requiring that the pivotal question of "integration" be resolved initially and as a matter of law, provides the courts, including the appellate courts, with a very considerable measure of flexibility. This, however, may also explain why the rule is commonly characterized as "murky".

In *Mitchill v. Lath*,[4] the plaintiff entered into a written contract to buy the defendants' farm for $8,400, intending to use the property as a summer vacation home. The contract, which contained "various provisions usual in such papers", appeared complete on its face, but plaintiff asserted and apparently could prove beyond a doubt that defendants had orally promised, as part of the transaction, to remove an "ice house"—an unsightly ramshackle structure—which belonged to defendants and stood in

---

4. 247 N.Y. 377, 160 N.E. 646 (1928), discussed in Weiskopf, *Supplementing Written Agreements: Restating the Pa-* *rol Evidence Rule in Terms of Credibility and Relative Fault,* 34 Emory L.J. 93 (1985).

plain view on a neighbor's land across the road. Having received their money and delivered a deed to the farm, however, defendants refused to keep their promise as to the ice house, and plaintiff sued for specific performance.

Holding for the defendants, the Court (with two dissents) found that the oral agreement was inadmissible—really, unenforceable—under the parol evidence rule. The rule, said the Court in effect, permits admission in evidence of an oral agreement made prior to the adoption of a written contract only if (a) such oral agreement is collateral in form (i.e., capable of being expressed in a separate agreement) and does not contradict the terms of the written contract, and (b) the written contract fails to fully integrate and embody the parties' understanding. A prior oral agreement to sell separate property for an independent consideration is obviously admissible; a prior agreement to pay more or less than the price named in the written contract for the very thing conveyed thereby is obviously not. The hard case, of course, is one in which the prior oral agreement *adds* to the obligations of one of the parties rather than contradicting a written term, but at the same time plainly falls within the scope of the written contract because it relates to the same subject-matter. Such was the case at hand: defendants' promise to remove the ice house could have been expressed in a separate agreement and it did not directly contradict anything in the written contract; yet it would have added materially to the defendants' costs by depriving them of the value of the ice house, which they apparently operated as a business, plus the expense of removing the structure itself. Ultimately, the issue depended on whether the detailed written contract would naturally appear to an "inquirer" to be complete and final with respect to the conditions governing the sale of the farm. At least to one inquirer—the Court majority—the contract did indeed appear to be complete and final; hence, the oral agreement could not be admitted in evidence. Pretty clearly, the majority felt that an outcome favorable to the plaintiff would signal a substantial relaxation of the parol evidence rule. That rule was "a wise one," however, and it should not be abandoned, "[n]otwithstanding an injustice here and there . . . ."

The words last quoted describe the result in *Mitchill* all too aptly, since it is (i) certain that the Laths did in fact promise to remove the ice house and (ii) very unlikely that the written contract was intended to eliminate that undertaking. The majority really questioned neither proposition. Rather, its concern was to support the safeguard-function of the parol evidence rule by emphasizing the preeminence of written over oral contracts even though the result might well be unjust. Read strictly, *Mitchill* holds that prior oral agreements are enforceable only if they entail separate consideration on the part of the promisee; if not, the written contract is nearly always decisive of the parties' obligations.

The *Mitchill* case can be compared with an equally well-known California decision, *Masterson v. Sine,*[5] which appears to treat the parol evidence rule more as an opportunity than a limitation. Masterson in 1958 sold his ranch to the Sines—his sister and brother-in-law—for $50,000. Under the terms of the deed by which the property was conveyed, Masterson reserved an option to repurchase the property at any time within the next 10 years for an amount equal to the original purchase price, $50,000, plus the cost of any ranch improvements made by the Sines. Masterson having subsequently been adjudged a bankrupt, the present action was brought by his trustee in bankruptcy to establish the trustee's right to exercise the option and obtain title to the ranch, now undoubtedly worth much more than $50,000. The Sines, with loyal support from Masterson himself, asserted that the parties had orally agreed that the repurchase option was non-assignable. It could be exercised by Masterson personally, according to the alleged oral agreement, but it could not be transferred to or exercised by Masterson's creditors (or by the trustee on their behalf) or indeed by any other third party.

Speaking through Justice Traynor, the Court held that evidence of the non-assignability restriction was admissible under (or despite) the parol evidence rule. The Court conceded that when a written contract is completely integrated, parol evidence cannot be admitted to vary its terms. However, it explicitly rejected the idea that admissibility depends on whether the written contract appears complete on its face. Even if it does, evidence of a collateral oral agreement should be excluded only when the fact finder is likely to be misled. The credibility of the proffered evidence, therefore, not the appearance of the written document, is the basis for decision. If under the circumstances the oral agreement could, or might naturally, have been entered into separately from the written agreement, then proof of such oral agreement should be permitted so as to avoid frustrating the parties' real intent. To be sure, the deed which Masterson delivered to the Sines specifically set forth the terms of Masterson's repurchase option. Hence an inquirer might well suppose that any additional terms, such as non-assignability, would naturally appear in the same place. Here, however, the writing was in a

5.   68 Cal.2d 222, 436 P.2d 561 (1968).

standardized form which did not readily lend itself to the insertion of additional terms, and this made it less likely that the special conditions agreed to would necessarily be included in that document. Moreover, the parties to the sale were family members who would presumably feel confident that they could rely on the spoken promises; they were, as well, inexperienced in land transactions and unaware of the disadvantages of failing to put their whole agreement in the deed. Given these circumstances, the case was one in which it could be said that a collateral understanding such as that alleged might naturally have been added through the medium of a separate agreement.

The decision in *Masterson* reflects an understandable solicitude for the Sines. A contrary outcome would have meant that the ranch—which may have been the Sine family's principal source of livelihood—would have been swallowed up in large part by Masterson's business creditors, persons with whom the Sines had had no dealings and to whom they owed nothing whatever. The Court viewed Masterson's repurchase option as a clumsy device for keeping the property in the family—more in the nature of a right of first refusal than a true option—and it does not appear that Masterson ever represented to his creditors that the value of the option could be regarded as part of his personal net worth. On the other hand, if you really believe that brother and sister overtly and consciously agreed that the option was non-assignable, you will, I think, believe anything. Actually (or at least most likely), they never mentioned or thought about the question of assignability at all. If that question *had* been brought to their attention no doubt they would have so agreed, but then, surely, they would have taken the trouble to add the necessary few words—"The option reserved to the Sellers herein shall not be assignable without the express consent of the Purchasers."—to the written contract itself. Of course, neither I nor Masterson's trustee was present when the sale of the ranch was negotiated, so nobody will ever know for certain. The plaintiff-trustee presumably gave up his attempt to draw the option into the bankrupt's estate once the Court had decided that evidence of the oral agreement should be admitted and made no subsequent effort to contest the factual issue at trial. Such a contest would have been useless in any case, since all of the parties to the negotiations were on the defendants' side of the lawsuit.

The Court in *Masterson* evidently didn't (or wouldn't) share my doubts about the credibility of the prior oral agreement. Instead, having determined as a first step that the evidence of such prior agreement was credible, it then went on to conclude that the written contract could not be regarded as an integrated document. As suggested, the approach thus adopted is essentially contrary to that taken in *Mitchill,* where the question to be decided *first* was whether the written contract appeared to be completely integrated: since it did so appear, proof of the prior oral agreement, although entirely credible, was held inadmissible as a matter of law.

In evaluating the two cases, I think many would feel that the *Masterson* decision, however desirable in outcome, renders the parol evidence rule somewhat circular in application. A prior oral agreement must be excluded if the written contract is found to be a complete integration; whether the written contract *is* completely integrated, however, depends on whether there is credible evidence of a prior oral agreement. Complete integration thus becomes a function not of the written contract but of the quality of the parol evidence—evidence which the written contract, if completely integrated, would effectively exclude. The *Mitchill* decision avoids the same element of circularity by assuming that the written contract is normally complete with respect to obligations falling within its scope (i.e., not supported by a separate consideration), so that evidence of a prior oral agreement must be excluded no matter how credible. As the case itself well illustrates, however, there is a price to be paid for whatever certainty and clarity is thus achieved: the Laths plainly did agree to remove that miserable ice house, and it is hard to respect an exclusionary rule which, in effect, allowed them to break their promise.

Choosing between *Masterson* (which admitted a prior agreement that was probably never made) and *Mitchill* (which excluded a prior agreement that was almost certainly made) is not a comfortable task. In making that choice, however, I suppose we should remind ourselves that the larger aim of contract law is to support and implement the common process of exchange by which private persons seek to generate welfare gains. The enforcement of contracts is the principal contribution that the law makes in this connection and nothing could be further from the purpose than a discharge rule that operates to withhold enforcement when the parties really have agreed. It is also true that the existence of an agreement needs to be verified before it can be enforced. Agreement by spoken rather than written word often makes the task of verification troublesome and costly—especially so when the oral contract appears to compete with a written contract—and it is fair enough to impose a heavy burden of proof on the proponent. But a rule of automatic exclusion—which, as in *Mitchill,* minimizes enforcement costs at the cost of enforcement itself—elevates the less important value of the two and hence, on balance, seems undesirable. Accordingly, one opts for *Masterson* in the end, though not without misgivings.

Written contracts frequently contain an explicit merger or integration clause stating, for example, that "this contract embodies the entire understanding between the parties, and there are no verbal agreements or representations in connection therewith". Despite such language, courts following the *Masterson* concept have been willing to admit evidence of a prior oral condition on the ground that the "true intent" of the parties is always the ultimate touchstone. In determining intent, "it is necessary to look not only to the written instrument, but to the circumstances surrounding its execution", which may of course show that a prior oral understanding was intended to survive. Justice Traynor himself indicated that if a merger clause had been included in Masterson's deed, this *might* have helped to resolve the assignability issue in the trustee's favor. Perhaps; yet one's intuition is that nothing short of an express contractual provision stating that the option was freely assignable would have won the day for the trustee.

The parol evidence rule has no application to oral agreements made *subsequent* to the execution of a written contract, although there may obviously be similar problems of proof. The parties to a contract (whether written or oral) are always free to modify their obligations by mutual agreement if they choose, or to terminate the existing contract and make a new one containing terms and conditions that better suit their present interests. As shown in Section A of Chapter 4, the principal legal issue in this context is whether the agreement to modify was freely entered into by both parties—or whether, in some sense, one of the parties imposed the modification on the other through an exercise of duress.

B. Filling the Gaps: "Best Efforts" and Other Flexible Commitments

Contracts for the sale of goods are usually specific as to vital terms—price, quantity, date of delivery—so that the question of whether the parties have "performed" can be answered in a straightforward way. Under certain circumstances, however, it may be preferable, even necessary, to avoid specificity and to leave one or more terms at large. Exclusive dealing agreements, and likewise requirements and output contracts, are major examples. Such contracts typically obligate the parties to buy or sell certain goods or perform certain services at a stated price, but intentionally omit to specify the *quantity* of the goods to be purchased or delivered or the extent of the services to be performed. There may be good reasons for the omission—it is not merely an oversight—but the problem which then arises is how, indeed whether, the courts can enforce an undertaking or commitment that is indefinite on its face.

Exclusive dealing contracts, including distributorships and licensing agreements, are common commercial arrangements. A manufacturer, for example, enters into an agreement with a distributor (say a wholesaler) for the sale of a particular product. The distributor is to pay the manufacturer a flat price or perhaps a percentage of the sale price for each item sold. The distributor's right to sell the product is exclusive—the manufacturer cannot sell through any other distributor within a defined geographical area—and in turn the distributor agrees to use its "best efforts" or "reasonable efforts" to generate a high volume of activity. The agreement might be for a specific period or it might be left open as to duration with the manufacturer having a right to terminate on giving timely notice.

The business motives that lie behind an exclusive dealing agreement of this sort are easily inferred. From the manufacturer's standpoint the agreement has the advantage of providing instant distribution facilities, including a sales organization, advertising and other promotional know-how, without an out-of-pocket investment on the manufacturer's part. Sharing profits with the distributor, all things considered, is seen as less expensive than creating a sales division internally. From the distributor's standpoint the exclusivity feature makes it worthwhile to allocate funds for advertising and sales promotion without having to worry about the possibility that other sellers of the same product will enjoy the benefit of those outlays and, in effect, get a free ride at the distributor's expense. For the same reason the distributor would want to be sure that the manufacturer's termination right was exercisable only after enough time had passed to allow the distributor to earn back its initial expenditures. The larger those expenditures, therefore, the longer the notice period demanded.

The unquantified element in an exclusive dealing agreement of this sort is, obviously, the distributor's promise to use best efforts in selling the product. Just how much the distributor will spend on advertising and precisely what proportion of its sales force will be employed in pushing this (as opposed to some other) manufacturer's product is nowhere specified, and it is conceivable that the distributor might determine that "best efforts" really means very little effort or at least much less than the manufacturer anticipated. Taken at face, the arrangement appears to be somewhat one-sided, which raises the threshold question whether the *fully* committed party—the manufacturer—has received a return promise that properly qualifies as "consideration."

In *Wood v. Lucy, Lady Duff-Gordon,*[6] the parties entered into a contract under which the plaintiff was given the exclusive right to license the use of the defendant's name in connection with the manufacture of dresses, hats, fabrics and the like. Defendant's opinions on women's fashions were then much in vogue, and it was expected that manufacturers and designers would pay handsome fees for her endorsements. The parties agreed to share all revenues equally. At some point, despite the grant of exclusive marketing rights to plaintiff, defendant began placing endorsements independently—in effect, went into the licensing business on her own—and plaintiff sued. The defense was that the contract lacked mutuality. Although the document said a great deal about how endorsements would be handled once they were placed and how revenues would be divided once they were received, it did not actually obligate the plaintiff to take any positive action whatever. Nowhere in the agreement, defendant argued, did plaintiff bind himself to do anything of an affirmative nature—his promise, if any, was illusory—and hence the grant of exclusive rights was without consideration.

Holding for the plaintiff, the New York Court of Appeals found that a promise on plaintiff's part to use "reasonable efforts" to generate license revenues was properly to be implied. While it did not appear in the contract in so many words, the promise and resulting obligation were unmistakably implicated by the document and by all the surrounding circumstances. That being so, there was a contract. "The law," said Judge Cardozo, "has outgrown its primitive stage of formalism when the precise word was the sovereign talisman, and every slip was fatal . . . A promise may be lacking, and yet the whole writing may be 'instinct with an obligation,' imperfectly expressed . . ."

Having thus concluded that a promise to use reasonable efforts could be inferred, the Court apparently also agreed that such a promise succeeds in supplying the needed element of mutuality. It follows that a *failure* on the part of a promisor to use reasonable efforts would be an actionable breach from the promisee's standpoint, which necessarily entails the further conclusion that "reasonable efforts" represents an enforceable standard of conduct. The latter, in a sense, is the boldest element in *Wood v. Lucy.* Having rather easily condemned the defendant for "primitive formalism," the Court might still have hesitated to

6. 222 N.Y. 88, 118 N.E. 214 (1917).

accept as legally sufficient an implied duty that lacked quantification or other specific character. But it did not, and it appears that the courts now generally agree that a promise, express or implied, to use "reasonable efforts" or "best efforts" to merchandise products or pursue some other business objective creates an obligation that is substantial and legally enforceable.

The holding in *Wood v. Lucy* is adopted by UCC 2–306(2) and presumably reflects the perception that the parties to an exclusive dealing arrangement—especially one that stretches out over an extended period—often wisely prefer to deal with future uncertainties through a process of flexible rather than fixed obligation. The distributor wishes to avoid being tied to a specific sales quota, because demand for the product—possibly a new product—is difficult to estimate. Accepting this, the manufacturer is prepared to allow the distributor to adapt to market conditions as they develop, but then counts on the distributor to perform in "good faith" by exerting its "best efforts" to promote sales. All of this seems sensible as far as it goes. It does, however, leave unanswered the question of how to measure or quantify the distributor's obligation when an actual dispute arises. As suggested above, the probable occasion for dispute is easy to imagine: the product sells poorly or, at least, not as well as expected, and the distributor, facing losses, decides to halt or reduce its sales and promotion activities. The manufacturer sues, and the issue is whether the distributor's good faith promise to use "best efforts" has been breached.

In *Bloor v. Falstaff Brewing Corp.,*[7] the Ballantine Beer Company sold its operating business—trademarks as well as various tangible assets—to Falstaff for $4 million plus a royalty of 50 cents for each barrel of Ballantine beer sold over the next six years. Falstaff promised to "use its best efforts to promote and maintain a high volume of sales" of Ballantine products and agreed also that if it should discontinue the sale of beer under the brand name "Ballantine" it would pay Ballantine liquidated damages of $1.1 million a year for the balance of the six-year period. Three years later, however, having sustained heavy operating losses, Falstaff came under new management which proceeded to slash its advertising outlays in an effort to return the company to profitability. That effort proved highly successful, but in the process of converting to a sort of generic beer operation Falstaff allowed the sale of Ballantine products to shrink very drastically in volume, though not to the point of triggering the liquidated damage clause.

7.   601 F.2d 609 (2d Cir.1979).

Speaking through Judge Friendly, the Second Circuit affirmed the trial court's finding that Falstaff had breached its best efforts covenant. The 50–cent royalty, it said, was an essential part of the original purchase price and could not be slighted even if the defendant showed that there had been no discrimination in its treatment of the Ballantine label and that advertising outlays for the Falstaff label had been curtailed in the same fashion. Falstaff was not required "to spend itself into bankruptcy to promote the sales of Ballantine products," but it could not excuse or justify its failure to use best efforts to maintain a high volume of sales merely by asserting that it could *make* money by operating in a different way. As to the difficult but critical question of damages, the Court approved the trial court's finding that a reasonable estimate of lost sales could be made by comparing the sales of other actively advertised local beers, and then computing what Ballantine sales would have been if its brand had suffered no more than the same relative decline in volume.

The emphasis in Judge Friendly's opinion, as noted, is on the circumstance, or at least the supposition, that Falstaff's management had ruthlessly sacrificed Ballantine's interest to its own lust for profits. "Falstaff," the Court said, "simply didn't care about Ballantine's volume and was content to allow this to plummet so long as that course was best for Falstaff's overall profit picture . . . ." The Court said nothing directly about the apparent fact that Falstaff would have suffered further operating losses if it had continued to spend money on television advertising for Ballantine, and we are left to wonder just how far in the direction of financial disaster Falstaff would have been required to go before the Court would concede that its "best efforts" obligation had been satisfied. Putting it differently, while the *Falstaff* opinion is plausible and even slightly ingenious, it really offers nothing more than an *ad hoc* solution to the particular dispute at hand. Best-efforts promisors are warned, in effect, that they cannot simply abandon their obligations when a better opportunity offers itself, but neither they nor their promisees get much in the way of guidance or instruction about how to identify the relevant limits.

Is there or can there be a determinate measure of "best efforts"? Suppose we assume that the parties actually sat down and bargained over the issue in advance. If they did, perhaps they would agree that the wisest course is for the best-efforts promisor to continue to promote and sell the product as long as the promisee's profits exceed the promisor's losses.[8] The promisee

8. Goetz & Scott, *Principles of Relational Contracts*, 67 Va.L.Rev. 1089, 1149 (1981). And see, Macneil, *Econom-* ic *Analysis of Contractual Relations*, 75 Nw.U.L.Rev. 1018 (1981).

can then reimburse or compensate the promisor and still have something positive left over for itself. If, for example, Ballantine beer can be sold for $5.00 a barrel, and if the cost of manufacture and distribution is only $4.90, Falstaff ought to be willing to continue its efforts even though it will also have to pay Ballantine a 50-cent royalty—*provided* that Ballantine is prepared to reimburse Falstaff for the resulting 40-cent loss. Since Ballantine would then be left with a 10-cent profit, it would presumably accept the reimbursement obligation pretty gladly. Ballantine would be better off as long as the royalty it received exceeded the reimbursement that it had to pay. Falstaff would be no worse off, and the customary test of economic efficiency would be met. Using the same criterion, once Falstaff's production and selling costs increased to $5.00, its best-efforts obligation would be deemed exhausted. At that point its reimbursable loss—50 cents a barrel—would exactly equal the royalty, and there would be no benefit to either party in selling more Ballantine beer. Presumably, these results could be achieved even without a specific reimbursement requirement by providing for an appropriate scaledown of the royalty as production costs approached market price.

The contracting parties in *Falstaff* did not of course include any such carefully calibrated measure of "best efforts" in their contract. It is just possible, however, though if so only accidentally, that the Court's reliance on comparable brand activity produced a roughly equivalent result.

It is also possible, I think, given the Court's emphasis on "profits," to approach the *Falstaff* case from a slightly different perspective—one that concerns itself less with the meaning of "best efforts" than with the mutual obligations of partners. Thus, the contract between Ballantine and Falstaff can be regarded as an agreement to pool certain resources in a joint enterprise, with Ballantine contributing a (then) valuable brand-name and Falstaff contributing production and distribution facilities. Falstaff was to be responsible for management, with all the judgment and discretion such responsibility entails. The understanding between the two co-venturers was that they would share the revenues of the enterprise. Ballantine's share was to be measured by gross sales at the rate of 50 cents per unit, Falstaff was to receive the remainder. Unanticipated changes in the market led Falstaff to determine that the original business plan—to sell brand-name beer—should be discarded and a substitute plan—to sell generic beer—adopted in its place. In itself this decision seems to have been entirely sensible and realistic and not at all an act of bad faith. It did, however, reveal a painful "gap" in the partnership agreement, because that agreement simply failed to provide a rule or mechanism by which the parties' shares would be redetermined if the manager decided that the brand-name plan should be abandoned. Plainly, however, the act of substituting one business plan for another ought not to have the consequence of terminating the sharing arrangement between the parties or of eliminating or reducing one party's interest to the advantage of the other. But the question then would be how to adapt the partners' original understanding to an altered business setting in which the sale of Ballantine-brand products was irrelevant. Resorting to comparable brands as a measure of Ballantine's continuing participation arguably represents the Court's solution to that difficult problem. In effect, Ballantine's claim on the revenues of the "old" enterprise (had it been carried forward as originally planned) was recast and expressed in the form of an equivalent claim to the revenues of the "new" enterprise.

Looked at this way, the *Falstaff* decision is really a somewhat heroic effort to fill out the terms of the co-venture agreement, with the "best efforts" provision serving merely as a handy contractual peg.

Requirements and output contracts raise issues that bear a resemblance to those presented by exclusive dealing arrangements, but on the whole such contracts appear to be less problematic for at least two reasons. The first is that the element of indeterminacy—how much the requirements-buyer will actually demand, how much the output-seller will actually tender—is more readily controllable by agreement than is the promise of a distributor or licensee to use "best efforts." Thus, requirements and output contracts frequently provide for maximum and minimum limitations on the quantity of goods entitled to be required or produced, either in specific terms or by reference to stated estimates based on prior experience. As a result, the risk to either party of being inundated or starved by the other is largely eliminated. Even where contractual limitations are not expressed, the UCC itself operates to fill in the blanks. Thus, UCC 2–306(1) provides that an agreement "which measures . . . quantity by the output of the seller or the requirements of the buyer means such actual output or requirements as may occur in good faith, except that no quantity unreasonably disproportionate to . . . any normal or otherwise comparable prior output or requirements may be tendered or demanded." By contrast, UCC 2–306(2), while it codifies the rule of *Wood v. Lucy,* says nothing about how *much* effort "best efforts" might consist of.

In *Feld v. Henry S. Levy & Sons, Inc.,*[9] the plaintiff, doing business as the Crushed Toast Company, entered into an agreement to purchase "all bread crumbs produced" by defendant at 6

---

9. 37 N.Y.2d 466, 373 N.Y.S.2d 102,
335 N.E.2d 320 (1975).

cents a bag. Bread crumbs, it appears, were not merely a by-product of defendant's much larger bakery operations, but were produced in quantity by running stale or imperfect loaves through a pair of grinders and then toasting the crumbs in an oven specially adapted for the purpose. The contract, which was for one year, provided for automatic annual renewal but allowed either party to cancel on six-months notice. Defendant made substantial shipments for some months, but then determined that the 6–cent contract price was "very uneconomical" from its stand-point. Accordingly, it quite abruptly and without formal notice of cancellation dismantled its oven, stopped producing bread crumbs in any quantity, and began selling the stale loaves otherwise used for that purpose to animal feed manufacturers. Defendant appar-ently indicated that it would put the equipment back in place and resume shipments if plaintiff would agree to a rise in price per bag, but plaintiff refused and sued, claiming breach. Defendant responded by arguing that "all bread crumbs produced" meant all bread crumbs produced, and that as bread crumb production had been terminated it had no further obligation under the contract.

While affirming the lower court's denial of summary judg-ment to either party, the New York Court of Appeals plainly concluded that the defendant's conduct was lacking in good faith within the meaning of UCC 2–306(1). Bread crumbs were obvi-ously a minor part of the defendant's much larger baking busi-ness, which continued to generate rye-bread, onion rolls and other good things just as before. Bread crumb losses, if there really were any, could hardly have been great enough to threaten the whole enterprise. Presumably dog-food packagers were offering more for stale loaves than the equivalent of 6 cents a bag, but the realization of less profit than expected, even the absence of profit, would not be sufficient to justify cessation under the good faith standard. Lacking good faith, defendant would have to rely for protection on its right of cancellation, which had been included in the contract for the very purpose of giving either party an oppor-tunity to terminate its obligations in an orderly manner. Al-though the Court somewhat confusingly intermixed the two sub-sections of UCC 2–306, its view of the merits was quite clear and one assumes that the defendant settled in the end instead of going on to trial.

The implication of the *Feld* decision, and likewise of the UCC provision, is that requirements and output contracts are essential-ly subject to the same enforcement standards as conventional contracts in which quantity is a fixed rather than a flexible term. In a fixed-quantity deal, the seller and buyer are obligated to deliver and accept goods in the amount agreed upon even if market changes or raw material costs have made the commitment "very uneconomical" to one or the other. Flexible-quantity deals differ chiefly in the respect that contract obligations are deemed satisfied if the quantity tendered or demanded falls within an expectable range, with upper and lower limits being determined on the basis of what was reasonably anticipated at the time the agreement was entered into. In addition, while the requirements-buyer or output-seller can reduce or even discontinue its participation as part of a general withdrawal from the business itself, it cannot escape the contract by diverting the same materials or facilities to a more profitable use, e.g., dog-food instead of bread crumbs. Elasticity exists, therefore, but the degree of stretch is limited by the overall obligation of good faith.

Exclusive dealing arrangements, by contrast, largely defy the same conventional analogue. The promisor's obligation to use "best efforts," though not regarded as too indefinite to be accepted as consideration, is obviously very difficult to quantify, even by prior agreement. Customary standards of performance are therefore hard to apply. One way to resolve the apparent ambiguity is to simply discard the idea that the parties are dealing with each other as wholly separate entities and instead to regard their relationship as a kind of partnership or co-venture. Perhaps, as suggested, the *Falstaff* decision can be understood as an effort to combine the interests of the parties in an equitable manner as if they were indeed co-venturers. But the statute and the cases admit no similar approach where requirements and output contracts are concerned. Although flexible, the quantity term is assumed to be definable within limits and the conventional framework of obligation applies.

Chapter 6

PERFORMANCE AND BREACH

The legal problems discussed in preceding chapters—consideration, offer-and-acceptance, capacity and unconscionability—have largely been concerned with the formation of a binding contract. In the main, the question that has been asked is whether there is a promise that is enforceable by legal process. The present Chapter can be regarded as commencing a new or at least a subsequent phase of our subject, in which the issue, generally stated, is whether the promisor has *kept* her promise. Thus, a contract has been formed—there are undertakings on both sides that are reasonably well specified—but one of the parties refuses to perform for the asserted reason that her contractual obligations have been excused or terminated. The other party claims breach, and the question for decision is whether the non-performing party's refusal was legally defensible under the terms of the agreement.

In general, a non-performing promisor can justify her non-performance on either of two related grounds. The first such justification is that the promisor's duty to perform was conditioned upon the occurrence of some event and the event never took place. Example: A agreed to buy B's house if a mortgage loan could be obtained at an interest rate not exceeding 10%; no mortgage loan was offered to A at less than 11%. The second is that a performance by the promisee was due in advance of the promisor's performance and the promisee did not perform. Example: A agreed to buy B's house if B completed certain repairs by a stated date; the date passed and B had not completed the repairs. In either case, and depending on the circumstances, the promisor may suspend her own performance under the contract or may regard her contractual obligations as wholly discharged. In some instances—as where the promisee's prior performance is not merely a condition but a duty—the promisor can sue the promisee for breach.

The rules thus summarized seem undebatable as a matter of principle. People being what they are, however, it is foreseeable that promisors may sometimes be inclined to behave opportunistically in this connection—may be inclined, that is, to go out and *look* for legally excusable reasons to avoid their contract obligations. Unless our justification rules are fairly carefully calibrated, we might expect a promisor who finds her contract duties burdensome to seize on any minor circumstance, or on any shortcoming in the promisee's performance, as a ground for suspending or terminating her performance. Behavior of that sort, or the threat of it, obviously adds to the risks of contracting and ought not to be encouraged or rewarded. As a practical matter, therefore, we need to distinguish between significant or "material" grounds for non-performance and grounds that are trivial or merely formalistic.

The point can be taken further. Even if we rule out opportunistic behavior, I think we would agree that there is both a social and a private interest in discouraging the precipitous collapse of existing contract relationships, particularly in the case of agreements that call for continuous and varied performances by one or both parties over a lengthy period of time. Thus, A agrees for a stated price to do extensive renovation work on B's house—first the roof, then the porch, then the basement. In turn, B agrees to make monthly percentage payments as the work progresses. While the common sense of the agreement is evident—house-repairs are to proceed and be paid for on a step-by-step basis—it is not unlikely that there will be disputes from time to time about the quality of A's work or about the amount that is due from B. If such disputes occur frequently and become rancorous, then at some stage, patience and goodwill exhausted, one or the other of the parties may be tempted to repudiate the entire undertaking— A by walking off the job or B by declaring that she won't pay A another dime. We might feel sympathy for either decision, but it is pretty clear that no one will benefit if a total break-down of relations occurs. There will obviously be litigation costs if a lawsuit follows, including a cost to the public which supports the legal system. And whatever the outcome of the suit, neither A nor B is likely to obtain what she regards as full compensation for the default of the other. Even if the plaintiff succeeds in establishing that a breach has occurred, the damage award will almost certainly fall short of making her whole when account is taken of delays and lost opportunities, the latter being especially difficult to prove. Finally, there may well be other persons—workers and suppliers, for example—who will have incurred non-compensable expenses in reliance on or in anticipation of the contract.

For these and related reasons, contract law reflects a preference for continuation of the contract relationship once it has been formed. Both common law and the UCC project a range of practical and doctrinal limitations which operate to restrain the parties from moving too quickly to the conclusion that contract duties have been discharged, whether by the failure of a condition or by a default of the other contracting party. Some of these limitations are discussed and particularized in the case-review that follows, though no attempt is made to exhaust the subject. Throughout, I think, we should bear in mind that the law imposes upon the contracting parties an obligation to act towards one another in "good faith". This extends not only to the performance of the contract but to the assertion and litigation of claims and defenses. "Subterfuges and evasions . . . failure to cooperate . . . conjuring up a pretended dispute . . . harassing demands . . . abuse of a power . . ." [1]—these and other venal acts of strategy are condemned as contrary to the good-faith requirement even though perhaps not technically beyond the bounds of the contract. As noted earlier, lay people sometimes imagine that the law favors literal construction and strict formalism in the interpretation of contract terms. Lawyers know (or soon learn) better, and the requirement of good faith, which can be gravely cited to one's client as a well-established legal principle, makes it easier to counsel decent conduct on occasion and to insist on caution and restraint.

A. Conditions of Performance

1. *Express Conditions.* Perhaps we should begin this topic with the traditional but somewhat confusing distinction between "conditions precedent" and "conditions subsequent". At stake, largely, are procedural matters such as burden of pleading and burden of proof. Yet the distinction may have substantive consequences as well. In *Howard v. Federal Crop Ins. Corp.,*[2] the plaintiffs, tobacco farmers, asserted that their crops, which were insured by the defendant, had been damaged by heavy rains, resulting in a loss of $35,000. Notice and proof of loss was promptly filed, but before an insurance adjuster could come and inspect the damage the plaintiffs plowed the tobacco fields under and prepared their land for another crop. Pointing to a provision of the insurance policy which stated that "The tobacco stalks on any acreage . . . with respect to which a loss is claimed shall not be destroyed until the Corporation makes an inspection", the defendant refused to pay and moved for summary judgment, which was granted by the lower court. Reversing and remanding, the Fourth Circuit held that the defendant's motion should have been denied for the reason that the inspection requirement was not a condition precedent to the defendant's duty to pay. Rather, that duty arose upon the filing of notice and proof of loss. While

---

1. Restatement Section 205, Comments d and e.

2. 540 F.2d 695 (4th Cir. 1976).

the defendant would afterwards be free to defend its refusal by proving that the plaintiffs' action had made it impossible to determine the extent of the loss, the plaintiffs might then respond by showing that the loss could have been evaluated without on-the-spot inspection, or that the plowing-under was necessary to prevent the spread of bugs. . . . or whatever. The larger aim of the insurance contract, in the Court's view, was to establish a right on the part of the insured to compensation for crop losses. That right having been established by the filing of a claim, the parties would then be left to determine the extent of such losses by inspection and other appropriate means. Treating the inspection requirement as a condition precedent would have meant that policy coverage was wholly forfeited even though there had in fact been rain damage; treating it as a condition subsequent properly placed the amount of the plaintiffs' damages in issue.

As there is no report of a decision on remand, I think we can assume that the defendant in *Howard* litigated the matter no further and simply paid or settled the plaintiffs' compensation claim.

In general, the function of a contractual condition is to place the risk of the non-occurrence of the critical event on one party rather than the other. One speaks of "risk" in this connection because the failure of a condition would often entail a loss, or at least a disadvantage, to one of the parties, with some sort of corresponding advantage or immunity to the other. If the parties bargained for that outcome—if the risk of non-occurrence was consciously assumed and priced into the deal—then, obviously, the law ought not to intervene and the disadvantaged party must simply take her lumps. Inevitably, however, there are instances in which the intention of the parties is less than clear. Where there is doubt about the meaning of the contract and the promisee has relied substantially on the expectation of the agreed exchange, the courts, as in the *Howard* case, usually seek an interpretation that avoids or minimizes the promisee's reliance loss. Supporting this effort, Restatement Section 227 states that in case of uncertainty with respect to the intended effect of a condition, the "preferred" interpretation is one that will reduce the risk of "forfeiture".

In *Gibson v. Cranage*,[3] the plaintiff was in the business of enlarging family photographs—presumably touching them up and coloring them in some ghastly manner. Having no doubt read about the death of the defendant's daughter in the obituary column of the local newspaper, plaintiff contacted defendant and

---

3. 39 Mich. 49 (1878).

offered to enlarge a snapshot of the daughter on the understanding that defendant would be obligated to pay for the work only if he was "perfectly satisfied" with the result. On being presented with the enlargement, defendant declared that he was *not* perfectly satisfied and declined to pay. Defendant apparently wouldn't state what his objections were, and he stubbornly refused to take a second look at the enlargement even after it had been returned to the "artist" for improvements. Left with a worthless photograph, plaintiff sued for his fee.

The Supreme Court of Michigan held for the defendant on the ground that defendant's personal satisfaction had been made a condition of his duty to pay by express agreement of the parties. Others might consider the portrait an excellent one, but the parties themselves had stipulated that the defendant was to be the only person with a right to decide that question. To be sure, the plaintiff had spent time and money on the project. Even so, said the Court, since the plaintiff took a deliberate risk in giving the defendant a right to reject the photograph at will, "there is no hardship whatever . . .".

The *Gibson* decision is generally regarded as correct, I think, although the notion that the defendant could arbitrarily declare himself dissatisfied and in that way impose a forfeiture on the plaintiff might in other circumstances seem unreasonable. Here, however, the forfeiture or "hardship" probably should be regarded, from the plaintiff's standpoint, as nothing more than an ordinary and necessary business expense. Allowing his customer to reject the product if not "perfectly satisfied" must be assumed to have been a marketing technique which the plaintiff consciously adopted as an aid to sales—in effect, the nineteenth-century equivalent of today's familiar money-back guarantee. Based on experience with customers, the plaintiff would have been able to predict quite accurately what percentage of his sales would ultimately fail of completion. The loss on uncompleted sales would simply be accepted as a cost of promotion and, like any other advertising outlay, would be reflected in the price at which the plaintiff regularly offered his services to the public. Putting the same point differently, the plaintiff actually made history of a sort by losing the case: if the decision had gone the other way and the defendant had been compelled to pay for the portrait, the money-back guarantee, by now a time-honored marketing gimmick, would carry less conviction to consumers and would presumably have had to be abandoned (or, at least, clarified).

In *Gibson,* as suggested, the question of whether "perfect satisfaction" did or didn't operate as a condition precedent was

100

resolved by reference to the parties' intended allocation of risk: buyer and seller understood that the latter *meant* to offer his services on a money-back basis; hence, the buyer's "satisfaction" was a condition of his duty to pay. A similar analysis, but with a different outcome, was employed in *Peacock Construction Co. v. Modern Air Conditioning, Inc.,*[4] a casebook standby in this field. In *Peacock,* the defendant (Peacock) was the general contractor for a large building project and had entered into a subcontract (no doubt one among many) with the plaintiff to supply and install the heating and air conditioning. The subcontract provided that Peacock would make final payment to Modern "within 30 days after completion of the work . . . and full payment therefor by the Owner." The Owner having gone bankrupt without paying Peacock for the subcontractors' work, Peacock refused to make final payment to Modern and the latter sued. Affirming a grant of summary judgment for the plaintiff, the Supreme Court of Florida held that the clause just quoted was not intended to create a condition precedent to Peacock's duty to pay the various subcontractors, but served merely to fix a reasonable time for Peacock to make such payments, i.e., 30 days after the events named. While the contract language was admittedly open to more than one interpretation, the "fairest way" to deal with the issue was to recognize that small subcontractors would not ordinarily expect to take the risk of an owner's financial failure. Instead, presumably, the parties would expect the general contractor to assume that risk, because the general, having dealt directly with the owner, would be in the best position to appraise the latter's creditworthiness and to insist on such security measures as the circumstances seemed to require. The Court noted that an agreement might be written otherwise, but if so, the intention to shift financial risk to the subcontractor would have to be clearly expressed, not left to inference.

A promisor whose obligation truly is subject to an express condition may of course prefer that the promisee complete the contract despite the fact that the conditional event has not occurred. If the promisor freely executes a written waiver of the condition, then, obviously, the non-occurrence of the event cannot later be erected as a defense against the promisee's claims. But suppose the promisor takes no particular action in the face of a non-occurrence and the promisee simply continues his own performance. Does the promisor's inaction or forbearance constitute an implied waiver on which the promisee can and should rely, or is the promisee still subject to a defense based on the failure of a

4.   353 So.2d 840 (Fla.1977).

condition? Suppose the contract itself is within the Statute of Frauds. Since an implied waiver is necessarily unwritten, shouldn't the effect be to treat it as unenforceable and hence to reinstate the original contract terms?

In *Universal Builders, Inc. v. Moon Motor Lodge,*[5] the plaintiff-construction company had entered into a written contract with the defendant to build a motel and restaurant. Among other things, the contract provided that all "change orders" must be in writing and signed by Moon or its architect, and that all requests for extensions of time must be made in writing as well. At some point while the job was underway, having detected a defect in the quality of the masonry being supplied by a subcontractor, Moon "threatened" (the Court's word) to withhold progress payments and to kick Universal out unless the latter agreed to pay Moon $5,000 to make up for the defective masonry, to do certain additional work for nothing, and to pay liquidated damages if completion were delayed beyond July 1. Universal evidently felt compelled to accept all this and signed a supplemental agreement. The work was substantially completed on September 1, some two months late.

Contending that it had done a good deal of *extra* work on the job beyond that required by the supplemental agreement, and that the extra work had been done at Moon's oral request and with the approval or acquiescence of Moon's agent at the site, Universal (or, rather, its trustee in bankruptcy) sued Moon for the value of such extras, about $42,000. Moon denied liability, pointing to the express contractual condition that change orders be submitted and approved in writing; it also counterclaimed for delay damages. A majority of the Supreme Court of Pennsylvania held that Universal was entitled to compensation for its extra work. While the contract required change orders to be in writing, that requirement could be waived by action of the promisor (in the alternative, the parties could authorize the extras in an oral agreement separate from their written contract). It was reasonable here to infer that Moon *had* waived the requirement, because its agent both requested the extra work and watched while it was being performed. Citing the predecessor of Restatement Section 150, finally, the Court held that the Statute of Frauds was no bar to an oral (or a tacit) agreement waiving a performance condition, where the waiver was relied upon by the other party (Universal) and had resulted in a change in position.

On the matter of delay damages, however, which presumably involved a smaller dollar amount, the Court held for Moon. Al-

5. 430 Pa. 550, 244 A.2d 10 (1968).

though the two-month delay resulted from Moon's own act in ordering work changes, Universal never indicated that the extra work would actually occasion a delay in completion; hence, the contractual requirement that requests for extension of time be made and approved in writing could not have been waived. How both things could be true at once—how Moon could have ordered extra work, yet be unaware that it would take additional time— the Court never explained.

Justice Musmanno, in dissent, accused the majority of doing Moon "an injustice". Quoting affectionately from an earlier opinion of his own, the dissenter warned that "[c]haos would envelope the commercial world" if Universal's waiver argument were allowed to prevail, because the effect would be to treat written contracts as if they had been "penned in disappearing ink." Even more important, perhaps, Musmanno pointed out that the majority view in effect left Universal free to decide for itself just what should be regarded as a change order, and free also to make up its own unreviewed cost schedules without crediting Moon for items charged in the original contract but now allegedly changed and billed as extras.

Pretty plainly, Justice Musmanno thought that Universal was engaged in attempting to recoup its contract losses by fabricating extras long after the event. Almost equally plainly, the Court majority thought that Moon had behaved towards Universal like a schoolyard bully and had driven the latter into bankruptcy. The "waiver" issue simply provided a legal framework within which these conflicting perceptions about the conduct of the parties— whether good faith was more (or less) in evidence on one side than the other—could be advanced.

2. *Constructive Conditions of Exchange.* We have no difficulty today in recognizing that the promises made by the parties to a bilateral contract are in almost every case "dependent". Each of the contracting parties regards performance by the other party as a condition of its own obligation to perform; failure to perform on one side obviously furnishes an excuse for non-performance on the other. Some contracts—those involving sales of real estate or securities, for example—plainly contemplate simultaneous performances by the parties. Thus, X and Y agree to the sale of Blackacre for $10,000, the closing to be held on June 1. On the closing date, X, the seller, is expected to deliver appropriate title documents and Y, the buyer, is expected to hand over her check. Check and title documents cross the table at one and the same moment; neither party would expect to surrender her property without equivalent action by the other. In other situations—sales

of services, typically—one party, usually the buyer, would expect to become obligated to perform only after the other party's performance had been completed, whether in whole or part. Thus, A promises to pay B a stated sum for painting A's house, and B promises to paint. Apparently, B is expected to "go first"—B's performance is an implied or constructive condition of A's duty to pay—and it is plain that A is excused if the job is never done.

But while the idea of dependent promises now seems apparent to common sense, prior to *Kingston v. Preston,*[6] decided by King's Bench in 1773, the law evidently lacked a constructive conditions doctrine and instead treated the parties' promises as independently enforceable. Thus, unless the contract expressly provided otherwise, the courts generally held that the failure of one party to perform did not, of itself, justify the other in withholding her own performance. X, above, could therefore seek payment from Y even though the deed to Blackacre was never delivered. Y might afterwards commence a suit against X to obtain title to the property, but of course there would be a fair chance by then that X would possess neither Blackacre nor other resources sufficient to meet Y's claim—to say nothing of the sheer waste of time and money involved in bringing multiple lawsuits.

Kingston v. Preston, which changed the law in this respect, appears to have involved a kind of small-scale leveraged buy-out. The defendant, in business as a silk merchant but eager to retire, had apparently induced the plaintiff to join the firm as an employee by entering into a contract with the plaintiff under which the latter (together with the defendant's nephew) was to purchase the assets of the business at the end of a year. The plaintiff agreed to pay for his share in monthly installments of £250, which presumably represented some portion of the anticipated cash-flow from inventory turnover. As assurance, the plaintiff further agreed, at or before the closing, to provide the defendant with "good and sufficient security" for his payment obligations, the same to be approved by the defendant himself. On the defendant's refusal to convey title at the closing date, the plaintiff sued, stating that he stood ready to make the installment payments as promised. In reply, the defendant asserted that he had no duty to perform, because the plaintiff had breached by failing to furnish the "good and sufficient security" that the contract required.

Not that it matters much at this late date, but I suppose we could wonder just what, beyond the inventory and accounts receivable of the business itself, such "sufficient security" was ever expected to consist of. Apparently, the defendant wanted the

6. 99 Eng.Rep. 437 (1773).

plaintiff to obtain additional collateral from other parties—a bank, perhaps, or another investor. The plaintiff, however, who conceded that his own net worth was zero and who had no outside source of capital, may well have assumed from the beginning that giving the defendant a security-interest in the firm's balance-sheet assets would satisfy the contractual condition; in effect, the defendant, like a mortgagee, would have a right to repossess those assets if the monthly installments were not paid. But this issue (if it was an issue) never got debated. Electing simply to demur, plaintiff argued that the defendant's obligation to sell the business was independent of the plaintiff's duty to furnish additional security; if defendant *had* a remedy, he could pursue it in a separate action.

Holding for the defendant on the ground that the plaintiff's duty was a condition precedent, Lord Mansfield rejected the notion that the defendant's promise to transfer "his stock and business" was independently enforceable. The "greatest injustice" would result, his Lordship thought, if the defendant were required to trust to the "personal security" of the plaintiff, who was admitted to be "worth nothing". In effect, the purpose of the transaction, together with the "evident sense and meaning" of the agreement, indicated that the parties, even without expressly so stating, had intended their promises to be conditional and mutually dependent. Without entirely discarding prior law, Mansfield quite clearly signalled that, for the future, a contract formed on the basis of an exchange of promises would be read to require an exchange of performances as well. Since, here, the plaintiff-purchaser had failed to perform by furnishing adequate security, the defendant-seller's performance obligations were excused.

As Lord Mansfield observed in *Kingston* (and as noted above), bilateral contracts can generally be divided into two subclasses— those that contemplate a simultaneous exchange of performances and those that assume a performance by one party in advance of, and as a condition to, performance by the other. The agreement in *Kingston* presumably belonged to the former subclass: evidence of the purchaser's security (e.g., a bank letter of credit payable to the seller in the event of default) and the seller's title documents were to change hands at the same moment in time, neither party being expected to act before the other. But in some cases the intention may not be quite so clear. In *Stewart v. Newbury*,[7] the plaintiff, a contractor, offered to do the excavation and concrete work on a mill building to be constructed by the defendants. The plaintiff submitted a written bid containing price quotations for

7.   220 N.Y. 379, 115 N.E. 984 (1917).

various elements of the job, and the defendants accepted by telephone and then in writing. Neither the bid nor the acceptance said anything about *when* the plaintiff would be paid for his work, but the plaintiff testified that in their phone conversation he had said, "I will expect my payments in the usual manner," and the defendants had replied, "All right, we have got the money . . ." After working for two months the plaintiff asked for payment, claiming that the "custom" was to bill and be paid for 85% of the value of work performed on a monthly basis, with 15% being retained until the job was completed. The defendants, asserting that the work done was not in accordance with specifications, declined to pay anything at that point and apparently urged the plaintiff to get busy and complete the job. The plaintiff refused to proceed without payment and the defendant notified the plaintiff that it considered the contract at an end, whereupon the plaintiff brought suit for the work billed to date, $896, plus $95 for loss of profits. Following a trial, the judge instructed the jury that "if there was no custom that was understood by both parties, and with respect to which they made a contract, then the plaintiff was entitled to payment at reasonable times." So instructed, the jury returned a verdict awarding the plaintiff the amount stated in his bill, though not the lost profits, and the defendants appealed.

Finding the trial court's instructions erroneous, the New York Court of Appeals reversed and remanded. The agreement between plaintiff and defendant was "an entire contract", meaning, presumably, a contract that called for a single completed performance, not a performance rendered in monthly installments. Absent anything in the agreement to the contrary, the common-law rule was that "the work must be substantially performed before payment can be demanded . . ." It followed, in the Court's view, that if the jury reached its verdict on the ground that the plaintiff was justified in abandoning the work because the installment had not been paid, then the verdict could not stand. While such verdict might be left intact if it simply reflected a finding that the defendant had breached the contract by preventing the plaintiff from going forward with the job, the jury's failure to have awarded loss-of-profits damages suggested that the former was true rather than the latter. The Court could not be certain, however, and hence a new trial was ordered.

Insofar as it pertains to service contracts generally, I suppose the *Stewart* decision is correct. Under ordinary circumstances, service providers are paid after their services have been performed. Thus, employees get their pay-checks at the *end* of a pay-period—a week or a month—for services performed during that period. In effect, the employee "loans" the value of his services to the employer until pay-day, and while this may sometimes be a bit tough on the employee, the alternative—payment in advance—is not likely to be acceptable to the employer, which would have no practical way of assuring itself that the employee will actually show up and perform. Employees with unique and highly valued skills—athletes, law-review editors—do occasionally receive advance signing bonuses, but for most service-providers the performance comes first and the compensation afterwards.

Restatement Section 234(2) reflects the rule of the *Stewart* case by providing that where the performance of one party to a contract requires a period of time, that party's performance is due at an earlier time than that of the other party, unless the contract "or the circumstances" indicate the contrary. This no doubt, as stated, is the general understanding as far as employees and employers are concerned; employers are not expected to finance their employees' living and consumption expenditures by paying salaries in advance of services. The plaintiff in *Stewart*, however, was an employer himself with a crew of workmen and a monthly payroll to meet. In asking for periodic payments as the work progressed, the plaintiff sought to shift that payroll burden to the defendants—quite understandably given that the job would take considerable time to complete and would require a substantial outlay for labor and materials. Indeed, having been denied such payments, the plaintiff (had he continued the project) would apparently have had to finance the entire cost of the building's exterior structure. He would thus have become a lender to the defendant on a relatively large scale, a status which the parties probably never contemplated.

Though not mentioned by the Court in *Stewart*, the challenged jury instruction—"if there was no custom . . . then . . ."—allows yet a third interpretation of the jury's verdict; namely, that it *was* the custom for owners to pay builders on a periodic basis for work performed, and that the jury so found. One would think it must have been so, even as early as the year 1911. Today, at all events, the practice where construction contracts are concerned is to make *express* provision for progress payments; financing costs are almost invariably assumed by the owner, who will have borrowed the necessary funds on a short-term basis from a bank or other lending institution. Hence, whatever its value as a legal abstraction or in other fields, the *Stewart* decision probably has little continuing importance in the context in which it arose.

B. Material Breach

1. *Substantial Performance.* In *Kingston,* as noted, the transactional setting was one that contemplated simultaneous performances by the parties—title documents to be exchanged for cash and debt—at a given date in the future. In that circumstance, presumably, the parties have ample time to prepare themselves to meet the conditions expressed in the contract, and one would suppose that a fairly high degree of conformity would be expected of each. Even so, Lord Mansfield thought it relevant to emphasize the *importance* of the "sufficient security" requirement—"the essence of the agreement," he said, "was that the defendant should not trust to the personal security of the plaintiff"—and perhaps we might infer that Mansfield had made a kind of mental distinction, obviously one of degree, between conditions that go to "the essence" and conditions that appear to be trivial or incidental.

The need for such a distinction is evident, I think, in the case of an extended service contract under which the service-provider obligates himself to meet a long list of contractual requirements, of which, however, some are plainly more important than others. *Jacob & Youngs v. Kent* [8] presents the issue in classic form. The plaintiff, a contractor, agreed to build a large country residence for the defendant for a price of $77,000 (the year was 1914) of which $3,400 remained unpaid at the time the work was completed. Having moved in, the defendant discovered after about a year that the water pipes which the plaintiff had installed were not "of Reading manufacture" as the plumbing specifications clearly required, but had been made by "Cohoes" and other pipe manufacturers. Apart from brand-name, however, the quality, value, cost and appearance of Cohoes and Reading pipe were exactly the same; moreover, the mistake (using Cohoes pipe instead of Reading) was unintentional on the plaintiff's part. Although the Cohoes pipe was enclosed in the wall in many places, the defendant demanded that it be ripped out "from cellar to roof", presumably at great expense, and Reading pipe put in its place. When the plaintiff refused, the defendant's architect similarly refused to issue a certificate for final payment and the plaintiff sued.

Finding that there had been substantial performance of the contract, the New York Court of Appeals held (4–3) for the plaintiff. Writing for the majority, Judge Cardozo accepted that the plaintiff's default had been inadvertent rather than willful or fraudulent. That being so, it was appropriate to draw a line

___
8.   230 N.Y. 239, 129 N.E. 889 (1921).

between "the important and the trivial" in the context of the overall contractual undertaking. If the default were found to be trivial—as, in the Court's view, the use of Cohoes instead of Reading pipe plainly was—then it ought not to be treated as the breach of a condition "to be followed by a forfeiture". Instead, the default would be "atoned for" by an award of damages for the resulting difference, or diminishment, in the value of the property. In many cases, perhaps most, the distinction wouldn't matter, because the difference in value would be measured by the actual cost of replacing the wrong item with the right one. Here, however, it obviously mattered very much, since the "cost of replacement"—tearing out all the plumbing—would be substantial. By contrast, "difference in value"—the effect on the market price of the house of having used Cohoes instead of Reading pipe— was "either nominal or nothing".

The outcome in *Jacob & Youngs* seems entirely reasonable on the facts given, but of course one's view of the decision does, ultimately, depend on whether one accepts the proposition that the brand-name on a water pipe (the two brands being otherwise identical) is indeed a "trivial" matter. The dissenting judges didn't think so: "Defendant contracted for pipe made by Reading . . . He wanted that and was entitled to it . . . The rule, therefore, of substantial performance, with damages for unsubstantial omissions, has no application." Cardozo himself conceded that the permitted "margin of departure" on a sale of "common chattels"—a car, a TV set—would be less than with respect to "the construction of a mansion or a 'skyscraper'." Thus, an auto-dealer cannot substitute a Dodge for a Chevrolet even though the two cars have the same market value and even though mechanical characteristics are virtually identical. Advertising and brand-name preferences are basic to the choices that consumers make, and whether prompted by real or imagined distinctions among competing products, such preferences obviously cannot be set aside in the name of "substantial performance". Aware of this, Cardozo nevertheless, as noted, lumped "mansions" and "skyscrapers" together. Both are large, to be sure, and in that respect they have something in common. There, however, the resemblance ends. Skyscrapers are built by investors whose interest in the property is exclusively financial and who truly do not care whether the builder installs Reading or Cohoes pipe. But houses, even mansions, are built to live in, and, as with other consumer choices, personal preferences count.

In a sense, therefore, the essence of the *Jacob & Youngs* decision resides in a kind of "finding" by Judge Cardozo that *some* consumer preferences are simply too remote and idiosyncratic to be taken seriously. We all care deeply about brand-names when it comes to beer, breakfast cereal and even bathroom fixtures. As to the water pipes in the basement, however, Cardozo evidently concluded that no reasonable consumer feels anything but total indifference about competing brands, provided that one brand is as durable and functional and costs the same as the other. But how could he actually know that? How could he have been so sure about prevailing consumer attitudes, so confident that a reasonable consumer would be indifferent as between Reading and Cohoes pipe? The probable answer: self-scrutiny. On reflection, Cardozo realized that he himself didn't actually know what brand of plumbing had been installed in his *own* house—and even more important, that he did not wish to know. Thoughtfully consulting his own preference on the question of pipe-brands, the good judge found that the choice was one that left him (and by extrapolation other sensible home-owners) absolutely cold.

In *Jacob & Youngs,* as stated, the defendant's home was a mansion. In *Plante v. Jacobs,*[9] yet another familiar home construction case, the residence in question was part of a standard suburban development—not very different, one supposes, from other homes in the same neighborhood. The plaintiff had contracted to build the residence for the defendants in accordance with "a stock floor plan" for the sum of $26,000. Having paid the plaintiff $20,000 during the course of the construction, the defendants finally declared themselves dissatisfied with the work done and refused to continue payment. The plaintiff thereupon halted construction and sued for the unpaid balance, claiming that the contract had been substantially performed. In reply, the defendants pointed out that the wall between the living room and the kitchen had been misplaced, narrowing the living room by more than a foot. To tear the wall down and put up a new one would cost $4,000. There were, in addition, a number of minor items— cabinets, closet poles, gutters and downspouts—which still remained to be furnished. Since the wall plus the minor items amounted to more than 25% of the total contract price, defendants argued that there had been no substantial performance on plaintiff's part and, hence, that the full cost of replacement—the wall as well as the minor items—should be offset against the balance otherwise due.

The Supreme Court of Wisconsin held for the plaintiff on the central question of substantial performance. The Court did not

9. 10 Wis.2d 567, 103 N.W.2d 296 (1960).

appear to deny or dispute that the defendants might reasonably have been dissatisfied with the placement of the living room wall. This, however, was outweighed by the "economic waste" that would result if the wall had to be torn down and rebuilt, because the plaintiff would then have to replaster and redecorate the walls and ceilings of at least two rooms, viz., the living room and the kitchen, at a cost that was "unreasonable and unjustified". Accordingly, while defendants would be compensated for the minor items on a cost-of-replacement basis, the misplacing of the living room wall fell "under the diminished value rule". All of the expert witnesses having testified that the market value of the house was the same whether the living room was a foot wider or a foot narrower, the defendants were entitled to no offset whatever for the builder's default in this respect.

Assuming the reader agrees with the writer that living room dimensions are a good deal more important than the brand-name on a water pipe, the decision in *Plante* may be hard to accept. The Wisconsin Court appears to have taken the view that the consumer's preference can be disregarded if (a) the cost of satisfying that preference is relatively high and (b) the market value of the product is the same either way. But that line of reasoning leads ultimately to a rule that would allow builders to freely substitute one home-design for another if the experts say that they have equal value, which obviously goes too far. The Court, to be sure, announced no such "rule", although, as stated, it did not seem to challenge the legitimacy and sincerity of the defendants' preference for a wider living room. In the end, perhaps, the Court may have felt that it simply had to recognize the fact that developers of serviceable, middle-income housing face significant cost constraints with respect to labor and materials, and that those constraints make it difficult to furnish a product that is totally without shortcomings. As noted, the plaintiff built his homes on the basis of "a stock floor plan . . . There were no blueprints. The specifications were standard printed forms . . ." Under these limiting circumstances, the defendants would have to regard the contract as substantially performed despite some disappointment with the final product. The Court conceded that there "may be situations"—the reference, presumably, is to sales of higher-priced homes—in which buyers can properly insist on precise room dimensions and other features "of great personal importance". But if what you want is a decent house for a mere $26,000, you will have to settle for "[s]omething less than perfection . . .", no matter how strongly you may feel about the size of your parlor. In effect, you cannot get hand-tailoring if the suit you buy is off-the-rack.

2. *Sales of Goods and Perfect Tender.* Contracts for the sale of goods—between "merchants" or between merchant and consumer—also present issues generally relating to shortfalls in performance, but here, as Cardozo observed in *Jacob & Youngs,* the tolerable "margin of departure" is likely to be much narrower than in the case of service agreements. One reason for this, perhaps, is that "goods" are more or less unitary in character; they present themselves as physical objects whose characteristics combine to create a single tangible article that either *is* the thing described in the contract or is something else. The article is either T or it is not-T; logically, no other categories exist. The nature of a service, by contrast, is less susceptible to categorical definition; whether the work done on the portrait of the late Miss Cranage was or was not artistically satisfactory would be a harder question to answer than whether a coffee-maker holds six cups or ten. Often, of course, services and goods are mixed together in a single contractual setting and there is uncertainty as to which predominates. *Jacob & Youngs,* I suppose, would be a fair example. Cardozo chose to regard the great water pipe question as one that involved the rendering of a service rather than a sale of "common chattels"; on that basis he was able to locate a third category—call it nearly-T—that qualified as substantial performance. The dissenters evidently viewed water pipes as "articles" like any other and, since Cohoes wasn't Reading, thought the contract had been breached.

At common law, a buyer of goods possessed a legal right to insist upon "perfect tender" by the seller. If the goods failed to conform exactly to the description in the contract—whether as to quality, quantity or manner of delivery—the buyer could reject the goods and rescind the contract, which meant that the parties would be returned to the positions they occupied before the contract was entered into. By contrast, as has been seen, the doctrine of substantial performance would entitle, but also limit, the buyer to damages measured by the difference between the value of the goods promised and the value of the goods delivered. If the market price of the goods happened to have dropped between the contract date and the delivery date, the buyer would obviously prefer to rescind and purchase the goods at the lower market price from other sources. Thus, suppose the contract price is $20 a widget but the market price of widgets has fallen to $5 at the date of delivery. If the seller delivers widgets that deviate from the contract description and have a market value of only $4.90, the buyer will be exceedingly pleased to rescind under the perfect tender rule and save $15, as compared with a damage recovery of only 10 cents a widget if the substantial performance rule applies.

Under these circumstances, quite obviously, the buyer will resort to the remedy of rescission even though the defect in the seller's tender is altogether trivial. Yet a change in the market price of widgets is the very contingency to which the agreement between buyer and seller is addressed: in agreeing to a $20 contract price, the parties' aim is to protect themselves against a later adverse change in the market price of widgets—the buyer against a later rise, the seller against a later fall. In effect, however, the rescission remedy deprives the seller of his contract protection and, for the same reason, enables the buyer to do better than he would have done if the contract had been performed to the letter.[10]

On this analysis the common-law approach appears somewhat faulty and the reader may therefore be slightly surprised to learn that the perfect tender rule, with accompanying right of rejection, is in fact adopted by UCC 2–601—at least purportedly.[11] The reason for this, presumably, is that despite the danger of opportunism on the buyer's side, there is an equal or perhaps a greater concern about how sellers would behave if buyers *lacked* a right to reject imperfect merchandise and were limited to a claim for damages (10 cents a widget in the illustration above). With little to lose, sellers would be expected to be less concerned with the need to conform precisely to the requirements of the contract; some, indeed, hoping the buyer will find it too burdensome to pursue a damage claim, might be tempted to deliberately substitute non-conforming goods for the goods described. A careless or a bad-faith seller who knows that he can defend on grounds of substantial performance might therefore seek to enforce a sale even though the goods delivered depart from the contract description and even though the seller was aware of the non-conformity at the time the goods were shipped.

The UCC attempts to resolve the conflict between buyers' and sellers' interests in this context through a kind of strategic compromise. As indicated, UCC 2–601 provides that a buyer may reject the goods supplied by his seller "if the goods or the tender of delivery fail in any respect to conform to the contract". Thus, facially, no distinction is to be made between more important and less important deviations from the contract or between a material and a non-material failure to conform. But while expressed in absolute terms, the buyer's right of rejection is actually somewhat

---

10. Priest, *Breach and Remedy for the Tender of Nonconforming Goods Under the Uniform Commercial Code: An Economic Approach*, 91 Harv.L.Rev. 960 (1978). And see, Wiseman, *The Limits of Vision: Karl Llewellyn and the* *Merchant Rules*, 100 Harv.L.Rev. 465, 526 (1987).

11. White and Summers, *Uniform Commercial Code* 303 (2d ed., 1980).

less than absolute. Under 2–602(1), a rejecting buyer must "seasonably" notify the seller of his intention. Such notice having been given, 2–508 provides that the seller may respond by notifying the buyer of his intention to "cure" and may then make a conforming delivery if the time for performance has not yet expired. Presumably, then, in the widget case above, while the seller cannot prevent the buyer from treating the non-conformity as grounds for rejection, he can avoid the loss resulting from the slump in market price by promptly making delivery of conforming goods. The effect, roughly, is to protect the buyer from having defective merchandise dumped in his lap with no recourse other than a damage claim, while at the same time affording the seller a kind of second chance to meet his contract obligations.

A buyer's right to reject non-conforming goods may even survive his acceptance of the goods in question, "acceptance" being defined as a failure to reject after a reasonable opportunity for inspection. Here, however, the buyer encounters additional statutory limitations which presumably reflect a further effort to balance the parties' legitimate interests. Under 2–608(1), a buyer who has accepted non-conforming goods may subsequently revoke his acceptance and reject the merchandise only if (a) the non-conformity "substantially impairs its value to him" and (b) either he had reason to assume that the non-conformity would be cured by the seller (but it hasn't been) or the defect could not have been discovered on initial inspection (e.g., the widgets looked great but they shrank after washing). Moreover, a buyer who decides to accept and perhaps even use the non-conforming goods for some purpose cannot simply change his mind at a later date. Under 2–608(2), revocation of acceptance must occur within a reasonable time after the defect was or should have been discovered and before any alteration occurs in the condition of the goods other than that resulting from their own defect. In effect, then, while a buyer is not bound by his acceptance of non-conforming goods, he can thereafter revoke only if the non-conformity is substantial, only if he accepted without knowledge of the defect or in expectation of a cure, and only if the revocation is prompt and timely.

If non-conforming goods are accepted and the acceptance is not revoked, the buyer obviously loses his right to reject and must keep and pay for the goods. He does not thereby give up his right to conventional contract damages, however. The terms of the contract describing quantity, quality, function, etc., together constitute an "express warranty" on the seller's part that the goods delivered shall conform to such terms in all respects. If they do not, there is a breach. Under 2–714, the buyer may recover as damages the difference in value between the goods described in the contract and the goods actually delivered, plus incidental and consequential damages as provided in 2–715.

3. *First Breach and Repudiation.* As noted earlier, there is an apparent opposition between the strict rule that failure to perform constitutes a breach which properly excuses the injured party from her own performance obligations and, on the other hand, a fairly strong sense that the law should do what it reasonably can to prevent or deter the break-down of contract relations. Like the UCC, the Restatement seeks to achieve a practical balance of interests by (a) asserting the absolute right of the injured party to treat non-performance as a breach, but then (b) calibrating the legal consequences by reference to the gravity of the offense. Thus, Restatement Section 235 provides that when performance of a duty under a contract is due, "any" non-performance by the obligor is to be regarded as a breach. If the obligor's failure to perform is not "material" in character—a minor departure from plan-specifications by a builder, for example—the injured party is required to continue performance but may claim damages for whatever loss has been sustained. If the failure *is* material, then, under Sections 225 and 237, the injured party may treat the failure as equivalent to the non-occurrence of a condition and, depending on the circumstances, either suspend her own performance or regard herself as having been discharged in full. If it is reasonable to expect that the party failing to perform will "cure" her failure in a timely fashion, the injured party's duty to perform will be suspended until a cure takes place; but if no cure is possible, or if none is effected, then, at last, the injured party may regard her obligations as discharged. In the latter event, the injured party is entitled to damages for "total breach"; in the former, to damages for "partial breach", meaning, presumably, any loss incurred by reason of the obligor's delay in effecting a cure.

In applying these (or similar common-law) rules to particular cases, the important questions, quite obviously, are: what constitutes a "material" as opposed to a non-material failure to perform, and when is the injured party justified in considering her own performance duties discharged rather than merely suspended? *K & G Construction Co. v. Harris*,[12] decided by the Maryland Court of Appeals, furnishes an illustration of the issues. In *K & G*, the plaintiff, owner and general contractor for a housing subdivision, entered into a contract with the defendant to do the excavation

12. 223 Md. 305, 164 A.2d 451 (1960).

and earth-moving work for the project. The contract called for the plaintiff to make monthly progress payments to the defendant (less a retainage of 10%), with each such payment being due on the 10th day of the following month. The defendant agreed to perform "in a workmanlike manner, and in accordance with the best practices", and further agreed to carry liability insurance for any property damage that might occur while the work was in progress.

Excavation proceeded satisfactorily through the month of July, but on August 9 a bulldozer operator employed by defendant drove his machine too close to a house, causing the collapse of a wall and other damage. The defendant, and more particularly its insurer, refused to repair the house and denied liability for the damage—presumably on the ground that there had been no negligence in the operation of the bulldozer. The plaintiff thereupon refused to make the payment otherwise due on August 10 for work that had been done during the preceding month. The defendant nevertheless continued to work on the project until September 12, at which date it stopped work and left the site because the plaintiff again refused to make payments either for July or for August. Although the defendant notified the plaintiff (by registered letter) that it was willing to return to work if the overdue payments were made, the plaintiff finally hired another excavating firm to complete the job and was obliged to pay the latter $450 above the contract price.

Plaintiff sued for the property damage caused by the bulldozer and for contract damages of $450. Defendant counterclaimed for the back payments plus its own lost profits, a total of $2,824. In a separate proceeding before a jury, the plaintiff was awarded $3,400 for the bulldozer damage, which defendant's insurer apparently paid. The parties' contract claims were then submitted to the trial judge, who held for the defendant and allowed its counterclaim in full.

Reversing the trial court on the contract issue, the Court of Appeals denied the defendant's counterclaim and awarded damages of $450 to the plaintiff. The Court found that negligent operation of the bulldozer by defendant's employee constituted a material breach of defendant's duty to perform "in a workmanlike manner. . . ." This, in turn, left the plaintiff with an option to regard the defendant's failure as a "total breach", in which event the plaintiff would have been discharged and free to sue for damages, or to treat the defendant as being in "partial breach" only, in which event the defendant, though unpaid, would be expected to continue its work and complete the contract. Plaintiff obviously chose the latter course. Accordingly, the defendant *again* breached the contract—this time totally—when it walked off the job on September 12, and it thereby became liable to the plaintiff for the increased cost, $450, of having the excavation finished by another subcontractor.

Despite the jury's finding of negligence on the defendant's part, the decision in *K & G* seems questionable. While "workman-like" performance was plainly a condition precedent to the plaintiff's duty to make monthly progress payments, it seems well arguable that isolated accidents were not intended to be regarded as violating that condition since such occurrences (if found to be due to negligence) would be covered by the defendant's repair obligation or by insurance. In any case, the defendant's overall performance *was* workmanlike; the bulldozer accident was not part of a pattern of careless job-performance and one would not have supposed that a single event, by itself, would amount to a breach. Even if it were so regarded, there would be a real question as to whether it should be considered "material" given that in all other respects the excavation was proceeding in a wholly satisfactory way. Finally, even assuming that the bulldozer accident was a material breach, it appears that a "cure" was assured to the plaintiff through resort to the insurance fund if and when the defendant should be found liable for negligence. From the standpoint of orderly conduct, one's impression is that plaintiff and defendant should have gone forward with their respective contract responsibilities—as defendant declared itself ready to do if progress payments were resumed—and that the parties should have treated the damage issue as one to be resolved separately, whether by suit or settlement, after the excavation work had been completed and paid for.

The plaintiff's decision to suspend progress payments on August 10—the day after the bulldozer accident—was undoubtedly taken in haste and without consulting counsel. This was fortunate as it turned out, because plaintiff's lawyer, had she been consulted, would very likely have found the legal and factual questions too close and too numerous to feel safe in advising her client that it would be legally proper to withhold the payment otherwise due. As has often been observed, the lawyer's counselling job in these and similar circumstances is somewhat chancy. If she advises her client that the latter may suspend performance because the other party has committed a material breach, and if that advice is acted upon but turns out to be wrong, then it will be the client who will have committed the first breach and the other party who will have a claim for contract damages. No doubt with this risk in mind, the defendant in *K & G* adopted what most would say was the better and more cautious tactic when it chose to continue working without pay for a second month and then—almost certainly on the advice of counsel—indicated its willingness to complete the job if payments were resumed. Defendant's aim, pretty clearly, was to leave it to the plaintiff to repudiate the contract and take responsibility for the final rupture. Ironically, this wise and well-considered strategy didn't succeed . . . though it probably should have.

The legal and factual issue in *K & G*, as has been seen, was whether the plaintiff or the defendant should be held to have breached by failing to render performance at the time such performance fell due. A slightly different and seemingly simpler question is presented if one of the contracting parties expressly repudiates her contractual obligations in *advance* of the time performance is due, in effect advising the promisee that no such performance will be forthcoming. Thus, A and B enter into a contract on April 1 under which B agrees to work for A for a three-month period beginning June 1. A is planning a trip abroad and wants B to come along as a kind of messenger boy and all-around flunkey. On May 11, A informs B that he has changed his plans and will not need B's services after all. On May 22, B brings an action against A for breach. Should B's suit be dismissed as premature? Viewed in strictly formal terms, the answer might be yes: A has promised to employ B on June 1 and he cannot logically be found to have broken that promise until the June 1 date has come and gone. Statements made by A before the June 1 date, however ominous, do not in themselves constitute a failure on A's part to perform his duty under the agreement. Practically speaking, however, it is plain that in repudiating his obligation to B, A has impaired, indeed destroyed, B's employment expectations and has made it necessary for B to scurry about and find other employment without delay. B cannot wait until June 1 to find out whether A might still provide him with a paycheck, and he obviously cannot live on the distant prospect of a damage recovery.

In *Hochster v. De La Tour*,[13] on the facts stated in the preceding paragraph, Queen's Bench held that A's repudiation operated to discharge B's duties under the employment agreement, which left B free to find himself another job for the three-month period and in effect precluded A from changing his mind yet again and repudiating his repudiation. Apparently deeming it

13. 118 Eng.Rep. 922 (1853), discussed in Jackson, *"Anticipatory Repu-* *diation" and the Temporal Element of Contract Law*, 31 Stan.L.Rev. 69 (1978).

a necessary corollary, the Court held also that the plaintiff had a right to commence an action for damages immediately, that is, prior to the scheduled beginning of performance on June 1. The latter holding, as many have pointed out, was something of a *non sequitur:* the Court could have dismissed B's suit for damages as premature, while still confirming his right to rely on A's repudiation by treating his obligation to work for A as having been cancelled. This quibble notwithstanding, the twofold rule of the *Hochster* decision is generally followed by the courts and is adopted by Restatement Section 253. In the end, the rather unsurprising point is that the anticipatory repudiation of a promise to perform, no less than a failure to perform at the time performance is due, may constitute a total breach. In either case the injured party has a claim for damages and may assume that her own performance obligations have been discharged.

In *Hochster* the promisor expressly repudiated the contract, but of course repudiation may be inferred from the promisor's conduct even if no statement is made. Thus, A agrees to sell a house to B, the deed to be delivered and the purchase price to be paid on June 1. On May 1 A sells the house to C. The latter act is obviously a repudiation even though A says nothing to B directly. Complicating the issue slightly, suppose B learns (on May 1) that various mechanics liens have been filed on the property which, unless satisfied before June 1, would violate A's obligation to transfer clear title. Assume further that B has reason to doubt whether A can find the money to satisfy the liens. At least arguably, the resulting uncertainty "impairs the value of the contract" from B's standpoint and leaves B in rather a quandary as to how she should proceed—e.g., whether she should or shouldn't commit herself to a lender, whether she should or shouldn't spend time looking for another house to buy, and so on. Restatement Section 251, which echoes UCC 2–609 in this respect, offers B a practical solution by providing that a promisee who has "reasonable grounds" for believing that the contract will be breached may "demand adequate assurance of due performance" from the promisor. Failure to provide such assurance may be considered by the promisee to be the equivalent of a repudiation, in which event the promisee, like the messenger-boy in *Hochster,* may sue for damages and regard her duties under the contract as discharged.

What qualifies as "reasonable grounds" for insecurity on the promisee's part, and what should then be taken as "adequate assurance" by the promisor, must of course depend on the particular facts and circumstances of the case at hand, which suggests that the parties and their counsel, like the litigants in *K & G*, will sometimes find themselves in the uncomfortable position of having to make nice judgments in a hurry. Thus, a promisor may decide not to respond to a demand for assurance because she or her counsel consider that the promisee lacked "reasonable grounds" for making that demand; similarly, a promisee who has received an assurance of some sort from the promisor may decide that such assurance is less than "adequate" and conclude that her own contractual obligations are cancelled. In either case, of course, the decision could turn out to be "wrong" in the later view of a court or jury, which would be asked to decide not whether there had been an *actual* failure to perform on the promisor's part, but whether the prospect of such a failure was sufficiently threatening to justify the promisee in taking self-defensive action in advance.

In *Pittsburgh–Des Moines Steel Co. v. Brookhaven Manor Water Co.,*[14] a case arising under UCC 2–609, the plaintiff, PDM, had contracted to build a tank for the defendant for $175,000, payment to be made 30 days after construction. The parties evidently understood that the defendant would obtain a loan to pay for the facility. Having learned that the defendant had been unable to complete arrangements with one prospective lender, the plaintiff advised the defendant that it would suspend performance unless the defendant placed the purchase price in escrow or unless the defendant's president gave his personal guarantee of payment. Subsequently, neither action having been taken, the plaintiff charged the defendant with repudiating the contract and sued for damages. The defendant, charging repudiation on the plaintiff's part, entered a counterclaim.

The Court held for the defendant. The issue, in the Court's view, was whether there had been a change for the worse in the defendant's financial condition after the contract was entered into sufficient to establish "reasonable grounds for insecurity". The defendant's inability or unwillingness to borrow money from a particular lender did not prove that such a worsening had occurred, and in fact the defendant's credit status, of which the plaintiff's comptroller conceded that he had had complete information, was no different, and no weaker, than it had been at the contract date. In effect, the Court surmised that the plaintiff-seller had simply changed its mind about extending credit to the defendant-buyer and had decided that it did not wish to go forward without additional security. On this view, the demand for "adequate assurance" lacked good-faith and was nothing more than a back-door attempt to rewrite the terms of the original agreement.

14. 532 F.2d 572 (7th Cir.1976).

Chapter 7

MISTAKE AND IMPOSSIBILITY

The question of contract breach most often arises by reason of the conduct and behavior, overt or implicit, of the parties themselves. One party is complained of by the other either for actively doing something he shouldn't have done or, more commonly, for refusing to do something he should have done, and the issue to be resolved is whether the circumstances reasonably support the complaining party's position. In the cases considered in this Chapter, by contrast, it is some exterior event—one that lies beyond the direct control of either party—that is said to explain and justify the apparent breach. The non-performing party admits his non-performance but argues, in effect, that facts or events not known to him at the time the agreement was entered into, or that took place afterwards, made performance impossible or impracticable both actually and as a matter of law.

The discussion that follows is divided into two sections, as the title implies. The two topics relate in the sense that the element of demonstrable fault is lacking in each. Thus, the cow in *Sherwood v. Walker* was not the cow, or at least not the kind of cow, that buyer and seller had in mind; but neither party intended to mislead or deceive the other (apparently). Similarly, while the big parade never took place in *Krell v. Henry,* neither landlord nor tenant could be blamed for the King's appendicitis. In both cases, however, there were losses—including actual out-of-pocket expenditures—that would have to be suffered by someone. Yet if no one was to blame, how do we decide which party should be made to take the consequences?

A. Mistake

Discussing the good ships *Peerless* in Chapter 2, above, it was observed that parties who misunderstand each other's initial intentions may find that they have no contract at all, that their apparent relationship does not exist and never did. The formation of a contract presupposes mutual assent, so that if each party assents to a different proposition, there is nothing to enforce and the contract is void.

But *Peerless* -type cases are surely rare. Somewhat more common, I would guess, are cases in which the contracting parties fully agree as to the identity of the particular property to be exchanged, but one or both are mistaken in what they understand that property to be. When the reality finally emerges and the nature of the property is seen in its true light, one party finds it advantageous to seek enforcement, the other to resist. Minds (however misguided) met at one level, so that at least conceptually the threshold question of whether there ever *was* a contract appears to be answered. Yet the fact that the parties (either or both) erred in making a basic assumption about the character of the transaction obviously raises doubts about whether such a contract merits enforcement.

Sherwood v. Walker,[1] long a vehicle for weary classroom humor, presents the issue in the context of what appears to have been a *mutual* mistake. The defendant, an importer and breeder of Angus cattle, offered to sell a certain cow (known by name and pedigree) to the plaintiff, a local bank executive. Defendant advised plaintiff that the cow in question was barren and could be purchased for $80, which represented her value as sirloin steak. By contrast, had the cow been capable of breeding her market value would have been $1,000. Plaintiff made a visit to defendant's cattle-pen, looked at the cow and liked what he saw, and therefore promptly accepted defendant's offer. Before plaintiff could take delivery, however, defendant learned from his ranch foreman that the cow was in fact "with calf" and refused to hand her over. Plaintiff then brought an action in replevin seeking to obtain possession of the animal, now known to be a breeder, at the $80 contract price.

Reversing a lower court judgment for the plaintiff and remanding the case for a new trial, the Supreme Court of Michigan held that if at the time they entered into their agreement both parties did in fact believe that the cow was barren and forever useless for breeding, then the defendant had a right to rescind and refuse delivery. Under well settled law, said the Court, a contract cannot be enforced if the "whole substance" and "very nature" of the merchandise sold is different from that which the parties bargained for, the mistaken identification was mutual, and the dollar consequences to the disadvantaged party are significant. Apparently each of those criteria was satisfied in the Court's view, and one assumes that the plaintiff abandoned his claim once the decision was announced. A dissenting Justice argued that the majority opinion overstated the strength of the parties' original convictions: defendant "thought" the cow would never breed, but plaintiff "thought" she might, neither being perfectly sure. The parties were not mistaken in a legal sense, merely ignorant or

1. 66 Mich. 568, 33 N.W. 919 (1887).

uncertain, and each took his chances. Accordingly, the banker should have his cow.

There are, I think, dark shapes and suspicions running through the *Sherwood* case.[2] Taking the facts presented by the Court at face, however, the decision is hard to accept. Certainly we must have a doctrine of "mistake". If B agrees to buy the contents of boxcar # 306 from S at a price which reflects the assumption that the boxcar carries a shipment of soybeans, when in fact it carries a shipment of gold bars, no sensible legal rule would deny S's right to rescind or reform the contract by showing that what he intended, and what B understood him to intend, was boxcar # 206, which happens to contain the soybeans. A contrary position would convert administrative and other quasi-clerical errors into acts of forfeiture and would be appropriate only if the law were viewed as a mindless ritual. Where, however, as in *Sherwood,* the transaction relates to property that has been particularized by the parties (the cow had a glorious name, as noted), and where appraisal of the property's value is a function of the seller's professional expertise, a different conclusion seems proper. The circumstances in *Sherwood* really suggest a misjudgment on the defendant's part rather than a mistake, and it is that, I think, that leaves the reader feeling doubtful about the outcome.

Perhaps even the term "misjudgment" concedes too much. A dealer in specialized property—antiques, paintings, pedigreed cattle, real estate—invests what he regards as an appropriate amount of time and money in ascertaining the value of his inventory. The dealer operates on the assumption that in general sales are final and cannot be reversed, but presumably he recognizes the possibility that he may, occasionally, arrive at too low an appraisal for some article and give some lucky customer a bargain. He knows from experience, however, that this will happen only rarely. To be sure, the number of such mistakes or misjudgments could be reduced even further, perhaps wholly avoided, by spending still more time and money on the appraisal process, but as a business

---

2. Sherwood was not a butcher but, as noted, a banker and perhaps a gentleman farmer. As such, why would he want to purchase a single head of beef cattle from Walker, i.e., just one non-producing cow? Whatever the reason, one marvels at his luck at having picked this particular cow out of a number of non-breeders that were being offered for sale. But was it luck? My own guess (just a guess) is that Sherwood paid a "fee" to someone at the cattle-pen who knew very well that the cow was with calf and was looking for a way to turn that inside information into cash. If the Michigan Court suspected such a thing ("She was evidently sold and purchased on the relation of her value as beef, unless the plaintiff had learned of her true condition, and concealed such knowledge from the defendants. . . ."), then the decision might possibly be explained as an exercise in judicial realism (upper Midwest variety).

matter it really isn't worth it. Quite simply, the dealer calculates that he will lose \$X through misappraisals unless he spends \$X *plus* \$Y to hire another appraiser. Since the cost of employing additional personnel exceeds the expected benefit, the dealer wisely decides not to take that step. But having made that decision, he cannot also claim that he has made a "mistake" and should be permitted to rescind when the rare event occurs. In effect, he *figured* it would happen (sometime) and rationally chose to assume the risk rather than pay to avoid it. If, nevertheless, he *is* allowed to rescind, then the dealer gets a financial benefit that is undeserved—very much as if he somehow became entitled to the proceeds of an insurance policy (call it "misappraisal insurance") without ever having had to pay any insurance premiums.

The best reason for allowing rescissional relief in a mutual mistake case, I suppose, is that otherwise one party would receive a windfall while the other would suffer a penalty. This is certainly true in the case of boxcar # 306, mentioned above. In *Sherwood,* however, as I have tried to argue, there really is no element of penalty, and the "windfall" is entirely up for grabs. Enforcing the contract would have given buyer an unexpected benefit, but rescinding did just the same for seller. With neither party having any moral claim to the difference between the contract price and the true value of the property, the fact that the seller could have "insured" but didn't, together with a general preference for treating transactions as final rather than reversible, pretty strongly suggests that enforcement would have been the better result.

Though largely disregarded in *Sherwood,* the factor of risk-assumption is treated by most modern authorities as an integral feature of the doctrine of mistake. Restatement Section 152 provides that a contract based on mutual mistake is voidable unless the adversely affected party bears the risk of the mistake under a reasonable view of the circumstances, and the Supreme Court of Michigan, indicating that *Sherwood* might be decided differently today, has expressly accepted the Restatement position. As suggested below, the question of which party *should* reasonably be said to bear such risk might be thought debatable in some cases, but where the seller is a professional dealer and the buyer is a mere customer the question, once raised, would seem to answer itself. Briefly put, experts dealing with non-experts cannot make "mistakes" as to the intrinsic value of the property being sold.

What about experts dealing with experts? In the *Beachcomber Coins* [3] case, the plaintiff, a retail dealer in rare coins, sought to

3. Beachcomber Coins, Inc. v. Boskett, 166 N.J.Super. 442, 400 A.2d 78 (1979).

rescind the purchase from defendant, another dealer, of a dime that bore a certain mark—"D" for Denver mintage—which, if genuine, gave the dime special value to collectors. Having completed the purchase, the plaintiff, on the point of reselling the dime at a profit to a retail customer, submitted the coin for certification to the American Numismatic Society in accordance with regular practice. In due course the Society reported that it was counterfeit. Finding that the transaction reflected a "mistake" on the part of both dealers, the Supreme Court of New Jersey held for the plaintiff and allowed the transaction to be rescinded. The mistake was mutual, apparently, because the defendant had paid a high price for the coin when *he* bought it, obviously supposing it to be the genuine article.

The outcome in *Beachcomber* can be explained, somewhat mechanically, by pointing to the circumstance that plaintiff and defendant were equally expert in appraising coins; hence, neither was more "at fault" than the other and neither bore the greater burden of risk. The case then presents itself, almost uniquely, as one of pure mistake. Yet even here one is left to wonder why the plaintiff didn't check the coin with the Numismatic Society at the time of sale, or make the sale contingent on certification, or require a representation of some sort from defendant as to genuineness . . . or *something*. Presumably, an expert purchaser should be expected to exhaust the available means of inspection and authentication before crying "mistake" (as opposed to fraud and misrepresentation, from which even he deserves protection), whether his seller is another expert or an amateur. As suggested in discussing the *Sherwood* case, a professional dealer would be presumed to spend as much on self-protection as his business experience appeared to justify; if he still gets stung on rare occasions, he deserves it. While the doctrine of mistake might literally apply to the facts in *Beachcomber,* there is surely something odd in extending relief on that ground to a coin dealer whose very occupation consists of distinguishing between the true and the false.

Searching for another explanation for the outcome, I might suggest that the Court in *Beachcomber* was really using the doctrine of mistake as a rule of prophylaxis or prevention. Its aim, perhaps, was to stop or deter worthless objects from being passed from hand to hand under cover of apparent authenticity. The Court was not in a position to identify the very first vendor of the phony dime—the counterfeiter, presumably—so as to place responsibility where it actually belonged. It did the next best thing, however, by halting the chain of transactions at the point of earliest discovery. In effect, *no* purchaser, however expert, bears the risk of unmasking a counterfeit; and I assume that the seller could now rescind as to *his* vendor if that person could be located. And so on back to the source. The "rule", then, is that you cannot shed yourself of a counterfeit coin (painting, precious stone, etc.) by passing it along in ignorance or by citing the buyer's expertise. What you can do, however, is return it to the person you got it from. Whether on grounds of fraud or misrepresentation (when that can be shown) or mistake (when it can't), sales of counterfeit articles are simply void.

Sherwood and *Beachcomber* are cases of mutual mistake— buyer and seller shared the same error—leading, as has been seen, to voidable contracts. The same result may follow, however, where the mistake is confined to one of the parties only. The notion, presumably, is that there can be no contract unless the minds of both parties coincide on a single subject-matter. A fundamental mistake may therefore result in a voidable contract even though the mistake is unilateral, provided, as usual, that the mistaken party does not bear the risk of the mistake under the circumstances. Once again, clerical error would be the typical instance of voidability. Thus, where a contractor submits a winning bid on a construction contract but inadvertently omits a major cost item from the total, the courts almost always allow the contractor (provided he acts before the other party has relied on the contract in some substantial way) to rescind or reform his bid on the ground that enforcement would be unconscionable.[4] The outcome would, of course, be otherwise and the contractor would be bound by his bid if the "mistake" was really a business misjudgment, e.g., underestimating the cost of the material and labor required for the job.

A much more interesting case of unilateral mistake—also easily resolved, but worth brief comment—is that of a seller who simply doesn't know as much about his property as the well-informed buyer to whom he sells it. Thus, suppose a farmer sells 100 acres of farmland to a shrewd purchaser who, based on geological tests that he has performed on neighboring tracts, believes—perhaps knows—that the land contains valuable mineral deposits. It in fact does, but the price paid to the farmer reflects the farmer's basic assumption that the land was useful for farming only. Can the farmer rescind? Certainly not, the reason commonly given being that the "adversely affected" farmer bore the risk of the "mistake". This, however, seems rather fanciful:

4. Elsinore Union Elementary School Dist. v. Kastorff, 54 Cal.2d 380, 6 Cal.Rptr. 1, 353 P.2d 713 (1960).

the farmer is hardly in a position to discover the true value of the property by carrying out the same geological tests for himself. He knows about seeds and fertilizer, but geology he's never heard of.

Probably, though, the real reason for barring rescission has as much or more to do with the geologist's interests and outlook as with the farmer's. The geologist, obviously, is in the business of converting low-value farmland into high-value mining property. Although most of us, as we drive along the turnpike, would rather gaze at a green and pleasant farm than an ugly mining operation, the plain fact is that people in general, otherwise known as the "market," have a greater need for copper and sulfur than they do for lettuce and tomatoes. It follows that the purchaser performs a socially valuable service, one from which we all benefit, when he does his geological survey, and he has to be rewarded for his time and effort. It may be odd, even slightly repellent, to say that the reward should come from the poor benighted farmer, but there appears to be no ready alternative. If, for example, we required the purchaser to share the value of his discovery with the seller in some measure, we would effectively discourage the purchaser from investing as much in research and discovery activities as he appears to be willing to invest, and we would then presumably have more lettuce and tomatoes, but less copper and sulfur, than we seem to want. While the farmer *might* go into the mineral prospecting business on his own, he can't do it by leaning on his hoe. He will have to make the same investment in skills and equipment that the purchaser has made, and if he does that he will quickly cease to be a seller and become a purchaser in his own right. The conclusion, which is really inescapable under present arrangements, is that we cannot allow contract rules—and certainly not the modest doctrine of mistake—to reduce or eliminate the rewards claimed by those who invest in information gathering[5]. Like an inventor's patent, the purchaser's information can be viewed as *his* property and, as such, entitled to the same protection as the farmer's title to his land.

The decided cases and the Restatement appear to confirm that the farmer would be treated as having made a "mistake" when he sold his land at a bargain price, but then deny his claim for relief on the ground that he assumed the risk. Taking a longer view of the matter, the farmer's mistake, if you want to call it that, was in deciding to grow lettuce rather than study geology in the first place. He made his bed, however, and the law leaves him with nothing but a feeling of regret (plus the proceeds of the sale).

5. Kronman, *Mistake, Disclosure, Information, and the Law of Contracts,* 7 J. Legal Studies 1 (1978).

Actually, the term "mistake," which implies an error or an over-sight rather than a fundamental career choice, is altogether mis-leading in this context.

Summarizing the obvious, it is plain that contract law needs a rule or principle that affords relief in cases involving clerical mistakes, arithmetical blunders, misidentification of persons or property, and the like. The rule itself, however, needs to be confined to cases of *just* that sort, and the question is how to express and then apply an appropriate limitation—one, roughly speaking, that separates inadvertent errors from misjudgments. The law attempts to answer that question by stressing the notion of risk-assumption, which appears to be correct as a policy matter, though somewhat ponderous and uncertain in operation. If we were drafting a statutory provision in this area, or yet another restatement, we might consider whether we would not do better to *reverse* the structure of the rule, i.e., by declaring that "mistake" shall not, in general, be grounds for relief, *except* in the case of clerical or arithmetical error, misidentification, etc. The chal-lenge, of course, would be to enumerate our exceptions so as to eliminate the ambiguity present in the risk-assumption concept, but without denying relief to those "adversely affected parties" to whom we really think it ought to be extended.

B. Impossibility and Frustration

The "impossibility" problem is a remarkably persistent one in contract law, going steadily back from the fairly recent *Transat-lantic* litigation, which involved the closing of the Suez Canal, to the destruction of the rickety old music hall in *Taylor v. Caldwell,* and far beyond. The reasons for this, alluded to earlier, have mostly to do with the limitations of human foresight and with the fact that the negotiation of contract details has to come to an end at some point. Every future contingent state of the world cannot be predicted, and lawyers are often faulted for spending too much of their clients' time and money quibbling about risks and hazards that will probably never materialize (although, as the reader may one day learn, that is absolutely nothing to the criticism they hear when contingencies *not* covered by the contract actually fall in). But even if the contract is planned and drafted with the greatest care and patience, "things" may happen that are not explicitly dealt with and that make performance difficult or impossible to carry out. And, of course, many routine transactions are expected to begin and end quickly—the two-day apartment rental in *Krell v. Henry,* for example—so that detailed and extended negotiations by batteries of lawyers would simply be too costly to justify.

The inevitable question is: who pays? In *Taylor v. Caldwell*[6], decided by King's Bench in 1863, plaintiff rented the Surrey Gardens—a music hall and outdoor dining area—from defendant for four separate days during the summer months at a rental of £100 a day. Plaintiff, who seems to have been a sort of roving impresario, planned to stage musical events and other entertainments for the local folks and with this in view spent a substantial sum on promotion, advertising and general preparation. Before any of these entertainments could be offered, however, the Surrey Gardens caught fire and burned to the ground. The disaster was no one's fault; it just happened. Claiming that defendant had breached by failing to make the Gardens available on the agreed dates, plaintiff sued to recover an amount equal to his promotional expenditures and related outlays, now wasted. Defendant responded by arguing that he should be excused as a matter of law, performance having obviously become impossible.

The Court held for the defendant. The central question, it indicated, was one of intent. To be sure, the contract itself said nothing about what should happen in the event of disaster, and evidently neither party raised the issue in the course of negotiations. Even so, the parties must have known that the contract could not be fulfilled if the music hall was destroyed by fire. They undertook their mutual obligations on the assumption that the Surrey Gardens would be there, physically, when the time came to use it. That circumstance was plainly essential to performance on either side. Looking at the contract as a whole, therefore, and in the absence of any express provision to the contrary, the continued existence of the music hall must be regarded as a condition "by law implied." Since without fault the premises had ceased to exist, the contract was discharged and both parties, but especially defendant, were legally excused.

The decision in *Taylor v. Caldwell* appears correct, but nothing in the Court's opinion really helps very much in resolving the critical issue of "intent." It is certainly true, as the Court says, that the defendant could not have been expected to make the Surrey Gardens available to the plaintiff once the facility had perished. But it does not necessarily follow that defendant's *financial* obligation to plaintiff was expected to perish as well. Thus, suppose we took a contrary position and insisted that the intention of the parties—somehow divined—was to require defendant to perform at all events. This would *not* mean that defendant must by some magic rebuild the Surrey Gardens in time for

6. King's Bench, 1863, 3 B. & S. 826,
122 Eng.Rep. 309.

the first of the scheduled entertainments—that indeed would be impossible and, hence, could not have been intended. Rather, the inference would be that defendant, finding himself unable to furnish the music hall as promised, must do the next best thing, which is to sit down and write a cheque to cover plaintiff's losses. Nothing could be easier and "less impossible" than that, and the question, therefore, is whether the parties intended that he should.

Lacking any clear affirmative evidence that they did so intend, I think the fairly clear presumption is that they did not. Like any contract, the music-hall lease was intended to protect each of the contracting parties against self-favoring conduct on the part of the other. The defendant had to make his property available at the rent agreed upon even if rents rose sharply thereafter, and the plaintiff had to pay the rent even if ticket sales turned out to be terrible. Either party might find it in his own interest to withhold performance, but if he chose to do so, then, obviously, the injured party would be entitled to compensation. Thus, if the defendant had breached by deliberate act because (for example) he got a better offer from another tenant, he would surely have been liable for the plaintiff's promotional outlays, assuming such outlays were reasonably foreseeable at the time the contract was entered into.

The question in *Taylor*, by obvious contrast, was whether the music-hall lease was intended to protect against a contract failure that was *not* attributable to self-favoring conduct but, rather, resulted from an accidental event which neither party willed and over which neither had any control. In a sense, the fire had an even-handed impact on the two parties: just as it destroyed the defendant's music-hall so it destroyed the intangible property interest—call it customer goodwill—that the plaintiff had created through his promotional expenditures. If fierce enough, it might also have consumed various tangible assets belonging to the plaintiff—say, costumes and stage-sets that had been stored nearby. In effect, plaintiff and defendant *both* suffered a casualty loss, in each case without fault or conscious intent on the part of the other. As suggested, therefore, the issue in the case was whether the defendant's promise to make the music-hall available at the rent provided for in the contract (or else pay compensation) carried with it an undertaking to reimburse the plaintiff for casualty losses as well.

One would hardly think so. The defendant presumably had fire and casualty insurance covering the value of the music-hall, and for that he paid premiums to an insurance company. I

130

suppose he *might* have been willing to increase the amount of such insurance to cover the value of his tenant's property as well, but that would be unusual. Normally, a tenant would be left to make his own individual insurance arrangements. In any case, if there *had* been such an undertaking on the defendant's part, the plaintiff would surely have been required to specify the amount of the insurable loss and to add the premium-increase to the rent. No evidence was offered by the plaintiff to suggest that such a premium adjustment had been made or even discussed, and without such evidence I think it would be difficult, if not quite impossible, to resolve the critical issue of "intent" in the plaintiff's favor.

Young v. City of Chicopee [7], another slightly antiquated decision in this field, follows the rule of *Taylor v. Caldwell,* but with the parties reversed, plaintiff being the seller of a service and defendant being the buyer. Briefly, plaintiff had contracted to make extensive repairs to a wooden bridge owned by defendant and in order to avoid delays agreed to store his construction materials, mostly timber, at the bridge site. After part of the work (which apparently consisted of laying one wooden plank beside another) had been completed, a fire broke out and consumed not only the bridge itself but the unused building materials that were kept nearby. As usual, the fire was nobody's fault.

The Supreme Court of Massachusetts held that plaintiff was entitled to recover for the repair work already performed—the bridge to that extent was usable before the fire—but not for the value of the unused building materials, even though the latter had been brought to the bridge site at defendant's request. Its opinion is somewhat gnarled and cryptic, but the Court evidently accepted the principle that destruction of the subject-matter of a contract— here the bridge—discharges the agreement on both sides. Hence, the outlays made by plaintiff in reliance on defendant's promise to pay for bridge repairs, like the impresario's advertising expenses in *Taylor,* were simply not compensable; defendant was excused. To be sure, there is a notable factual difference between *Chicopee* and *Taylor.* In *Taylor,* the advertising expenses were incurred solely to promote the plaintiff's business; the music hall owner was presumably unaffected by the level of ticket sales, provided only that he got his £100 a day. In *Chicopee,* by contrast, the construction materials were to be used directly in repairing defendant's bridge and were being stored at the bridge site at defendant's insistence. There was thus an element of proximity or

7. 186 Mass. 518, 72 N.E. 63 (1904).

relatedness that was lacking in *Taylor,* which makes the denial of plaintiff's damage claim especially striking.

But the ultimate rationale, though differently expressed, may be the same. While defendant knew that plaintiff would have to purchase timber and other supplies in order to carry out the repair work, it would not have been likely to assume the risks associated with fire and casualty. It was, of course, like any other promisor, responsible for losses occasioned by its own self-favoring conduct. If, for example, the defendant had repudiated the contract after the plaintiff had purchased materials that could not be used for another purpose, the defendant would almost certainly have been liable for plaintiff's reliance expenditures. But unless the defendant had actually committed itself to do so, its performance duties under the contract would not include an obligation to provide the plaintiff with casualty insurance as well.

The plaintiffs in *Taylor* and *Chicopee* made no claim for expectation damages, but if they had the analysis and the result would be the same. Once again, the parties are unlikely to have intended that fire or other disaster would render the music-hall owner or the bridge-owner liable for lost profits without a specific understanding to that effect. Deliberate breach at some point during the life of the contract would, of course, be another matter.

The so-called impracticability or frustration-of-purpose cases have a good deal in common with *Taylor v. Caldwell* but also differ in important ways, and the question is whether the similarities or the differences ought to count most in the result. *Krell v. Henry*[8], one of the famous coronation cases, will serve to make the point. Queen Victoria having at long last gone to her reward, the coronation of her son, soon to be Edward VII, was jubilantly planned for the end of June, 1902. The coronation procession, in all its magnificence, was to pass along Pall Mall on June 26 and June 27, so that individuals having apartments overlooking the procession route were greatly envied. Apparently caring more for money than pageant, Krell, the owner of a flat so situated, agreed to let his chambers to Henry for the two daytime periods at a fee of £75, of which £25 was paid in advance as a deposit. To everyone's disappointment, Edward suffered a sudden attack of appendicitis and the coronation had to be postponed. Henry, in consequence, refused to pay the balance of the rent, and Krell sued.

Finding the issue controlled or at least dominated by *Taylor v. Caldwell,* the Court of Appeal held for the defendant. Concededly, Krell's apartment, unlike the Surrey Gardens, continued to exist,

8. Court of Appeal, 1903, 2 K.B. 740.

and Henry could have gone in and spent two days looking at the vacant streets if he wanted to. But the undebatable purpose of the agreement was to provide a view of the great procession. That goal having been frustrated by the King's illness, the foundation of the contract was eliminated. Performance effectively became impossible; hence the contract was discharged.

Edward VII's coronation, including the procession along Pall Mall, did take place in August, just six weeks later. While one might suppose that the parties would have agreed to transfer their arrangement to the later date, they obviously didn't. Henry may have lost interest in the meanwhile (the August ceremony was apparently less well attended than the earlier one would have been), or, of course, Krell, then considering himself free to let his chambers for a second time at the same premium, may have rejected any idea of a rain-check.

Restatement Section 265 specifically approves the result in *Krell v. Henry,* treating the case as one of "supervening frustration". Writers on the subject are not unanimous, however, and a contrary decision was reached on related facts in another of the coronation cases.[9] The reason for feeling doubt about the Court's decision, I suppose, is that the two-day lease of Krell's apartment *could* be viewed as nothing more than a speculation in Henry's hands. The lease was apparently transferable, and if things had turned out differently, it might have been Krell rather than Henry who wound up suffering the bitter pangs of frustration or, at least, of lost opportunity. Thus, demand for a vantage-point overlooking the big parade might have increased stupendously as coronation day approached, so that Henry could have found himself holding a very hot ticket indeed. In effect, Henry was "long" 1 two-day lease on a flat in Pall Mall. Whatever his original aim might have been, if the coronation had gone forward as scheduled and the day had been especially fine, he might finally have chosen to sell his lease at a profit—say double his purchase price—and then contented himself with reading about the coronation in the Times. Even a spectator can become a speculator if the price is right.

Putting the same point more generally, it might be argued that the situation in *Krell v. Henry* was really just a very special instance of a common configuration with which the law deals swiftly under ordinary circumstances. Thus, a typical buyer and seller agree today upon a price for goods or services to be delivered in the future. Each of the parties knows that the actual market

9. Chandler v. Webster, 1 K.B. 493 (1904).

price on the delivery date may be higher or lower within some predictable range, with the upside and downside probabilities being roughly symmetrical on either side of the contract price. The contract will, of course, be enforced *whatever* the outcome—the law is properly indifferent between the parties—and indeed, as explained much earlier, the willingness of the parties to enter into a contract in the first place depends on a legal remedy being available if performance is refused. Why should Krell and Henry be treated differently? While the King's illness was certainly unexpected, star performers do get sick from time to time. Such a development can never be regarded as entirely remote—"unexpected" is not the same as "unforeseeable"—and I would imagine that a modern insurance company could tell you exactly what the chances were that a person of the King's age (and habits) would get sick today, next month or a year from now. Neither Henry nor Krell was a modern insurance company, but this does not mean that they were wholly incapable of weighing relevant contingencies, including the very familiar contingency of illness and mortality.

The effect of all this argumentation is to leave one in some doubt about whether it really is correct to place *Krell v. Henry* within the general ambit of the impossibility doctrine. If we take the position, as the Court apparently did, that Krell was simply the seller, and Henry simply the buyer, of a ticket to the big parade, then, perhaps, the parade having been called off, the ticket price should be refunded or forgiven. The difficulty, of course, is that Krell was not the sponsor or producer of the event and had no responsibility for anything except the availability of his well-situated flat.

As a final observation, it might be noted that Henry cross-claimed (successfully in the court below) for the return of his £25 deposit, but for reasons not given withdrew that claim on appeal. A possible inference is that Henry was prepared to view the deposit as a kind of liquidated damage figure—as if the parties had agreed that Krell could retain that amount (but would receive no more) even if the big parade was cancelled—and that the Court, in effect, approved what it took to be a reasonable settlement of a difficult controversy.

Transatlantic Financing Corporation v. United States [10], which arose on the seller's rather than the buyer's side of the equation, is a well-known modern illustration of the "impracticability" prob-

10. 363 F.2d 312 (D.C.Cir.1966), discussed in Posner & Rosenfield, *Impossibility and Related Doctrines in Contract* *Law: An Economic Analysis,* 6 J. Legal Studies 83 (1977).

lem. The plaintiff, a shipping company, had entered into a contract with the United States to carry wheat from Galveston to a port in Iran. The contract price for the shipping service was $305,000, a figure that reflected the parties' shared assumption that the cargo ship would make the voyage—some 10,000 miles—by way of the Suez Canal, which was the customary and the shortest route. While the ship was on the high seas, Egypt was attacked by Britain, France and Israel and responded by closing the Canal and blocking passage to all vessels. Following inconclusive discussions with the Department of Agriculture, plaintiff's ship was rerouted around the Cape of Good Hope, arriving in Iran several weeks later than expected, and having added 3,000 miles to the trip. Plaintiff never sought to be excused from its contract obligations—the ship did go on to Iran—but it subsequently asked the government for an additional $43,000 to cover the expense of the longer voyage. The government refused. Arguing that performance of the original contract had become "impossible" because of the Canal closing, plaintiff sued in *quantum meruit* for the sum just mentioned.

In an opinion much-admired for its thoughtful treatment of the topic, the D.C. Court of Appeals held for the government. Three elements, said the Court, were necessary to justify the plaintiff's impossibility claim. These were (i) an unexpected occurrence, (ii) a failure to have allocated the risk of that occurrence by agreement or by custom, and (iii) "commercial impracticability" with respect to the performance of plaintiff's obligations. Running down the list, Judge Wright agreed with plaintiff that both parties expected the ship to follow the usual and customary route, which, as stated, was through the Canal. Hence the need to travel around the Cape qualified as an "unexpected occurrence". As to risk-allocation, however, the Court felt that tensions in the Middle East, which were present long before the joint attack on Egypt, must have alerted plaintiff to the presence of "abnormal risks" in any voyage that was routed through Suez. To be sure, the United States would have been no less aware of those risks and tensions; hence it would be difficult to say that one party rather than the other was in a better position to make predictions about the possibility of war. But assuming that the parties were equal in that respect, it would still follow that the plaintiff, as an experienced shipping company, would be better able to estimate the added cost of performing by alternative routes. In effect, both parties knew that there was some risk of a Canal shutdown. But only plaintiff would know exactly how much its own additional expenses would amount to if a trip around the Cape became necessary. In any event, the actual variation in cost was fairly modest—only $43,000, less than 15% of the total contract price of $305,000—so that performance could not be said to have been "commercially impracticable" from a purely financial standpoint. "While it may be an overstatement to say that increased cost and difficulty of performance never constitute impracticability, to justify relief there must be more of a variation between expected cost and the cost of performing by an available alternative than in the present case, where the promisor can legitimately be presumed to have accepted some degree of abnormal risk, and where impracticability is urged on the basis of added expense alone."

The Court noted, finally, that there was an inconsistency in plaintiff's litigating position. Thus, plaintiff sought to enforce the basic contract itself—it still wanted $305,000 for carrying the freight from Galveston to Iran—but then also demanded non-contractual relief in the form of *quantum meruit* to cover the additional cost. The claim of "impossibility," however, is all-or-nothing. Either the contract should be treated as wholly discharged—in which event the entire voyage would be compensated at a *quantum meruit* rate—or the contract should be viewed as binding and the plaintiff should be limited to the contract price for its services. Apparently, however, as the Court slyly observed, the contract price was just too good to give up. The *quantum meruit* rate seems to have been a little more than $14 a mile ($43,000/ 3000 miles). The extended voyage, Cape route included, was 13,000 miles in total, so that *quantum meruit* for the whole trip would have been only about $182,000.

Although steadily supported by the Restatement, the doctrines of "supervening frustration" and "supervening impracticality" have not often been invoked by our courts to excuse performance by a disadvantaged buyer or seller. In crude terms, the reason is that post-contractual change in the market price of promised goods or services is generally an expected element in any forward exchange. Once again, the odds that the buyer or the seller will turn out to be the advantaged party must be assumed to be about equal, with the contract price representing something like a midpoint between the foreseeable high and low. Future events that "merely" affect the market value of the thing promised—whether a two-day right of occupancy or an ocean carriage contract—would almost always be presumed to have been anticipated by the parties when they settled on their terms initially, even if the particular event is both unexpected and impracticable or frustrating.

By contrast, *Taylor* and *Chicopee* are true "impossibility" cases. The subject-matter of the contract having been destroyed, no market substitute is available at any price. The question then is whether the non-performing party (non-performance being involuntary, of course, and without deliberation) should be liable for the other party's out-of-pocket expenses and, perhaps, for expected profits. The answer given by the cases is no, and the reason, most probably, is that the promisor, though responsible for losses resulting from his own self-favoring conduct, is not also a casualty insurer merely because the casualty event has made it impossible for him to perform.

In an effort to delimit the grounds for excuse in the event of an unexpected occurrence, the parties to a contract calling for the future delivery of goods or services will often include a so-called *force majeure* provision in their agreement. Such provisions are chiefly designed to protect sellers if a delay or default in delivery occurs that is due to "causes beyond Seller's control and not occasioned by its fault or negligence." Typically, an attempt is made to specify the classes of events that are to be regarded as excusable—governmental prohibition, strikes, failure to perform by another vendor, and so on. When applicable, a *force majeure* provision will of course operate to excuse the defaulting party even if the common law would not. Often, however, a listing of excusable events is followed or preceded by an inclusive reference to Acts of God or the like, so that the parties can still be expected to resort to general legal principles when the event at issue is not referred to by specific description in the contract itself.

Chapter 8

REMEDIES

Assuming a failure or unwillingness to perform on the part of a promisor, the law customarily provides a remedy to the promisee in the form of money damages based upon the promisee's expectation interest. As suggested in Chapter 1, the aim and the effect of the prevailing damage rule can be described as forward-looking as well as remedial. Two parties contemplating an exchange obviously need to be assured that their commitments are mutual and that neither party will be free to receive the performance of the other while withholding his own. Lacking such assurance the parties might well be reluctant, perhaps unwilling, to make deals on the basis of mere promises and would find themselves unable to project their plans into the future with the necessary degree of confidence. The larger purpose of contract law is to supply that assurance by requiring each party to meet the expectations of the other, if not through willing performance then by forced surrender of the equivalent in hard cold cash.

Calculating expectation damages is easy in theory, though not, I think, always so in practice. The object of the exercise, once again, is to give the injured party the benefit of his bargain, that is, to put him in as good a position as he would have been in had the contract been performed in accordance with its terms. Briefly stated, this formulation means that the injured party is entitled to a damage recovery equal to (a) the value he has lost by reason of the other party's default, plus (b) the expenditures he has made (if any) in carrying out his own obligations under the contract. To illustrate simply, suppose that C, a contractor, agrees to build a house for O for $100,000. C figures that the job will cost him $80,000 and hence looks forward to a $20,000 profit. After the house is partly built and C has spent $50,000 on wages and materials, O repudiates the contract. C is entitled to damages of $70,000—$20,000 for the lost profit, plus $50,000 to compensate for the expenditures he made in reliance on the contract. Another way of reaching the same result is to measure C's damages by reference to the difference between the full contract price of $100,000 and the $30,000 of "cost avoided" by C in not having to complete the work. I should add that C would have a damage claim even if O had repudiated before C spent anything on the project, but then, of course, C's recovery would be limited to his $20,000 profit expectation.

Turning the illustration around, assume that it is C who repudiates the contract and O who has a claim for damages. Since O is entitled to a house for $100,000, O's recovery would be measured by the difference between the contract price and any greater amount that he might have to pay another builder to do, or to finish, the work. If, for example, O had already made progress payments to C of $50,000, and if O now has to pay a second contractor $55,000 to get the house completed, then O has suffered a loss of $5,000 in the value of his expectation interest and would be entitled to recover that amount from C.

The UCC applies essentially the same damage rule to the purchase and sale of goods. Thus, assume Seller agrees to deliver certain merchandise to Buyer at price of $1 a unit but subsequently fails to make delivery or repudiates the contract. Under Section 2–712, Buyer may "cover" by making a purchase of substitute goods and have damages from Seller equal to the difference between the "cost of cover" and the contract price. If Buyer (without unreasonable delay) acquires like merchandise by paying another seller $1.50, his damage claim is obviously 50 cents a unit. Buyer thus obtains the goods that he requires at a net cost of $1 a unit just as if Seller had performed as promised. A seller's remedies in the event of breach by a buyer are largely parallel. If it is Buyer who breaches by repudiating the contract or refusing to accept the goods when tendered, Seller may resell those goods to other buyers "in a commercially reasonable manner" and, under 2–706, claim damages equal to the difference between the contract price and the resale price. The matter does not quite end there, as our discussion of the "lost volume" seller at p. 148, infra, will suggest. In general, however, the effect of the Code provision, at least the aim, is to put the injured seller in as good a position as he would have been in if the buyer had accepted the goods and paid the price called for by the contract.

The availability of a substitute transaction—an owner hiring another contractor after the first has defaulted, a buyer resorting to "cover" after the seller has failed to deliver—makes the damage calculation look pretty straightforward, but in some cases the simple act of substitution may not be possible or feasible. Suppose, for example, that A agrees to sell B certain specialized equipment which is not available, or at least not readily available, from other sources. Although eager to perform, A finds that he cannot obtain the equipment, or cannot make timely delivery, and hence is compelled to breach. If B is not able to cover or to ascertain the cost of substitute equipment by reference to "the market," B's damage claim will have to be measured by looking at his own individual expectations with respect to the value of the promised performance. This, however, seems somewhat open-ended and, depending on the circumstances, one might have some concern for the extent of *A*'s financial exposure, even though A is the non-performing party and presumably took a conscious risk when he entered into the contract. The problem would not seem too serious if B were a jobber whose aim was simply to resell the equipment to end-users at a conventional mark-up. Assuming A was aware of B's role as a middleman, the net profit that B would have realized on resale would be a proper measure of B's expectation interest and A's liability. But suppose B himself is the end-user and asserts that A's failure to deliver the equipment resulted in the shut-down of a major manufacturing division and the loss of 6 months' operating income. Although B's loss of earnings is plainly a consequence of A's breach, the scope and extent of B's potential loss might not have been known, or even have been reasonably foreseeable, by A at the time the transaction was agreed to. The question, then, is whether A's state of expectation should serve as a limitation on B's recovery rights, though A is the party in breach and B is the victim of A's default. This issue, which is one of some conceptual importance in the contracts field, is discussed at p. 150, infra, in connection with the famous case of *Hadley v. Baxendale.*

Moving briefly to a more general policy level, I think students are sometimes troubled by the rather stark fact that the law does not actually require a promisor to keep his promise, but instead treats the payment of money damages as a wholly adequate remedy for breach. In effect, the law says that a party to a contract is free either to perform or not to perform, provided only that if he breaches he shall be obliged to pay the injured party an amount in cash sufficient to give the latter the benefit originally expected. In everyday life, to be sure, we regard breaking promises as more or less dishonorable. By contrast, in the largely commercial setting with which contract law is concerned, keeping or breaking one's word appears to be an ethically neutral event, of which the proof, perhaps, is that punitive or exemplary damages are not recoverable by an injured promisee.[1]

The explanation generally given for this apparent state of moral indifference is that the law, in permitting (even encouraging) a promisor to breach and compensate the promisee with money, promotes an efficient disposition of material resources.

1. Restatement Section 355. And see, White v. Benkowski, 37 Wis.2d 285, 155 N.W.2d 74 (1967). On damages generally, see Kornhauser, *An Intro-* *duction to the Economic Analysis of Contract Remedies*, 57 U.Col.L.Rev. 683 (1986).

Assuming the breaching promisor has acted rationally, there is, or should be, a net social gain to the parties; yet no one is left worse off after the breach than before. The point is customarily illustrated in the following way. Suppose Ursula contracts to sell Gerald a certain customized machine for a price of $100,000, delivery and payment in 60 days. The machine is worth $120,000 to Gerald, who intends to use it in his business. Prior to the delivery date, Rupert offers Ursula $150,000 for the machine. Assume that Ursula reacts by deliberately breaching her contract with Gerald and selling the machine to Rupert. To be sure, Ursula then owes damages of $20,000 to Gerald. Even after paying Gerald's damage claim, however, Ursula nets $130,000 instead of the measly $100,000 she would have had if she had kept her promise. In the end, Ursula is better off to the tune of $30,000, Gerald is as well off as he expected to be when the contract was entered into, and the machine is ultimately acquired by the person for whom it has the highest economic value, namely, Rupert. Accordingly, there is a net social gain, and no harm to anyone, as a consequence of Ursula's deliberate act of breach.

One's doubts about Ursula's morality in breaking her promise are thus overcome by awe and admiration for the elegance of the result. Or are they? Actually, a rule of specific performance that absolutely *required* Ursula to sell the machine to Gerald for $100,000 would lead to an equally efficient outcome, but the $30,000 of overplus would wind up in Gerald's hands rather than Ursula's. Thus, Rupert, on learning of Gerald's contractual right to pay $100,000 for the machine, would be just as glad to offer Gerald (rather than Ursula) $150,000 for a transfer of title to the machine (or to offer Gerald $50,000 for an assignment of his contract rights). Assuming he accepted, Gerald would obviously be $30,000 richer than he expected to be, Ursula would be no worse off than *she* expected to be, and the machine would go to the highest-value user just as above. What is more, our moral faces would be saved, because Ursula, now operating under a specific performance rule, would have no inducement to break her promise. Finally, specific performance would make it unnecessary to put a dollar value on Gerald's expectations—Ursula simply has to go ahead and deliver the machine. Hence, the quite considerable danger that a court might miscalculate the injured party's actual damages would be avoided.

As a practical matter, Ursula, being in the business of selling machines, would be more likely than Gerald to receive an inquiry from Rupert and may be in a better position than Gerald to get Rupert's highest bid. If so, the effect of a specific performance rule would simply be to prompt Ursula to negotiate with Gerald for a buy-out of his contract rights. Gerald would then get some portion of the $30,000 in question—just how much would depend on how good he is at haggling—with Ursula retaining the balance as a reward for her superior market expertise. Efficiency goals would be met—Ursula and Gerald would both be better off—but the legal rule would lead to a negotiated compromise rather than a breach.

All this argumentation should not, of course, be taken by the reader to suggest that there is any doubt about the state of the present law of remedies in this field. Both at common law and under the UCC, the remedy that is normally and generally available to a disappointed promisee is, quite simply, money damages, with specific performance being granted only if the contract involves "unique" property—land, typically—and only if damages would be inadequate to protect the injured party's expectation interest. The point, however—one that modern scholars have made with increasing emphasis [2]—is that the option to breach-and-pay may not always be the best or the only way to reach an efficient and a fair result.

The discussion that follows is divided into three sections. Section A describes the principal limitations on the expectation damage rule. Section B examines the chief alternatives to expectation damages, namely, damages based on the promisee's reliance and restitution interests. Section C, finally, considers whether and to what extent the parties may contract for a damage measure in advance of any breach instead of leaving the matter for judicial determination after a breach occurs.

A. Limitations on Expectation Damages

1. *Avoidability and Mitigation.* For reasons that seem apparent, an injured party cannot recover damages for losses that he could have avoided after the promisor's breach became known. So stated, the rule, or limitation, applies both to the reliance feature and to the lost-profit feature of the injured party's claim. Having become aware of the promisor's non-performance, the injured party is expected to suspend or terminate his own performance

---

2. Bishop, *The Choice of Remedy for Breach of Contract*, 14 J. of Legal Studies 299 (1985); Shavell, *The Design of Contracts and Remedies for Breach*, 99 Q.J.Econ. 121 (1984); MacNeil, *Efficient Breach of Contract: Circles in the Sky,* 68 Va.L.Rev. 947 (1982); Schwartz, *The Case for Specific Performance*, 89 Yale L.J. 271 (1979); Farnsworth, *Legal Remedies for Breach of Contract,* 70 Columbia L.Rev. 1145 (1970).

and has no claim for expenditures made in reliance on the contract beyond that point in time. Going further, the injured party is expected to minimize his lost-profit claim by making reasonable efforts to substitute other arrangements—another job, another seller or buyer—for those provided in the contract. In effect, he cannot recover the value of lost benefits if and to the extent that there are opportunities to mitigate the loss by doing similar worthwhile things with his time and resources.

In *Rockingham County v. Luten Bridge Co.,*[3] the plaintiff, Luten, in January entered into a contract with the County Board to build a bridge which was to be part of a newly constructed County road. There was public opposition to the project and in February, after one of the County commissioners had resigned (but then quickly attempted to rescind his resignation), the Board reversed itself (by a bare majority vote) and notified the plaintiff, which had by then spent $1,900 on labor and materials, that the contract was now regarded as unauthorized and invalid. The plaintiff, apparently believing that the later notice was itself invalid because the Board was illegally constituted, chose to disregard that notice and continued to build the bridge in accordance with the terms agreed upon. By November, the plaintiff had expended more than $18,000 and, its request for payment being refused, sued the County for that amount.

Reversing the trial court, which had held for the plaintiff, the Fourth Circuit found that the February notice possessed a kind of de facto legality and should have been taken by the plaintiff as a repudiation of the contract. At that point the plaintiff should have halted its own performance rather than piling up damages by "proceeding with the erection of a useless bridge." In the present action, therefore, the plaintiff was entitled to recover $1,900—its outlays up to the date of the notice—plus anticipated profit. It could not, however, claim reimbursement for expenditures made after it had become aware that the County had breached.

The rule of the *Luten* case—that the victim of a breach has a duty to avoid actions that increase the other party's damages—is well accepted and obviously correct. On the other hand, we might wonder what Luten's position would have been if it *had* halted performance on receiving the February notice and if the de facto legality question (to which the Court devoted four full pages of its opinion) had been decided differently. Then, perhaps, Luten itself might have been regarded as the party in breach and disentitled even to recover its $1,900 outlay (especially if the road project had

3. 35 F.2d 301 (4th Cir.1929).

finally gone forward). The February notice advised Luten that its contract "was not legal and valid", which was plainly false, and Luten might well have considered that the notice, hastily issued by a rump Board, could not be taken as definitive. As indicated, the Court held for the County by reciting the familiar and well-acknowledged rule that an injured party has no right to "pile up damages". But the real issue in the case, I think, was whether Luten faced an honest or a phony dilemma regarding the effect of the February notice, and if the former, whether its decision to continue working on the bridge was reasonable or capricious. As to this factual question, the Fourth Circuit had nothing whatever to say, although, as stated, one might suppose that it would have been seen as fairly critical.

Minimizing loss through mitigation is a self-executing obligation when the subject-matter of the contract is commodities or other fungible merchandise, because the injured party's damage claim is capped, in effect, by the market value of equivalent goods. In other situations, particularly where the contract calls for specialized services, the question of equivalence or substitutability may be much less certain. In what is perhaps the best known of all "duty to mitigate" cases—*Parker v. Twentieth Century–Fox Film Corp.*[4]—the plaintiff, Shirley MacLaine, in 1965 had entered into a contract with Fox to play the lead role in a movie version of the Broadway musical *Bloomer Girl.* The much coveted role would provide an opportunity not only to "act", but also to sing, dance and otherwise exhibit oneself to advantage. MacLaine's fee was guaranteed at $750,000 for 14 weeks' work. For reasons unknown, Fox decided to cancel *Bloomer Girl* before production had begun. In order "to avoid any damage to you," however, Fox offered in writing to employ MacLaine as the leading actress, at the very same fee, in a western film tentatively entitled *Big Country, Big Man,* giving her one week to say yes or no to the offer. The female lead in *Big Country* would presumably have involved little more than standing about in a flimsy frock tearfully begging Big Man to settle down and leave his guns at home. MacLaine said no and sued for her fee.

Holding (with one dissent) that MacLaine was under no legal obligation to mitigate damages by accepting the western role, the Supreme Court of California affirmed the trial court in granting her motion for summary judgment and awarding damages of $750,000 against the studio. The Court majority acknowledged the general rule that the measure of recovery for a wrongfully

4. 3 Cal.3d 176, 89 Cal.Rptr. 737, 474 P.2d 689 (1970).

discharged employee is the salary agreed upon *less* the amount that the employee earned or with reasonable effort could have earned from other employment. This, however, did not mean that the wronged employee must simply take any job in the economic universe; rather, the "other employment" must be comparable and not "of a different or inferior kind". By "no stretch of the imagination", said the Court, could a silly part in a cowboy movie be considered the equivalent of the lead in a major song-and-dance production. As to comparability, therefore, there was simply no factual issue whatever—no need to take testimony or to hear the views of experts—and hence the trial court's action was correct.

The dissenting Justice, concerned that the majority opinion might encourage plaintiff-employees to ignore the general duty to mitigate and thus increase the cost of contractual failure, thought that there should have been a trial to determine whether the differences between the two jobs really were substantial enough to justify MacLaine in treating the later offer as "inferior" in kind. One suspects that the dissenting Justice viewed MacLaine's conduct in rejecting the substitute role as distinctly egoistic. The dissenter may also have experienced a certain visceral shock when he perceived that MacLaine would now receive $750,000 (more than $2,000,000, I guess, in 1990 dollars) for sitting home and doing nothing.

The outcome in the Shirley MacLaine case obviously invites comparison with the result reached by the New York Court of Appeals in *Jacob & Youngs v. Kent,* discussed in the preceding Chapter. In the latter, the promisor's breach—installing Cohoes instead of Reading pipe—was dealt with under the diminished value rule, presumably because the cost of curing the defective performance would have been so much greater than the very small loss in economic value suffered by the promisee. In the Shirley MacLaine case, apparently, the Court majority made the opposite finding: the loss to MacLaine of professional standing and future career opportunities resulting from the cancellation of *Bloomer Girl* was so great that it could not be compensated by a dollar amount smaller than the entire fee that had been promised her. In effect, and by implication, the Court seemed almost to believe that MacLaine would not have substituted the female lead in *Big Country* at any price. That could not literally be true, one would think, even for the proud MacLaine; and while the task of proving otherwise in the face of her sworn denials would have been difficult, one might suppose (along with the dissent) that the defendant should at least have been given a chance to show the jury that the *Big Country* part was not so inferior as to be wholly non-substitutional. My guess is that the Court's willingness to let the issue go on summary judgment reflected a conviction (which the trial judge may have shared) that the studio was not in good faith when it offered MacLaine the role of a cowboy's cowgirl—*and* gave her just one week to take it or leave it. Did the studio people truly expect that she might take it? Perhaps; yet the language of the offer itself—"to avoid any damage to you"—sounds more like the conscious product of a legal mind intent on laying the basis for a mitigation defense than it does the gravelly voice of a movie executive eager to convince MacLaine that the role was exactly right for her.

As the above mention of *Jacob & Youngs* should suggest, the "mitigation" principle can be taken to refer broadly to the prevailing notion that the law ought to do what it reasonably can to minimize the cost of contract breakdown—subject, however, to the constraint that the injured party's expectations be fully compensated by the party in breach. *Groves v. John Wunder Co.,*[5] yet another casebook classic, provides a fairly challenging illustration both of the minimization goal and of the constraint. Groves (a corporation) owned 24 acres of suburban real estate which, though zoned as industrial property, was being used by it for the excavation of sand and gravel. In 1927, Groves leased the land, together with related equipment, to John Wunder Co., also engaged in sand and gravel excavation, for a 7–year term. Wunder paid Groves a lump-sum rent of $105,000 and agreed that when the lease expired it would restore the land to Groves "at a uniform grade, substantially the same as the grade now existing at the roadway. . . ." Seven years later, however, having turned the property into a choppy mess, Wunder refused to carry out its grading obligation and chose instead to deliberately breach the contract.

In the litigation that followed, Wunder conceded that Groves had a valid claim for breach, but it urged that the proper measure of damages was the difference between the current market value of the property if the grading work had been done as promised, $12,000, and its value as a choppy mess, roughly zero. Groves, by contrast, argued that damages should be measured by the actual cost of grading—doing the work itself—which, as it turned out, would have been more than $60,000. Using *Jacob & Youngs* terminology, Wunder sought the application of a "diminished

---

5. 205 Minn. 163, 286 N.W. 235 (1939). Compare Peevyhouse v. Garland Coal & Mining Co., 382 P.2d 109 (Okl.1962). And see, Farnsworth, *Your Loss or My Gain? The Dilemma of the Disgorgement Principle in Breach of* *Contract,* 94 Yale L.J. 1339 (1985); Muris, *Cost of Completion or Diminution in Market Value: The Relevance of Subjective Value,* 12 J. Legal Studies 379 (1983).

value" rule, while Groves sought "cost of replacement". Underlying the dispute, quite obviously, was the advent of the Great Depression: land values in suburban Minneapolis had simply collapsed between the commencement and termination of the lease.

The Supreme Court of Minnesota held (3–2) that Wunder was liable to Groves for an amount equal to the "reasonable cost" of grading the property, presumably $60,000. Groves, said the Court, was entitled to the promised performance (or its money equivalent) since that was what the contract called for. The diminished value rule would properly apply where the cost of remedying a defect in a completed structure was excessive relative to the loss in value attributable to the defect—that, indeed, would entail "economic waste"—but it could have no application to a contract to *construct* an improvement, "particularly where, as here, the delinquent [Wunder] has had full payment for the promised performance." In any case, as Cardozo emphasized in *Jacob & Youngs*, the doctrine of substantial performance and diminished value could not be appealed to by a promisor when the act of breach was willful and deliberate. In effect, therefore, Wunder must go ahead and spend $60,000 to generate property-value of $12,000—or else, of course, settle with Groves for a payment in cash. The dissenters urged, to the contrary, that the correct damage measure was Groves' loss ($12), not Wunder's cost ($60), and that willfulness had nothing to do with the question.

According to report, Wunder did in fact settle following the decision, paying Groves $55,000 cash in lieu of actual performance. What Groves did with the money one doesn't know, but if it still had faith in the future of suburban real estate it could have purchased nearly five times the acreage it started with at the depressed market price of $500 an acre. Should we therefore regard the Court's decision as having provided a "windfall"—that is, an undeserved benefit—to Groves and a corresponding penalty to Wunder? Answer: no. As the Court implied, Groves, as lessor, had really paid in advance for the grading work when it agreed to accept a rent of $105,000. If Wunder had *not* undertaken to grade the land at the expiration of the lease, then, obviously, Groves would have had to look forward to doing that job itself and at its own expense. In the latter event, the rent initially agreed to by the parties would necessarily have been higher. If, for example, Groves foresaw that the cost of grading at the end of 7 years would be about $60,000, it would have demanded an additional amount equal to the present value of the anticipated outlay (i.e., a sum which, at current interest rates, would grow to $60,000 in Groves' hands over the 7–year term). No one would regard that "fund" as a windfall to Groves; Wunder would have no claim to recapture any portion of it just because land values had fallen; and Groves would be free to use the fund for any purpose it chose, whether to grade the land, buy new property, or make unrelated investments. Having decided that the grading work would be carried out more efficiently by Wunder, Groves in effect forbore to demand additional rent and, in so doing, gave up an equivalent sum to Wunder for later expenditure on Groves' behalf. If the cost of grading varied from the parties' original expectation, one or the other would enjoy a benefit, so that they did indeed "gamble" with each other on that factor. But there was no evidence whatever that they intended their duties to be affected by ups and downs in the real estate market (or the stock market or the economy in general). Wunder had indeed received "full payment" for the work it agreed to perform, and hence there was nothing that could properly be identified as "economic waste" in requiring it either to repay or to carry out its performance obligation.

2. *The Lost–Volume Seller Exception.* Under UCC 2–706, as noted, where a buyer of goods repudiates or wrongfully refuses to accept delivery the seller's damages are measured by the difference between the contract price and the price—presumably lower—at which the same goods are or can be resold in the market. But suppose the seller resells at exactly the *same* price; the buyer's reason for repudiating is simply a change of heart—he no longer wants the goods in question—rather than a drop in market price. If the second contract is regarded as a substitute for the first, the seller would have suffered no loss by reason of the breach (apart from incidental expenses) and would apparently have no damage claim whatever. But how do we know that the second contract *was* a substitute for the first? Suppose the seller is a retailer—say a department store—and both the first and the second contract involved merchandise held for sale to customers in the ordinary course of business. Retailers are generally prepared to sell as many cars, TV sets and diamond rings as there are customers to buy them—the more the better, obviously—and there is something not quite right about the idea of regarding one customer as a substitute for another. If customer A, having agreed to buy, later repudiates his purchase agreement, the retailer would hardly feel that the profit he expected to realize from the sale to A had been recouped because customer B walked in a little later and purchased goods of the same sort at an identical price.

Recognizing that the contract-minus-resale measure may not be appropriate in these circumstances, UCC 2–708(2) establishes an exception for so-called lost volume sellers. In effect, if the standard damage measure is inadequate to put the seller in as good a position as performance would have done because the buyer's breach entails the loss of a profitable sale, then the seller's damages shall instead be "the profit (including reasonable overhead) which the seller would have made from full performance by the buyer . . ." *Neri v. Retail Marine Corp.,*[6] is illustrative. In *Neri,* the plaintiff contracted to purchase a new boat from the defendant, a dealer, for $12,500 and put down a deposit of $4,250. Within a week the plaintiff's lawyer notified the defendant that the plaintiff was rescinding the purchase contract because of illness, but the defendant, having by then ordered and received the boat from the manufacturer, refused to return the plaintiff's deposit. Four months later the defendant sold the same boat to another buyer at the same $12,500 price. The plaintiff sued to recover his deposit, and the defendant counterclaimed under 2–708(2) for lost profit of $2,500 plus incidental expenses.

The New York Court of Appeals held for the defendant. "The conclusion," said the Court, "is clear from the record—indeed with mathematical certainty—that 'the [contract-resale] measure of damages . . . is inadequate to put the seller in as good a position as performance would have done' . . . and hence . . . that the seller is entitled to its 'profit' ". The second customer would not be regarded as having replaced the first nor the later transaction the earlier. The defendant could have obtained sufficient inventory to supply all available customers, and it would therefore have had two sales instead of one if the plaintiff hadn't breached.

The lost volume exception has provoked a very earnest scholarly debate in recent years[7], with some writers taking the position that, by definition, a seller operating in a competitive market always attains an optimum volume of sales; in effect, he sells all the goods at the going market price that he can profitably dispose of. Additional sales, including the one "lost", would not be made, because the marginal cost of producing and selling one more unit of merchandise—the salary of another store-clerk, say—would exceed the revenue to be realized from the sale of that unit. Other commentators, somewhat more plausibly I think, argue that the typical retailer can probably expand sales with his *existing*

---

6. 30 N.Y.2d 393, 334 N.Y.S.2d 165, 285 N.E.2d 311 (1972).

7. See, e.g., Cooter & Eisenberg, *Damages for Breach of Contract,* 73 Calif.L.Rev. 1432 (1985); Goldberg, *An Economic Analysis of the Lost–Volume Seller,* 57 S.Cal.L.Rev. 283 (1984); Goetz

& Scott, *Measuring Sellers' Damages: The Lost Profits Puzzle,* 31 Stan.L.Rev. 323 (1979); Speidell & Clay, *Seller's Recovery of Overhead Under UCC 2–708(2): Economic Cost Theory and Contract Remedial Policy,* 57 *Cornell L.Rev.* 681 (1972).

sales force and store facilities and, hence, could have made the additional sale without increasing his costs beyond the wholesale cost of the article itself. On this view, the buyer's breach truly did deprive the seller of a profit equal to his mark-up—$2,500 in the *Neri* case—so that a recovery under 2–708(2) would be appropriate both in legal and in economic terms.

Whatever the merits on either side, my impression is that the issue presented in *Neri*—whether breach by a retail customer results in recoverable damages to the retailer—does not arise very often in practice. If that impression is accurate, the reason may be that retailers generally make their order-cancellation policy known to their customers in advance. A high-class department store might have a policy that not only permits cancellation prior to delivery but allows its customers to return merchandise within a specified period after delivery. A discounter, by contrast, sells for cash or requires a deposit for big-ticket items and permits no return or cancellation once you leave the premises. In either case, the terms of dealing are pre-announced, and in that sense pre-negotiated, by the retailer, and hence disputes that result in claims under 2–708(2) are rare. It goes virtually without saying that the department store with a "liberal" cancellation policy also has higher selling costs than the discounter and will recoup those costs at its customers' expense; the discounter has an "all sales are final" policy but obviously sells for less. The customer can presumably have it either way, depending on where he chooses to do his shopping. The Court in *Neri* made no determination with respect to the parties' understanding on this question, and of course it may be that they had none. On the other hand, the seller did require the buyer to make a cash deposit at the time of sale. While the amount, $4,250, slightly exceeded the seller's profit margin, the parties may well have intended thereby to establish both the existence and the limit of the buyer's liability in the event that he later changed his mind about the boat.

3. *Foreseeability.* In *Hadley v. Baxendale*,[8] decided by the Court of Exchequer in 1854, the plaintiffs, operators of a flour mill in Gloucester, sued the defendants, a firm of carriers, for their failure within the time promised to deliver a broken millshaft to the manufacturer in Greenwich, which needed the broken shaft to use as a model for making a replacement. Since the broken shaft was delayed in getting to Greenwich, its replacement was similarly late in getting back to Gloucester. As a consequence, the flour mill had to be shut down for five days, during which period the

8. 156 Eng.Rep. 145 (Court of Exchequer 1854).

plaintiffs paid wages and assertedly lost business profits.   From a jury verdict awarding damages to the plaintiffs for lost profits, the defendants appealed.

Speaking through Baron Alderson, the Court held that, although they had breached the carriage contract by their delay, the defendants were not liable for the very sizable losses that resulted from the five-day shut-down of the mill.   "Where two parties have made a contract which one of them has broken, the damages which the other party ought to receive . . . should be such as may fairly and reasonably be considered either arising naturally, i.e., according to the usual course of things, or such as may reasonably be supposed to have been in the contemplation of both parties, at the time they made the contract . . ."   The five-day shut-down would not have been considered as arising in the "usual course", the Court thought, since one's natural assumption, "in the great multitude of cases of millers sending off broken shafts", would be that the miller had another shaft in reserve or otherwise had made provision for continuing his business.   Here, as it turned out, there were "special circumstances"—plaintiffs *didn't* have another shaft in reserve, so that any delay in getting a replacement would cause a total shut-down of the mill.   No doubt the defendants heard a great deal about the need for on-time delivery *after* the breach had occurred.   At the time the contract was entered into, however, the plaintiffs said nothing, or at least not enough, to make the defendants aware of how dire the consequences would be.   Had there been sufficient communication at that time, the defendants might have done a number of things, of which one (and the most likely) would have been to insist that the contract contain "special terms as to the damages"—meaning, presumably, limitations on defendants' liability for breach.   And "of this advantage," the Court said, "it would be very unjust to deprive them."

The rule of the *Hadley* case—that damages are not recoverable for loss that was not reasonably foreseeable by the party in breach at the time of contracting—can be linked to the familiar proposition that "contract", unlike tort, is a species of absolute liability.   An unexcused failure to perform results in liability for the promisor even though such non-performance is unintended and inadvertent and cannot be blamed on the promisor's negligence or on his failure to meet an ordinary standard of care. Coupling absolute liability for breach with exposure to unlimited consequential damages, however, could be devastating to the promisor and especially in the case of routine over-the-counter transactions like the carriage contract in *Hadley* would impose a

151

risk upon the promisor which far outweighs the modest benefit that he might expect to realize from the transaction itself.

The point can be expanded slightly. Like any producer, a seller of goods or services—in *Hadley,* the carrier—needs to calculate his costs when he sets a price on his performance. Such costs would include not only the standard bookkeeping outlays (wages, fuel, docking fees), but also a reasonable reserve for contingent expenses where there really are adverse contingent events to worry about. If, for example, experience shows that Event X will occur 10% of the time and will result (if it does occur) in an unavoidable expense of $1,000, then, no doubt, the seller will add $100 to his cost estimate and price his performance accordingly. In the case of a freight-carrier, perhaps the adverse event that is most likely to occur would be the seller's own inadvertent failure to perform. If so, the seller's reserve for contingencies would have to reflect his potential liability to the buyer, discounted by the probability of occurrence. Quite obviously, the greater such potential liability the greater must be the seller's contingency reserve and the higher the price he will demand for his product or service. The buyer, who faces a similar set of considerations in dealing with his own customers, is of course aware of all this and, as a result, has an incentive not to disclose any unusual damages that might result from the seller's non-performance *until* the contract price has been agreed to and it is too late for the seller either to negotiate a higher figure or to insist on liability limitations. The effect, if this tactic succeeds, is to add a large insurance-like obligation to the seller's undertaking without his knowledge. But as that would be "very unjust," the Court in *Hadley* effectively eliminated the benefit of a non-disclosure strategy by excluding unanticipated losses from the final damage calculation.

Viewed from yet another angle, the foreseeability doctrine can be said to encourage the promisee to behave in an efficient, cost-saving manner *before* the promisor breaches. Thus, anyone reading the *Hadley* opinion will quite naturally find himself wondering why the mill-owner didn't have a couple of extra millshafts around the place somewhere. If the continued operation of the mill was entirely shaft-dependent, so to speak, then it seems imprudent not to have maintained an inventory of spare parts. The explanation, presumably, is that the mill-owner wished to avoid investing money in spare parts and preferred instead to rely on the shaft-manufacturer's ability to furnish a quick replacement when one was needed. Then, however, as the Court suggested, it became necessary to inform the carrier in the clearest terms that an on-time delivery was essential. Had the mill-owner made its "special circumstances" known, the carrier might have reacted (a) by adding extra personnel or by using a separate vehicle to assure that the shaft arrived on time, or (b) by refusing the contract unless the mill-owner obtained loss-insurance (whether from the carrier itself or from a third-party) in case delivery failed. Either alternative, to be sure, would ultimately be reflected in higher freighting cost to the mill-owner, but I think it is plain that neither would be as costly as the loss that might be expected to result from a prolonged shut-down of the whole mill operation. The finding in *Hadley* that the mill-owner's losses were "unforeseeable" is thus equivalent, in practical effect, to a finding that the mill-owner was in the best position (prospectively) to minimize damages, but that he failed to do so.

Put differently, the foreseeability doctrine creates what has been described as "an implicit duty to premitigate".[9] The mill-owner could have met that obligation either by carrying an inventory of replacement parts or by informing the carrier about his special circumstances "at the time they made the contract". Having done neither, recovery was barred.

4. *Certainty*. As a general rule of limitation, damages for breach are recoverable only to the extent that the injured party's loss can be established with reasonable certainty. The issue has arisen most frequently in connection with lost profit claims, presumably for the reason that determining the injured party's "profits" entails projections and predictions that are sometimes speculative and conjectural and are almost always open to debate. As in the *Village Plaza* case, discussed below, each of the parties is likely to produce an expert, often more than one, to testify in his behalf. Hired for the purpose, the experts are virtually certain to disagree with one another, and to do so at length and in the most positive terms, leading an exhausted court or jury to view the whole process with skepticism verging on mistrust. In the end, as the Restatement observes, reasonable doubts are likely to be resolved against the party in breach, since it is he who is responsible for generating the problem to start with.

In *Fera v. Village Plaza, Inc.,*[10] the Supreme Court of Michigan affirmed a jury award to the plaintiffs of $200,000 for lost profits. The plaintiffs had leased store-space in a shopping center, the lease to run for 10 years at a stated monthly rental plus a

9. Goldberg, *Relational Exchange, Contract Law, and the Boomer Problem* (in Goldberg ed., Readings in the Economic of Contract Law, 1989, p. 71). And see, Posner, *Economic Analysis of the Law* 107 (3d ed. 1986).

10. 396 Mich. 639, 242 N.W.2d 372 (1976). And see Restatement Section 352.

percentage of sales. The leased space was to be used by the plaintiffs as a "book-and-bottle" shop, whatever that may be, but through neglect or confusion on the part of the managers of the shopping center the space was leased to another tenant and the plaintiffs were refused occupancy. The Court held that the evidence on lost profit presented at the trial—after "days and days of testimony" from experts on both sides—was sufficient to sustain the jury's verdict. This was true even though the book-and-bottle shop was a new business with no past-earnings history on which to base an estimate of future earnings, even though it appeared doubtful that the lessees would ever have obtained a liquor license, and even though the Court itself "might have found plaintiffs' proofs lacking had we been members of the jury". Mathematical precision was not required in cases where precision is unattainable, said the Court, particularly when "it is the defendant's own act or neglect" that has created the problem.

Although it upheld the jury's verdict, the Court in *Village Plaza* may have been troubled by a sense that the award was exaggerated and perhaps vindictive. We are told next to nothing about the lessees' business outlook, yet $200,000 does seem rather a large number to attach to the "lost profit" of a humble book-and-bottle shop, and I suppose we might wonder how the jury arrived at that figure. My own suspicion—just a guess and admittedly unprovable—is that, in calculating the lessees' damages for lost profit, the jury, or the trial court, overlooked two important financial elements that should have been taken into account and that might well have reduced the award in size. The first such element concerns the definition of "profit", especially relevant here because the shop was a new business to which the plaintiffs had as yet committed neither services nor funds. The second concerns the purely mechanical process of discounting future earnings to present value.

First, then, what should we understand by "profit"? For accounting and tax purposes, the answer would be: total returns from the sale of books and bottles minus the firm's actual business outlays, which would typically include payments for inventory (the books and bottles), employees' wages, rent, utilities and various other "inputs" purchased from third parties. But while the balance—revenues less business expenses—is certainly "net income" in an accounting sense, it is not economic "profit". Thus, an economist would presumably argue that the accountant's "net income" is just a preliminary or midway figure and needs to be reduced by "implicit costs"—costs for which no obvious money payments are made—in order to determine whether the firm has truly realized a profit from operations. Such implicit costs would chiefly include (a) the value of the individual plaintiffs' services in running the shop (that is, the salaries they would be entitled to if they worked for an employer instead of for themselves) and (b) a normal return on their invested capital (that is, the interest they would earn if the plaintiffs put their money in a savings account instead of in their own business). In economic terms, "profit" is what is left after deducting these implicit costs from accounting net income. My hunch (unprovable, etc.) is that the jury in the *Village Plaza* case calculated the shop's "lost profit" by deducting money outlays only and ignoring implicit costs—and further, that if implicit costs *had* been taken into account the "profit" figure would have been pretty close to zero.

If that hunch is correct, then the effect of the jury's action would be not only to overstate the plaintiffs' loss, but—equally important for our purposes—to disregard the plaintiffs' legal duty to mitigate damages. Thus, once aware that the defendants had breached, the plaintiffs must be assumed, as a matter of law, to have sought substitute (non-inferior) employment as managers of somebody else's liquor store and likewise to have invested their capital in some other income-producing asset. The Shirley MacLaine case shows that the duty to mitigate is not always the same as the economist's notion of implicit opportunity cost; but where, as here, the injured party's service skills are routine in nature, the two constructs are very much alike and omitting one is roughly equivalent to omitting the other. To be sure, the State liquor license for which the plaintiffs had applied would have no close economic substitute, and I concede that the license (if it had ever been granted) would be an asset of premium value in the plaintiffs' hands. In addition, I suppose that the idea of combining books with bottles might have seemed to the jury to be a brilliant and innovative marketing concept from which the plaintiffs' were entitled to expect an unusually high return. Still, it is hard to believe that either the liquor license or the marketing concept could have been worth as much as $200,000 in the year 1965, and of course the Court did not suggest they were.

The other question that comes to mind is whether the jury's $200,000 figure represented the discounted value of 10 years' future earnings or was simply the *sum* of such earnings, that is, 10 times average earnings of $20,000. If the former, and if we assume a discount rate of (say) 15% on liquor store investments, then, to generate a present-value figure of $200,000, the expected annual earnings of the book-and-bottle shop would have to have been about $40,000. The number $40,000 seems rather high, however, even if the plaintiffs' implicit costs were ignored, and my suspicion is that the jury simply multiplied expected annual earnings by 10. If so, the result would be a substantial measure of over-compensation, but there would be nothing on the face of a general verdict that would tell you which "methodology" the jury had actually employed.

B.   Reliance and Restitution

While damages for breach of contract are generally based on the injured party's expectations, there are two well-recognized alternatives to the expectations measure; namely, reliance and restitution. The alternatives are elective in the sense that the injured party may choose to seek reliance damages or restitution instead of expectation damages, but as a matter of pleading and case-presentation there is nothing binding about the choice and a plaintiff may present his claim *in* the alternative—that is, under more than one heading—or may shift from one to the other if the defendant is not misled thereby.

Actually, expectation and reliance are not true alternatives since both assume that the contract is to be enforced against the promisor in accordance with its terms. The promisor being bound by his promise to perform and having breached, the remedy is money damages and the question becomes one of how best to measure the promisee's loss, that is, whether with respect to reliance only or with respect to expectations as well. Restitution, by contrast, though a fairly frequent form of relief in contract cases, is based upon the quite separate concept of unjust enrichment; recovery is measured by the value of the benefits conferred upon the promisor by the promisee rather than by reference to the loss resulting from the promisor's failure to meet his obligations under the contract as such.

What follows is a very brief discussion of the reliance and the restitution interests, with the latter being further divided into two sub-topics, namely, restitution for a breaching plaintiff and restitution for the injured party to a "losing" contract.

1. *Reliance Damages.* As amply noted, the customary damage claim for breach of contract seeks compensation both for the injured party's expenditures in reliance and for his lost profit. In some instances, however, the lost profit element may be uncertain or, at least, very difficult to establish, and the injured party may find it simpler and less burdensome to limit his claim to his expenditures. Expenditures in reliance would include outlays made in actual performance of the contract itself—the $1,900

spent by Luten prior to the County's repudiation, for example—
and also amounts spent on items that are incidental or collateral
to the contract—the cost of books and bottles, say, purchased by
the disappointed lessees in *Village Plaza*. Damages recovered
under a claim of promissory estoppel as in the *Red Owl* case
(supra, p. 51) may similarly be based on the injured party's
reliance, though the claim itself need not, strictly speaking, seek
contract enforcement in conventional terms.

Damages based on the reliance interest bear an obvious resemblance to damages for tort since the effect under either approach is to restore the victim to the position he would have
occupied if the event or transaction had never occurred. While
overlapping circumstances would be rare, there may be instances—*Sullivan*, below, is evidently one—in which an injured
party can frame his complaint both in tort *and* in contract. But
why would he bother to do that—why would he add a contract
claim to a tort claim if his potential damage recovery is the same
whether he is found to be the victim of a breach or is found to be
the victim of a tort? The answer, presumably, is that the injured
party's legal burden becomes considerably easier to carry if the
existence of a contract can be established. The reason, once again,
is that contractual obligation is a form of absolute liability. The
injured party—now a promisee—establishes his claim to damages
by showing merely that the wrongdoer—now a promisor—failed to
perform. That done, and the failure being unexcused, the case for
liability is complete. Fault, in the technical, tort-related sense of
wrongful or negligent conduct, is irrelevant and need not be
proved.[11]

In *Sullivan v. O'Connor,*[12] the Supreme Court of Massachusetts was obliged to review a jury verdict awarding contract
damages to the plaintiff, a self-styled professional entertainer, in
connection with an unsuccessful effort by the defendant, a plastic
surgeon, to reduce the length of the plaintiff's nose. The entire
procedure was expected to require two operations, but when the
second was completed the result was apparently so disappointing
that a third operation had to be undergone in an effort to undo the
effects of the first two. The third operation, however, made
matters still worse: the plaintiff's nose "now had a concave line to
about the midpoint, at which it became bulbous . . . flattened
and broadened . . ." and somehow asymmetrical. For all this
misery the plaintiff paid $622 in fees and hospital expenses.

11. See, Birmingham, *Notes on the*
Reliance Interest, 60 Wash.L.Rev. 217
(1985).

12. 363 Mass. 579, 296 N.E.2d 183
(1973).

In her suit against the doctor, the plaintiff sought damages principally on grounds of medical malpractice. As an alternative cause of action, she asserted that there had been a breach of contract by the defendant for having failed to improve the appearance of her nose as promised. The jury found for the defendant on the malpractice count, apparently concluding that there had been no negligence in the way he performed the several operations. On the contract count, however, it found for the plaintiff and awarded damages of $13,500, having been instructed by the trial judge that such a finding would entitle the plaintiff to recover (a) the $622 of out-of-pocket expenses, (b) compensation for the *worsening* of her appearance (i.e., the difference between the mildly regrettable "before" and the perfectly ghastly "after"), including the mental anguish she felt as a person with a professional stake in how she looked, and (c) compensation for the pain and suffering she experienced by reason of the third operation, though not the first two, but (d) nothing whatever for lost earnings, because there had been no proof that the plaintiff actually lost any. The trial judge refused the plaintiff's request to instruct the jury that she could also recover for the difference in value between the beautiful nose that the defendant had promised and the nose as it appeared before the operations. Both plaintiff and defendant appealed.

Sustaining the verdict and the damage award, the Supreme Court held that there had been no error in the trial court's jury instructions. In a carefully developed opinion, the Court apparently agreed that there was sufficient evidence of an exchange of promises between the doctor and his patient to justify an award of damages for breach of contract. To be sure, physicians would "seldom" be found to have made binding promises (as opposed to mere encouraging noises), and it would be appropriate to instruct juries that "clear proof" was required before a doctor could be held to have entered into a contract with his patient to achieve a particular result. "On the other hand," said Justice Kaplan, "if these actions [for breach of contract] were outlawed, leaving only the possibility of suits for malpractice, there is fear that the public might be exposed to the enticements of charlatans, and confidence in the profession might ultimately be shaken."

With respect to damages, the Court apparently rejected both "restitution" and "expectations" as the proper measure of the plaintiff's claim. Restitution would entitle her to recover no more than the $622 that she had paid to the doctor and the hospital, and this was "plainly too meager". Expectations, however—that is, the difference in value between a beautiful nose and the nose she started with—might prompt a compassionate jury to heave up a very large damage figure and thus, despite the absence of negligence, impose a liability out of all proportion to the fee the doctor had received for his services.[13] On the whole, therefore, although not obliged to rule finally on the issue (owing to the posture of the appeal), the Court appeared to view "reliance" as the best measure of the plaintiff's loss. This, in turn, meant that the plaintiff was entitled to recover her "detriments", that is, to be put back in the position she occupied before the parties made their contract. The trial court was therefore correct in instructing the jury that the plaintiff was entitled to the $622 paid out in fees, plus the loss caused by her worsened appearance, plus the pain and suffering associated with the third operation. Probably, it would have been proper to award damages for the pain and suffering she experienced from the first two operations as well since there would have been no pain and suffering at all if there had been no contract and hence no surgery; in effect, limiting P & S to the third operation was not consistent with the reliance measure, because the suffering associated with the first two was similarly "wasted" when the contract failed. As the plaintiff had not appealed with respect to that issue, however, the verdict as rendered could be sustained.

Having labored through this wearisome dissection, I think we might return again to consider the Court's larger premise, namely, that the doctor-patient relationship can sometimes, even if only seldom, be regarded as a contract with result specified. Thus, why should the Court have accepted the jury's finding that this—out of the multitude of malpractice suits that sound in tort only—was the seldom-occurring case? The Court made no effort to review the evidence on the contract question, and perhaps the opinion can be faulted on that ground. In the end, however, I suspect that the Court's attitude and sense of the situation was revealed by its rather startling reference to "the enticements of charlatans". Almost everybody feels aggrieved about some aspect of his or her appearance and most people are prepared to spend small amounts of money on remedial devices in an effort to feel a little better. If you feel bad to the point of despair, however, you are likely to be

---

13. Compare Hawkins v. McGee, 84 N.H. 114, 146 A. 641 (1929), in which the defendant-physician had promised by surgery to convert the plaintiff's damaged hand into a perfect hand but in fact made the hand worse than ever. Finding that there had been a contract and that the defendant had breached, the Court indicated that the jury should be instructed to award expectation damages equal to the difference between the value of a perfect hand as promised and the value of the hand as it emerged from surgery. Neither the defendant's fee nor the plaintiff's cost in pain and suffering could be recovered, however, since those "costs" would have been incurred even if the surgery had been successful. The Court in *Sullivan* obviously declined to follow the *Hawkins* decision, presumably for the reason given in the text.

willing to spend a great deal more, and I suppose nothing is quite so enticing as the sudden magic of a surgical procedure that promises to change your life completely—for example, by turning one's fantasy about being a professional entertainer into a dream-come-true. Sensitive to the pathos of it all, the Court in *Sullivan* no doubt wished to establish a constraint in this connection by warning practitioners that their promotional efforts might ultimately come back to haunt them as contractual obligations, particularly when, in the view of a sympathetic jury, the promotion had been too aggressive.

Essentially, though with a special twist, the Court treated the plaintiff's surgical disaster as equivalent to the breach of a consumer contract—the defendant being the seller, obviously, and the plaintiff being the disappointed purchaser. In the case of a conventional retail transaction, if a purchase contract is breached because the item purchased and paid for turns out to be unavailable, the retailer would meet its obligation to pay "damages" by simply refunding the customer's purchase price. Nothing is allowed for the pain and suffering of having shopped in vain, and nothing is allowed for unrewarded "expectations". As respects the latter in particular, the customer might assert that she, personally, placed a greater value on the item than its actual cost—the item was so pleasing and attractive (she says) that she would have bought it even if the price had been much higher. Arguably, therefore, her expectation interest remains uncompensated unless the store gives back (say) twice the price she paid. Plainly, however, it would be entirely impracticable to measure and compensate for the loss of so-called consumers' surplus, and hence the retailer's only legal responsibility is to make a dollar-for-dollar refund.

It follows also, in the ordinary case, that the customer's recovery is the same whether her damage claim against the store is measured by her reliance interest or her restitution interest. She gets her money back under either measure, but no more. In *Sullivan,* by contrast, the Court's evident purpose was to give added protection to consumers of cosmetic surgery by allowing recovery not only for the price paid, but for physical injury and for pain, suffering and mental anguish as well. This made it necessary for the Court to pinpoint the reliance interest, because restitution, in the sense of benefit conferred, would have limited the plaintiff's recovery to her "meager" out-of-pocket expenditures. But, as with consumer transactions generally, such protection did not extend to the plaintiff's expectation interest; hence, nothing was allowed for the value (net of the surgeon's fee) which the plaintiff herself attached to the promise that she would one day have a nose to be proud of.

2. *Restitution.* As noted, while restitution is a claim that is based on a concept of unjust enrichment rather than contractual obligation, it does serve on occasion as an appropriate remedy in the contract setting. One example would be the case of a contract discharged by reason of mistake or impossibility. In *Young v. City of Chicopee* (supra, p. 131), the bridge-repair contract was held to be discharged when the bridge was destroyed by fire. While the plaintiff-builder was unable to recover for the value of the materials that he had brought to the site for later use, he did get restitution for repair work that had been completed before the fire occurred. The completed repairs increased the insurable value of the bridge in the defendant's hands—there was a transfer of benefit from plaintiff to defendant—and hence to that extent restitution was appropriate.

Yet another situation in which restitution rather than contract damages might be sought would be that of a buyer who has paid in advance for property or services. Logically, the choice of restitution would be made only if the market value of the property or service had fallen well below the contract price, although in such event, apart from special circumstances, one assumes that the seller would be eager to perform and unlikely to breach. If the property or service was clearly worth more than the contract price, then, restitution being the lesser claim, the injured buyer would presumably seek contract damages in the usual manner. However, establishing expectation damages through detailed proof can be a burdensome exercise, so that even in the latter case the injured buyer might find it simpler and less costly to claim restitution and, in effect, settle for his money back.

The discussion following takes up two problems in the restitution field that are of special note. The first is relatively uncomplicated and the solution is straightforward; the second is somewhat knottier and, in the words of the Restatement, "has engendered much controversy".

(a) *The breaching plaintiff.* We would not ordinarily think of the party in breach as having a right of recovery against the injured party, but on second thought it becomes apparent that such a right is built into the damage calculation itself. Thus, suppose S agrees to deliver a carload of widgets to B at a price of $1 a widget and delivers on schedule. B pays S at the contract rate but subsequently discovers that the widgets do not conform to the contract description—too small, let's say—and as such are worth only 90 cents apiece. B nevertheless elects to accept the non-conforming goods and sues S for damages. Under UCC 2–714(2), the measure of such damages is the difference between the value of the goods if they had been as warranted and the value of the goods as actually delivered—10 cents a widget, obviously, assuming no change in the market price of widgets between the contract and delivery date. In effect, although S is the party in breach, he gets credit for the value of the non-conforming goods and is liable only for the shortfall. One way to explain (really, over-explain) the result would be to say that it reflects two separate computational steps, the first being B's claim to recover the contract price ($1) of the widgets paid for but never delivered, the second being S's claim to restitution for the value (90 cents) of the non-conforming goods which B accepted and placed in inventory. The conclusion—that B's damage claim nets down to 10 cents a unit—is so plain that a two-step computation is unnecessary. Yet it (the conclusion) does embody a legal principle of sorts; namely, that a party's right to restitution may survive his own performance deficiency, or, to put it differently, that breach of contract does not validate unjust enrichment.

In *Britton v. Turner*,[14] decided by the Supreme Court of New Hampshire in 1834, the plaintiff agreed to work for the defendant for one full year—March to March—for a salary of $120, the entire salary to be paid at the *end* of the 12–month period rather than at weekly or monthly intervals. After about 9½ months the plaintiff quit his job for "no good cause" and the defendant refused to pay him anything. The plaintiff sued in *quantum meruit* for the value of 9½ months work and was awarded $95 by the jury, which obviously prorated his annual compensation over the 9½-month period. On appeal, the Court sustained the jury's verdict, holding that as the defendant had realized an economic benefit from the plaintiff's services which obviously couldn't be rejected or returned, the defendant was bound to pay for the value of those services even though the plaintiff had breached the employment agreement by quitting early. The defendant would be entitled to counterclaim for any damages he had sustained by reason of the plaintiff's breach—e.g., hiring another man at a higher salary for the 2½ months remaining—but in fact "no evidence [was] offered of any damage arising from the plaintiff's departure". Finally, since the plaintiff's claim was in *quantum meruit* rather than for contract damages, the defendant was liable for the "reasonable worth" of the plaintiff's services, which the jury might have found (but didn't find) to have been less than the contract rate. The defendant could not, of course, be liable for an amount in excess of

14. 6 N.H. 481 (1834).

the contract rate, since the plaintiff would then have succeeded in breaching the contract to his own advantage.

The rule of the *Britton* case—that restitution can be claimed by the party in breach—is obviously correct and is reflected in Restatement Section 374, which apparently also approves the Court's approach to the calculation of damages. Thus, Section 374(1) provides that the breaching party is entitled to restitution for "any benefit that he has conferred" on the injured party through part performance "in excess of the loss that he has caused by his own breach". In this context, the term "benefit" refers not to the cost of equivalent services, but to the actual increase in the injured party's wealth, which would sometimes be a lesser quantity. To illustrate, suppose that Builder agrees to repair Owner's building in return for Owner's promise to pay $10,000 on completion of the work. After spending $8,000, B abandons the job and O has another builder finish the repairs for $4,000. Suppose the value of the building has been increased by $9,000 after all repairs have been completed. How much can B recover from O in restitution? The answer given by the Restatement is $5,000, although just what that number represents is not too clear. Apparently, B's damage claim is to be pegged at a level such that, when added to the amount paid the second builder ($4), the total equals the resulting increase in the value of O's building ($9). Hence, B's recovery is $5. This, however, seems to mean that B is charged not only with the difference between the cost and value of his own part performance, but with the difference between the cost and value of the second builder's work as well. But why (unless we wish to punish him for breaching) should he be? The correct damage number, I think, is $6,000 ($8/12 \times $9,000$), which is evidently the value of B's part performance alone. Since that amount together with the $4,000 paid the second builder does not exceed the original contract price of $10,000, O will have sustained no "loss" as a consequence of B's breach and the pot would appear to be right from the standpoint of both parties.

Damage calculation aside, the *Britton* opinion tells us nothing directly about the nature of the plaintiff's employment or the reason for the once-a-year payment arrangement, and I suppose we might wonder how the plaintiff, who must have been an ordinary farm-hand, could have met his daily living expenses for 12 long months without pay. The explanation, no doubt, is that he did get paid for the day's work, not in cash, to be sure, but in the form of room-and-board and other necessaries which the defendant would have supplied to him and to the other workers on the farm. But of course farm-hands were wanderers—rootless non-cosmopolites—who came and went more or less at will in those days, and unless their shiftless habits could be restrained somehow the effect might be to disrupt the operation of the farm by confronting the defendant with a manpower shortage during some critical period. Slavery having been ruled out, the 12–month payment arrangement was obviously designed to promote job-loyalty and discourage abrupt departures. From that perspective, instead of being regarded as pro-ratable wages, the deferred payment could be looked at as a standard length-of-service award that was subject to a 1–year "vesting" requirement. A modern analogue would be the corporate employee's pension rights, which begin to build when employment commences but are forfeited if the employee fails to complete a stated period of service. No "restitution" or *quantum meruit* recovery is allowed to an employee who quits before his pension rights have vested, it being understood that the employer's aim is not (or not only) to compensate daily services as such, but to encourage continuity and minimize employee turnover.

The Court in *Britton,* which knew at least as much as the writer knows about the conditions of New Hampshire farm labor in 1834, certainly understood all this. Plainly also, however, it felt concern—probably more than a little—for the vulnerability of ordinary farm workers to oppressive tactics on the part of their employers. Thus, why *did* the plaintiff quit his job so near to the end of the 12–month period? Maybe he was just a heedless fellow, indifferent to his obligations and quite prepared "to desert his service before the stipulated time". On the other hand, perhaps the defendant cruelly "[drove] the laborer from his service, near the close of his term, by ill treatment, in order to escape from payment . . ." Which of the parties was at fault in this context, and where to place the blame, might be a close and complicated question. Looking for some way to balance interests, the Court conceded that the parties *could* "provide by an express agreement that nothing shall be earned if the laborer leaves his employer . . . before the expiration of the time" agreed upon. But in the absence of such "express agreement" the legal presumption would be otherwise, because the Court had "abundant reason to believe that the general understanding of the community is that the hired laborer shall be entitled to compensation for the service actually performed".

Just why "express agreement" was deemed lacking where the employee had been told that he would be paid *only* on the completion of 12 months' service, the Court in *Britton* did not say. Presumably the defendant failed to prove by sufficient evidence that the "general understanding" had been overcome in the present case; he probably did not realize he had to. This, however, left the Court free to extend some measure of protection to the plaintiff (and others in his position) by giving notice to employers who sought to tie their workers to the land through deferred payment arrangements that the burden would be on them to show (a) that the employee had expressly agreed to the conditions of vesting and (b) equally important, that the employee had not been driven from his job "by ill treatment" just as the term was coming to an end.

(b) *Losing contracts.* Damage claims for breach of contract normally arise in a setting in which the injured party expects to make a profit from completing the contract, while the party in breach anticipates a loss. The injured party's claim, under the customary formula, is equal to the sum of his expenditures in reliance plus his disappointed profit expectation. But suppose that the injured party *himself* anticipates a loss. A builder, for example, having done a portion of the work called for by a construction contract, realizes that his expenditures *already* exceed the contract price and that completion of the job will simply mean a further deficit from his standpoint. At this point, the owner—for its own special reasons—elects to repudiate the contract and directs the builder to discontinue his work. How should the builder's damages be calculated? Should the expenditures made up to the date of the breach be recoverable by the builder in full, or should the builder's recovery be reduced by his anticipated loss? Or is there some other measure? A completely satisfactory answer, as will be seen, is not so easy to come by.

An illustration—drawn from the venerable *Kehoe* case [15]—will be useful. Assume a builder-plaintiff agrees to pave a street for a price of $2,700. Having completed 60% of the work, the builder finds that his costs already amount to $3,000—$300 more than the contract price—and he estimates that he will have expended $5,000 by the time the job is done. The builder thus expects to incur a loss of $2,300 ($5,000—$2,700) overall. The owner-defendant, a municipality, suddenly decides to terminate the paving project and tells the builder to stop working. How much in damages can the builder recover from the municipality?

The Restatement and the decided cases offer a number of alternative solutions—three plus a variation, actually—and this in turn suggests that the problem here addressed is a bit more complicated than most. While each of the alternatives has some

15. Kehoe v. Rutherford, 56 N.J.L. 23, 27 A. 912 (1893).

measure of plausibility, in the end (as shown below) one realizes that the differences between them relate chiefly to the question of which of the two parties—builder or municipality—the inevitable loss falls on *first*. Our choice of rule might then boil down to a judgment as to whether "we" are better off if one party to a losing contract rather than the other takes the first hit or if they share the misery somehow.

Rule # 1: Restitution. Restatement Section 373 would apparently support recovery by the builder of the entire value of his work up to the date of breach. That amount—$3,000—necessarily equals the builder's reliance interest, though here expressed in terms of restitution of the benefit received by the municipality. Recovery is under *quantum meruit* rather than the contract, so that the builder's prospective loss becomes irrelevant. In effect, the contract is discharged in view of the municipality's breach, and the builder's recovery is measured by the market value of the services rendered. As stated in a leading case [16], "The measure of recovery for quantum meruit is the reasonable value of performance . . . undiminished by any loss which would have been incurred by complete performance."

Treating the builder's claim as independent of any contract limitation means not only that his loss expectation is disregarded, but also that his recovery will exceed the contract price itself. Thus, the restitution damage measure is $3,000, while the total contract price—the amount the defendant would have had to pay if it hadn't breached the contract—is only $2,700. The result (as has often been noted) is odd and anomalous. Since the builder thus recovers more in damages than the payment he would be entitled to under the contract itself, the municipality, once aware of the rule, would apparently be prompted to engage in "strategic" behavior in order to contain its own liability. If, instead of terminating the project at the time its undesirability became apparent, the municipality simply allowed the builder to go on and finish the job, the builder's entitlement would obviously be limited to $2,700. There would then be no breach and no damage claim—merely an obligation to pay the contract price. In effect, the municipality's potential liability for the unwanted paving work rises to a high of $4,999 just before the contract is completed, and then abruptly drops to $2,700 when the job is done. Although $2,000 ($5,000 – $3,000) of wasted expenditures are avoided if the contract is promptly terminated, the municipality can save $300

16. United States v. Algernon Blair, Inc., 479 F.2d 638 (4th Cir.1973). See Wolcher, *The Accommodation of Regret* *in Contract Remedies*, 73 Iowa L.Rev. 797, 809 (1988).

for itself alone if it permits the work to grind along pointlessly to completion.

To avoid this wasteful consequence, it might be best, in these special circumstances, to limit the measure of restitution damages to an amount not in excess of the contract price. The builder is still permitted to disregard his expected loss in calculating his restitution claim, but outlays above the contract price would be excluded from such claim and would not be reimbursed. The result, admittedly, is something of a conceptual hybrid, but perhaps we can give it dignity by calling it "constrained restitution". Taking this approach, the municipality in my illustration would be liable for only $2,700, with the builder being left to absorb the $300 balance.

The important thing to observe—especially in comparing the capped version of Rule # 1 with the alternatives described below—is that using restitution as the measure of damages in this context means that the *first* $2,700 of loss incurred by the parties falls on the municipality alone rather than on the builder or on both parties proportionately. The municipality is thus encouraged to minimize social and private costs by terminating the unwanted paving contract at the *earliest* possible date—that is, presumably, before the $2,700 outlay figure is reached. Given the cap, moreover, the municipality would have somewhat less inducement to engage in strategic behavior by allowing the work to continue beyond the point at which the project would otherwise be brought to a halt.[17]

Rule # 2: Contract Damages. Though unlikely to be elected by a losing-contract plaintiff, Restatement Section 349 offers a damage measure that permits the injured party to recover his reliance costs, reduced, however, by any loss that the injured party would have suffered had the contract been fully performed. As applied in my illustrative case, a reliance-minus-negative-expectations rule would entitle the builder to recover $700—$3,000 of actual outlays less $2,300 of anticipated loss. In effect, the first $2,300 of loss falls on the builder, with the balance—here $700— being absorbed by the municipality. Since the builder takes the first hit, the municipality has less incentive than it does under the restitution measure to effect an early termination of the contract.

---

17. But, I admit, only somewhat less. Once the builder's outlays had passed the $2,700 level, the municipality would have no further inducement to terminate and, indeed, could threaten to keep the contract going unless the builder agreed to settle on a favorable basis. Rule # 3, under which the loss is shared between the parties at all stages, avoids this defect, but by sharing the loss it provides less inducement to terminate the project early. While the choice is hard to make, as suggested below either approach seems better than that of Restatement Sec. 373.

For the same reason, perhaps, the builder is encouraged to make a more careful estimate of his own costs and risks when he submits his original bid; yet it seems unlikely that the builder would be led to relax his customary degree of care in the hope that an act of breach by the municipality might rescue him from error.

Rule # 3: Loss Sharing. Apparently alone among the decisions in this field, *Kehoe v. Rutherford,* mentioned above, permits the plaintiff to recover in damages a proportion of the original contract price equal to the percentage of the contract completed at the date the breach occurs. Having expended $3,000 out of a total foreseeable cost of $5,000, the builder's recovery would be $3,000/$5,000 × $2,700, or $1,620. The balance of $1,380 ($3,000 − $1,620) would be absorbed by the builder himself.

It will be recalled that the builder's total loss expectation is $2,300, while the municipality's total contract obligation is $2,700. Since the fraction $1,380 (builder's loss)/$1,620 (municipality's loss) is the same as the fraction 2300/2700, the effect of the *Kehoe* "principle" is simply to divide the burden between the two parties on a ratio of 23:27 throughout the entire term of the contract. In some cases—for example, where the defendant is a governmental agency whose appropriations have unexpectedly been terminated by the legislature—the act of breach might be viewed as faultless or as a kind of quasi-impossibility event, so that a sharing concept has some equitable appeal. The plaintiff would still have reason to make a careful estimate of costs and the defendant would still have an incentive to avoid delay in terminating the project, but now both parties take the risk of an abrupt change in underlying circumstances.

Which of the damage rules that have been described is best? Solely from the standpoint of fairness, the question seems rather evenly balanced. On the one hand, no very good reason exists for relieving the builder of the consequences of his bidding error. The municipality's breach is fortuitous as far as the builder is concerned and it is not obvious why that chance event should generate a windfall for him. On the other hand, the municipality's action in terminating the contract is "willful" in the sense of being deliberate and perhaps for that reason the financial consequences should fall more heavily on it. In the end, however, as suggested, our choice may depend less on fairness considerations than on what we want the damage rule to do in practical terms. Viewed from that standpoint, I think "constrained restitution"—the capped version of Rule # 1—can be seen as marginally preferable to any of the alternatives. Under this approach, as noted, the loss falls first on the municipality, which is presumably in the best position to bring what has become a wasteful undertaking to a speedy end. The street-paving job is a dead loss to everyone— unprofitable to the builder and unwanted by the municipality— and hence a damage rule that encourages early termination is clearly desirable. As conceded, there is an element of windfall to the builder under the restitution measure which one might otherwise prefer to withhold, but the fact is that a complete integration of goals is impossible and on balance the former objective— encouraging early termination—seems the more important of the two.

C.   Liquidated Damages

As an original matter, we might think it doubtful that the courts would ever be willing to give up the damage-setting function to the contracting parties themselves. It is true, as has been stated, that contract rules largely operate as default provisions in lieu of express provisions, and that the parties are free to contract around the legal rules if it suits their interests to do so. Still, we might suppose that the freedom to "contract around" would be denied when it comes to damage rules. Awarding damages is the principle means by which courts exercise their enforcement authority. Allowing the parties to agree upon their own damage award might be thought equivalent to allowing private persons to preempt that authority.

As it turns out, the law has taken a kind of mid-way approach in this area. Recognizing that a prior agreement on damages may avoid litigation costs and save the time of courts and juries, the rule in most jurisdictions, as reflected in Restatement Section 356(1), is that damages for breach may be "liquidated", that is, pre-determined by the contract. The amount of such liquidated damages, however, cannot exceed a figure "that is reasonable in the light of the anticipated or actual loss caused by the breach and the difficulties of proof of loss." If excessive, the liquidated damage provision may be deemed unenforceable as a "penalty", in which event, presumably, the injured party's damages will be determined under customary standards. In effect, the contracting parties may agree on damages in advance of the event and create their own "rule" in that respect. But unlike other self-created rules, this one is subject to review and to possible rejection on the ground that public policy prohibits private parties from imposing penalties on one another for breach of contract.

A very common illustration of liquidated damages would be a provision requiring a builder to pay a stated amount for completion delays. Thus, a contract to construct a store-building might provide that the builder shall pay the owner $1,000 for every day completion is delayed beyond a specified date. If $1,000 reasonably approximates the owner's anticipated loss of net rents, and if the actual loss would be difficult to prove, the contract provision fixing damages will be enforced. On the other hand, if the construction delay is harmless because the owner is obliged to delay renting the facility for some other reason—denial of an occupancy permit, say—or if the loss of rents is plainly less in amount than $1,000 a day, then the liquidated damage term is likely to be treated as a penalty and for that reason held unenforceable.

Lake River Corp. v. Carborundum Co.,[18] decided by the Seventh Circuit in 1985, offers a full work-out of the rules on liquidated damages (together with a brief lecture by Judge Posner on the infirmities of paternalism). In 1979 Lake River and Carborundum entered into a three-year contract for the local distribution of an abrasive powder used in making steel. Lake River would receive the powder in bulk from Carborundum, bag it, and then ship the bagged material to Carborundum's customers. Carborundum would pay Lake River a stated price per unit for this service. At Carborundum's insistence, Lake River purchased new bagging equipment at a cost of $89,000. Carborundum then promised to ship not less than 22,500 tons of powder to Lake River for bagging over the three-year term and agreed also that "if, at the end of the three-year term, this minimum quantity shall not have been shipped, Lake River shall invoice Carborundum at the then prevailing rates for the difference between the quantity bagged and the minimum guaranteed."

Demand for domestic steel declined sharply during the period covered by the contract, so that by the end of the three-year period Carborundum had shipped and paid Lake River for only 12,000 of the guaranteed minimum of 22,500 tons. Lake River thereupon sent Carborundum a bill for the balance of the amount guaranteed—$241,000, the contract price for bagging an additional 10,500 tons—and sued when Carborundum refused to pay. Carborundum's defense was that the above-quoted contract formula imposed a penalty and was therefore unenforceable under applicable Illinois law.

The Court, finding that "Illinois, untroubled by academic skepticism . . . ., continues steadfastly to insist on the distinction between penalties and liquidated damages", held for Carborundum on this issue. The reason, fairly obviously, was that the amount claimed as liquidated damages failed to reflect the cost avoided by

18.   769 F.2d 1284 (7th Cir.1985).

Lake River in not having been required to process the omitted 10,500 tons. Carborundum's breach at any point in the life of the contract, whether early or late, necessarily meant that Lake River would be spared the expense (labor, materials) of bagging from that point forward. A damage formula based on the full contract price would therefore compensate Lake River for costs that it never incurred, even assuming that the new bagging equipment had no salvage value whatever. Since damages so calculated must exceed Lake River's actual loss (the earlier the breach, to be sure, the greater the excess), the formula was a penalty provision and could not be enforced. Lake River was still entitled to its common law damages, however—$241,000 minus "cost avoided"—and that figure would be determined by the trial court on remand.

The basis for "academic skepticism" [19] regarding the wisdom of the prohibition against penalties in this context can probably be surmised. Carborundum was a seasoned and sophisticated business organization amply provided with legal and financial counsel when it entered into the distribution contract with Lake River, so that considerations of duress, capacity, adhesion and the like obviously have no application. If it was willing to commit itself to a damage obligation equal to the full contract price in the event it failed to deliver the minimum tonnage—without reduction for "cost avoided"—then the very strong presumption is that it saw an advantage to itself in making that commitment. The advantage, presumably, as the Court observed, lay in providing a "credible assurance" to Lake River—which was being asked to purchase new equipment and perhaps also to redirect other resources such as warehouse space and docking facilities—that the contract would be performed. To be sure, non-performance would entitle Lake River to damages for its reliance plus lost profits, but for various reasons it might well have seemed to Lake River that the customary damage measure would be inadequate and that it needed a promise of premium damages before it could accept the risks involved. For its part, Carborundum probably foresaw little likelihood that it would breach and in any event deemed the additional risk worth taking when compared with the certain costs that it would incur if it had to develop its own distribution services. Had the parties known at the time the contract was being negotiated that the liquidated damage provision would be rejected by a court, then either the contract price would have had

---

19. See Clarkson, Miller & Muris, *Liquidated Damages versus Penalties: Sense or Nonsense*, 1978 Wis.L.Rev. 351 (1978); Goetz & Scott, *Liquidated Damages, Penalties and the Just Compensa-* *tion Principle*, 77 Columbia L.Rev. 554 (1977). And see, Epstein, *Beyond Foreseeability: Consequential Damages in the Law of Contract*, 18 J. of Legal Studies 105 (1989).

to be increased in Lake River's favor or there would have been no deal at all. Neither of the latter alternatives, however, would then have seemed as desirable to Carborundum as its apparent obligation to pay premium damages if it should later choose to withhold performance.

Carborundum made a bet on the three-year market for domestic steel when it entered into the distribution agreement with Lake River. The bet turned out to be a loser but the Court's decision eliminated most of the adverse consequences. In effect, "public policy" produced a windfall to Carborundum and a penalty to Lake River, which is kind of an ironic reversal, and perhaps it is this that explains why some observers have been skeptical. There may be instances in which liquidated damage provisions are so extreme as to shock one's conscience, but by and large such instances are likely to involve individual consumers (see the *Walker–Thomas* case, supra p. 72) and are probably best dealt with through an application of the unconscionability doctrine. Carborundum, by contrast, breached its contract with Lake River because it chose to allocate its resources in a different way, and it was therefore hardly a candidate for special mercy.

Chapter 9

THIRD PARTY BENEFICIARIES

Commencing with the New York Court of Appeals' decision in *Lawrence v. Fox*,[1] the courts in this country, with support from successive Restatements, have exhibited a general willingness to recognize the contract rights of third party beneficiaries. The concept is easily expressed: where A, for a consideration, promises B to pay money or transfer property to C, then, in the name of procedural economy and convenience of remedy, C, no less than B, should be able to sue for damages if A fails to perform. To be sure, C has furnished no consideration to A (though, of course, B has), and C is not a party to the contract between A and B. But these shortcomings would appear to be largely formal. Thus, A's obligation to perform is the same whether it is B or C who receives the benefit, and A's exposure to liability for non-performance is the same whether it is B or C who asserts a claim against her. Given the simple outlines of the problem, perhaps the real question is why there should ever have been any hesitation about accepting the idea of third-party contract rights. In the alternative, one wonders whether the situation is really as straightforward as it appears.

In *Lawrence v. Fox,* the defendant, Fox, borrowed $300 from an acquaintance named Holly. As Holly owed the same amount to Lawrence, Fox promised Holly that on the very next day he would repay Holly, in effect, by paying Holly's debt to Lawrence. What all this was really about remains something of a mystery, though it has been suggested that the loans in question—Lawrence to Holly and Holly to Fox—were actually gambling debts which, as a matter of public policy, could not have been enforced directly.[2] Whatever the case, Fox ultimately refused to pay Lawrence and Lawrence sued. Fox defended on the ground that his promise had been addressed to Holly alone and not to Lawrence: while Holly (the promisee) might claim against Fox (the promisor) if he chose, Lawrence had no equivalent right. Fox, after all, had received no consideration from Lawrence, and as Lawrence was not a party to the contract between Fox and Holly, he (Lawrence) lacked standing to seek enforcement.

1. 20 N.Y. 268 (1859).   2. Waters, *The Property in the Promise: A Study of the Third Party Beneficiary Rule*, 91 Harv.L.Rev. 960 (1978).

The New York Court of Appeals held for Lawrence. While Lawrence could not, in traditional terms, be regarded as Fox's promisee, the fact was that Fox had received ample consideration from Holly and in return therefor had made an unequivocal promise to repay the amount borrowed in accordance with Holly's direction: ". . . . the consideration received and the promise to Holly made it as plainly his [Fox's] duty to pay the plaintiff as if the money had been remitted to him for that purpose . . ." It might be true (as fervently stressed by a dissenting judge) that Holly at some stage could have discharged Lawrence's claim against Fox either by settling with Fox directly or by assigning Fox's debt to someone else—say an even more insistent creditor of his own. In that sense Lawrence's claim, unlike that of a conventional promisee, could be divested by action of other parties and perhaps even without his knowledge.[3] This, however, in the Court's view, was not a damaging anomaly. Once Lawrence had recovered a judgment against Fox, Holly's legal power to make an independent settlement with Fox would disappear; indeed, such power might have disappeared when Lawrence commenced the present action, or even, possibly, at some earlier point. In effect, the danger that recognition of third-party rights might generate legal confusion—overlapping claims, say, or settlements without the consent of the affected party—seemed to the Court majority to be a manageable risk. In hindsight, as suggested below, the Court's confidence has largely proven to have been justified; on the other hand, the problems and difficulties that might have been foreseen were certainly not fully debated by Court or counsel, and hence the decision in *Lawrence v. Fox* must be admired (from one standpoint) as a leap of faith.

Having determined that Lawrence, whom we may refer to now as a "creditor beneficiary", possessed enforceable rights under a contract entered into by two other people, the New York Court had relatively little difficulty in according the same enforcement rights to contract beneficiaries occupying the status of "donee". In *Seaver v. Ransom*,[4] the plaintiff was the "beloved niece" of old Mrs. Beman, who, on her deathbed, was asked by her husband, the Judge, to sign a will leaving her property, a house and lot, to him for life, remainder to the ASPCA. Mrs. Beman feebly objected that she wished to give the remainder interest to her niece rather than the ASPCA, whereupon the Judge, with upraised hand, took

---

3. Lawrence's claim against Holly is, of course, unaffected by Holly's arrangement with Fox: if Fox fails to pay, Lawrence can still recover from Holly as Fox's "surety". See Restatement Section 304, Comment c. If Fox does actually pay Lawrence, then Holly's debt to Lawrence is obviously satisfied—Lawrence can't collect from both.

4. 224 N.Y. 233, 120 N.E. 639 (1918).

a mighty oath that if Mrs. Beman would sign the will already prepared, he would leave enough to the niece in his own will "to make up the difference". Mrs. Beman did as requested, then expired. When, however, the Judge himself later "came to die", it was found that he had left the niece nothing whatever. The latter, claiming breach, brought suit against the Judge's estate for the value of the real estate, which was found to be $6,000.

Echoing the proposition that the rule of *Lawrence v. Fox* was "progressive, not retrograde", the Court held for the plaintiff. The Judge had made "an unqualified promise on a valuable consideration" which the plaintiff, as "donee beneficiary", had standing to enforce in a suit for contract damages. The case would be clear, said the Court in effect, had the gift to the plaintiff been wholly testamentary. If Mrs. Beman had made a will leaving the house to the Judge on condition that he assume a debt to the plaintiff of $6,000, then the Judge's "debt" would be an asset of Mrs. Beman's estate and would simply be a bequest to her niece from Mrs. Beman herself. The distinction between the latter arrangement and the contractual obligation to which the Judge agreed was "discernable, but not obvious"; if one was enforceable, the other should be as well. The Court therefore approved the "tendency of American authority. . . . to sustain the gift in all such cases and to permit the donee beneficiary to recover on the contract."

The outcome in *Seaver*, insofar as it confirms the extension of third-party rights to donee beneficiaries, is hardly debatable. On the other hand, drawing an analogy, as the opinion does, between a testamentary gift and an oral contract for the donee's benefit is itself slightly breathtaking. Testamentary gifts (i.e., wills) are required by statute to be in writing and to be dated, executed and formally witnessed; oral dispositions made at the last gasp generally wouldn't, and I suppose shouldn't, qualify as legally effective substitutes. The Court's willingness, here, to give effect to a hasty, death-bed agreement—neither promisor (Judge) nor promisee (Mrs. B) being available to verify it—suggests either that the evidence in support of that agreement was powerful indeed [5] or else, perhaps, that the beloved niece made an eye-moistening appeal to judicial sentiment which the alternate takers under the

---

5. In addition to some rather shaky testimony from the attending physician, such "evidence" consisted of the lower court's finding that Mrs. Beman was simply not a pet-lover: "It does not appear that a dog, a cat, a bird or any animal at any time had a home in the Beman house, or that she ever showed any particular interest in animals. Unexplained, we cannot understand why she should. . . . practically overlook her favorite niece. . . . and throw her property to the dogs." Seaver v. Ransom, 180 App.Div. 734, 168 N.Y.S. 454, 456 (1917).

Judge's will (whoever they were) just couldn't match. Whatever the case, resort to third-party beneficiary "law" enabled the Court to make an end-run around the much stricter rules and requirements that otherwise apply to testamentary dispositions.

As indicated immediately below, the "tendency of American law" has been to expand the category of third-party beneficiary to include any person *intended* to be benefited by the contracting parties, whether or not such person would otherwise fit within the definition of "creditor" or "donee". Reflecting this approach, Section 302 of the Restatement distinguishes between "intended" and "incidental" contract beneficiaries, defining the former (somewhat tautologically) as anyone intended by the promisee to be benefited by the promisor's performance and the latter as anyone who is not the former. Section 304 then provides that a promise creates a duty in the promisor which an "intended beneficiary" may enforce. The aim, presumably, is to confirm that the parties to a contract shall be free, if it suits their interests, not only to confer economic benefits on non-parties but also to extend enforcement rights against the promisor to such non-parties, always assuming the promise is otherwise binding.

Broadly speaking, the problems of interpretation that arise under the Restatement and its common-law counterpart are two. The first, and perhaps the more challenging, is simply how to apply the terms "intended" and "incidental" where the promisee's aims are less explicit than they were in *Lawrence v. Fox* and *Seaver v. Ransom*. Having moved beyond "creditors" and "donees", the question, essentially, is who else might qualify as a contract beneficiary and whom to regard as a mere outsider. The second set of problems, as suggested, concerns the scope of the promisor's defenses to third-party claims and the ability of the contracting parties to terminate the beneficiary's claims without the beneficiary's consent.

1. *Intended Beneficiaries.* In *Lawrence* and in *Seaver* the third-party beneficiary was designated by name in the agreement between the contracting parties; hence there could be no doubt as to either (a) the intention of the promisee (Holly, Mrs. Beman) to give the beneficiary (Lawrence, the niece) the benefit of the promised performance or (b) the willingness of the promisor (Fox, the Judge) to assume an obligation to such beneficiary. The Restatement, however, does not restrict the status of "intended beneficiary" to persons named or otherwise specifically designated by the promisor and promisee. Rather, the beneficiary of a promise is to be recognized as an intended (not merely an "incidental") beneficiary if such "recognition . . . is appropriate to

effectuate the intention of the parties" and if "the circumstances indicate" that the beneficiary was expected by the promisee to receive the benefit of the promised performance. The implication, borne out, it would seem, by the decisions in the field, is that the question is one of interpretation and case-by-case analysis.

Third-parties who are money-creditors or donees obviously qualify as intended beneficiaries and presumably stand at one end of the spectrum. At the other end would be those individuals for whom the contract between promisor and promisee may have important consequences, but whose interests were simply not within the contemplation of the contracting parties at the time they made their agreement. Thus, suppose A agrees to erect an improvement on B's land which, if completed, will enhance the value of an adjoining tract that happens to belong to C. C licks her chops in anticipation of a windfall, but if A (for example) breaches the contract and the project fails there is obviously nothing that C can do about it as a matter of legal right. C cannot invoke A's contract duties as if she (C) were the intended beneficiary of A's promise, even though C would in fact have benefited had A performed her obligations. The reason (if any is needed) is that A and B could not have considered the expectations of myriad unnamed persons (e.g., C and other neighboring landowners) when calculating the risks of their original undertaking; nor, indeed, would they have worried much about the financial impact on such persons of any subsequent decision to breach. Generally, and as already much noted, contract law provides an enabling framework within which the contracting parties can generate financial benefits for themselves; it is not, however, directly concerned with the wealth effects on *non*-parties.

The hard case in this area—one that falls somewhere towards the middle of the spectrum—would seem to be that of a third party who has a specific contractual claim against the promisee which depends, as a practical matter, on the promisor's willingness to perform her duties to the promisee under a separate but related agreement. By way of common illustration, suppose G, a general contractor, agrees to construct a building for O, the owner. G then subcontracts with P to do the plumbing. Is P an intended beneficiary of G's contract with O? If O terminates the contract— say before any work has been done—can P recover lost profits from O? The answer—at least the answer given by the Restatement[6]—is no: O's obligation as promisor is to pay G for the construction of the building, but not to discharge G's obligation to

---

6. Restatement Section 302, Illustration 19.

P. O would have had no knowledge of the costs and profit-expectations of G's subcontractors (P and dozens of others perhaps) and might not even know the subcontractors' identity in many cases. O knew she might be liable for G's costs and profits when she entered into the original contract with G; but the liability *then* within O's contemplation would be different in amount from that claimed by P and other disappointed subs.[7]

Presumably the same answer and the same reasoning would apply if P failed to perform her contract with G, and O attempted to recover from P on a third-party theory. Thus, P's obligation as promisor is to do the plumbing, but not to erect an entire building. Hence P's work, even if completed, would not discharge G's duty to O. P would properly be liable to G for the difference between the price to which she had agreed and any higher price that G might have to pay for the same plumbing work, but P would not have assumed liability for O's profit expectations or other incidental costs, which would presumably exceed the value of the plumbing contract itself.

In effect, recognizing third-party claims in either of the above cases would impose risks on the promisor which the latter would not and probably could not have taken into account when the terms of the primary contract (between O and G in the first case, between P and G in the second) were negotiated and agreed upon.

Yet despite this rather cautious approach to third-party rights, the courts in a few instances have gone beyond the manifest aims of the contracting parties and have found the requisite "intention to benefit" even though promisor and promisee were, in fact, wholly indifferent to the third party's interest. In the *Lonsdale* case,[8] for example, Chesterfield Land, Inc., the owner of a tract of undeveloped land in Oregon, platted a portion of the land and sold residential lots to eighty-one individual purchasers for a cash down-payment (presumably) plus a promise to pay future installments. In its agreements with the lot-purchasers, Chesterfield promised to install a water system for the use of the entire development. Chesterfield then assigned the installment obligations (called "land purchase contracts") to the plaintiffs, a group of investors, for cash. Subsequently, Chesterfield sold the

---

7. State statutes, however, protect laborers and suppliers by allowing them to place so-called mechanics' liens on the owner's property in order to secure their rights to payment for services actually performed. To free her property from lien, the owner, in turn, may require the general contractor to furnish a payment bond obligating the issuing insurance company to pay all debts owed to sub-contractors if the general fails to do so.

8. Lonsdale v. Chesterfield, 99 Wash.2d 353, 662 P.2d 385 (1983). See also, Visintine & Co. v. New York, Chicago & St. Louis R.R. Co., 169 Ohio St. 505, 160 N.E.2d 311 (1959).

remaining undeveloped portion of the tract to the defendant, Sansaria, Inc., the latter promising as part of the deal to assume Chesterfield's obligation to install the water system. But in fact it never did: the residential land market evidently went sour, and Sansaria either suspended or abandoned its plans for further development. As a result, the individual lot-purchasers defaulted on the land-purchase contracts, which rendered the plaintiffs' investment in such contracts worthless. Claiming to be intended beneficiaries of the Sansaria–Chesterfield agreement, the plaintiffs sued Sansaria for the recovery of their investment.

The trial court, finding that Sansaria (the promisor) and Chesterfield (the promisee) had no intention whatever to confer a benefit on the plaintiffs, held for the defendant. On appeal, the Supreme Court of Washington reversed. Chesterfield, it found, had impliedly warranted to the plaintiff-investors that it would take no step (i.e., by failing to construct the water system) that would impair the value of the lot-purchasers' installment debts. Sansaria having promised Chesterfield to carry out Chesterfield's duty in this regard, the plaintiff-investors qualified as intended beneficiaries and, as such, had a legal right to enforce that duty against Sansaria. "Under the terms of the contract," said the Court, "Sansaria could not fully perform its promise to install the water system without directly benefiting [the plaintiffs]." Since the plaintiffs *would* have benefited from Sansaria's performance, they must be regarded as intended rather than incidental beneficiaries even though (as noted by the court below) nothing could have been further from the minds of the contracting parties than the preservation of the plaintiffs' investment in the land-purchase contracts.

All this, one assumes, must have come as a considerable surprise to Sansaria, which presumably understood that it had an obligation to the individual lot-purchasers, but probably never imagined that its failure to put in the water pipes would mean liability to the investors as well. Claims by the lot-purchasers could perhaps have been settled or compromised for a good deal less in total than the damages claimed by the plaintiff-investors, and indeed the latter sum, when added to the amount paid to Chesterfield, may have exceeded the entire value of the undeveloped land, which was all Sansaria acquired in the deal. Ultimately, perhaps, the question was whether the plaintiff-investors should be left to sizzle in their own grease for having neglected, at the time they bought the installment contracts, to require Chesterfield to *secure* its obligation to put in the water system—for example, by placing a portion of their investment in escrow until

179

the system had been completed. Pretty plainly, however, the Court felt that the investors had been lulled or misled in this connection and deserved to be bailed out of their predicament. Accordingly, the Court determined that Sansaria and Chesterfield had impliedly contracted for the benefit of the investors—not because they meant or intended to in any conscious sense, but simply because there would have been a benefit to the investors had the water system been installed.

2. *Defenses.* At least at inception, a third-party beneficiary's rights against a promisor (e.g., Lawrence's rights against Fox) derive from the rights of the promisee. In an action by the beneficiary, therefore, the promisor can presumably assert any contract defenses that could be raised against the promisee, unless for some reason the parties have otherwise agreed. In the *Rouse* case,[9] for example, Winston, a homeowner, purchased a furnace from Associated, giving the latter her note for $1,008 payable in monthly installments of $28. The note finally wound up in the hands of the Federal Housing Authority as guarantor. Winston subsequently sold the house to Rouse, the defendant, who (though he didn't sign the note) agreed in the contract of sale "to assume payment of $850 for heating plant, payable $28 per mo." The note being in default, the FHA sued Rouse for $850 as a third-party beneficiary of Rouse's contract with Winston. Rouse raised two defenses: first, that Winston had lied to him about the condition of the furnace, which apparently didn't work; and second, that Associated had failed to install the thing correctly to begin with. The lower court struck both defenses and Rouse appealed.

Reversing in part and affirming in part, the Court of Appeals held that the first defense—that Rouse had been cheated by Winston—should be reinstated. Conceding that the FHA was an intended beneficiary of the Winston–Rouse agreement, Rouse's liability to a third party could be no greater than his liability to the promisee. If Rouse could raise a fraud defense to a suit on the contract by Winston, then the same defense must be available in a suit by the contract beneficiary; in effect, "one who promises to make a payment to the promisee's creditor can assert against the creditor any defense that the promisor could assert against the promisee." With respect to the second defense—that against Associated for improper installation—the lower court's decision to strike was sustained. To be sure, the promisor (Rouse) would be entitled to show, if he could, that the promisee (Winston) was

9. Rouse v. United States, 215 F.2d 872 (D.C.Cir.1954).

under no enforceable liability with respect to the heating plant; if Associated (and the FHA as its successor) had no valid claim against Winston, its rights against Rouse would be no greater merely because Rouse had agreed to take over Winston's outstanding contractual obligations. Here, however, the obligation assumed by Rouse was to pay a specific amount of money—$850— rather than to take over a litigable claim. It was as if Winston had *already* settled with Associated and had conceded herself to be indebted in the amount of $850 at the time she sold the house to Rouse. In effect, Rouse assumed the burden of that settlement (which might have subsumed a variety of claims between Winston and Associated) and was not at this stage free to reopen it.

The *Rouse* decision thus confirms that a third party's claim is subject, generally, to the promisor's defenses against the promisee and to the promisee's defenses against the third party (unless already settled). What remains to be considered, briefly, is the related question of *post*-contractual modification or discharge—in effect, the question that seemed to trouble the dissenting judge in *Lawrence v. Fox* itself. As noted earlier, Judge Comstock, the dissenter, objected to the majority decision on the ground, among others, that the third party's claim might be subject to divestment or dilution through separate action of the promisor and promisee and for that reason occupied a sort of legal limbo. The answer given by the majority was that the third party's rights must "vest" at some appropriate point, though whether at the time the third party actually brings suit against the promisor, or earlier, was not made clear. The problem arises (one imagines) because dealings between the promisor and promisee may involve other matters and other issues than those involved in the contract affecting the beneficiary, so that the beneficiary's interest may ultimately be bargained away or compromised as part of a separate settlement or exchange between the primary parties. More simply, the promisor and promisee may decide, for reasons of their own, to rescind their contract or modify it in a way that eliminates the third party's claim.

On the whole, as stated, a third-party beneficiary's rights are derivative and rise no higher than those of the promisee himself. As a result, generally, the contracting parties retain control of their contract and are free to rescind or modify without the third party's assent. There are, however, reasonable and largely expectable limitations on such freedom. If the third party participated directly in the bargaining that led to the agreement, then either expressly or by inference his assent to any variance is likely to be required. Going further, if the third party learns or is advised of the agreement and changes his position in reliance on what he assumes to be the promisor's enforceable duty, modification or discharge without his assent may be precluded. Whether there has been "reliance" depends on facts and circumstances, but as to "creditor beneficiaries"—Lawrence himself—mere notification probably is sufficient.[10] Lawrence, we may assume, would have relaxed his efforts to collect from Holly once he learned that Fox had agreed to pay the debt. Having been told to expect performance from Fox (Holly meanwhile, perhaps, departing for another jurisdiction), the presumption is that Lawrence's rights become fully vested and are thereafter immune from any subsequent attempt by the primary parties to discharge or modify their agreement.

10. Robson v. Robson, 514 F.Supp. 99 (N.D.Ill.1981).

TABLE OF CASES

References are to Pages

TABLE OF CASES

References are to Pages

INDEX

References are to Pages

185

†